Behind
the Golden
Curtain

Behind
the Golden
Curtain: *A VIEW OF THE U.S.A.*

by Susan Cooper

CHARLES SCRIBNER'S SONS : New York

Library of Congress Catalog Card Number 66-23989

ACKNOWLEDGMENTS

The author thanks the following for permission to use quotations:
ANTHONY SAMPSON for passages from the 1963 edition of *Anatomy of
Britain,* published in New York by Harper & Row; JAMES BALDWIN
and Dial Press, New York, for an extract from *Nobody Knows My
Name* (1961); DWIGHT MACDONALD for an extract from *Against the
American Grain,* published in 1962 by Random House, New York;
the HELGA GREENE LITERARY AGENCY for an extract from *Raymond
Chandler Speaking* by Dorothy Gardiner and Katherine S. Walker,
published in 1962 by Houghton Mifflin Co., Boston; and MORTON
M. HUNT and DOUBLEDAY and COMPANY, New York, for passages from
The Inland Sea (1965).

For Denis Hamilton

and Patrick Murphy

PREFACE

"O books, O endless minatory books!
Explaining the barbarians to themselves . . . ."
—STEPHEN VINCENT BENÉT,
Western Star

But this isn't one of those. This is a book about an uneasiness. It puts forward one particular view of the United States, which is contained, more or less, in its title.

When I first traveled through the United States at the age of twenty-seven, I was hit very hard by a double astonishment: at my own reaction to the place, and at the Americans' reaction to everyone else. All the images of the U.S.A. which I had ever been given, as a reasonably well-informed foreigner, seemed in face of the reality to have been born out of ignorance; and the Americans themselves seemed just as ignorant—not only of every country but their own, but of their own place in the world. And although this first alarm of mine could have been easily enough dismissed as "cultural shock," in the neatly-packaged phrase with which some Americans explain away the initial babblings of foreigners, it didn't end there. Later I came to live in the United States for good, and I discovered so much more about the misunderstandings bouncing to and fro across the Atlantic that I began to feel there was another version of the Iron Curtain splitting the West in half. The Golden Curtain has these differences from the other: it is accidental; it

vii

encloses only one nation; and it is not guarded with guns. But it can be just as dangerous, if no one recognizes it is there.

I have tried here to write about this curious barrier; to show the things which go to make it up, and the effect which it has both inside and outside America. And since I suspect that British ideas and attitudes have something to do with the preservation of the Curtain from the other side, I have begun by writing about Britain in some detail. In any case, since so many of my assumptions are British-made, this is inevitably a book about two countries in relationship, rather than one alone. Even though both members may be wearing blindfolds, the relationship still exists.

I owe much gratitude on either side of the Atlantic: to *The Sunday Times* (London), who not only made my first travels in the United States possible but have allowed me to use material—and my title—from three articles I originally wrote for them; to the U.S. Government, who once rashly gave me three months as a "cultural exchange" import; to Paul Block, publisher, who was generous enough to employ me on his newspaper in America and I hope has not been put off foreigners by the experience; and to friends and informants in many parts of the U.S.A.

This is a revised version of the edition of *Behind the Golden Curtain* published in Britain, which contained more description of those aspects of America which foreigners tend to misunderstand. I have removed most of this, since there is obviously no point in giving an American reader a detailed explanation of, say, the American educational system; and I have replaced such passages, whenever it seemed useful for comparison, with explanations of their British equivalents. But I have let some of the original description stand; it can after all be illuminating sometimes to see familiar things through a foreigner's eyes.

Finally: there will undoubtedly be some who will think this book outrageously impertinent, if not sacrilegious, for not altogether approving of all American traditions and attitudes. We have such people in Britain, too; there, they are still talking about the qualities that built the *Empah,* and attacking anyone who suggests that Britannia no longer rules the waves. But in both countries there are many others of more objective views; and it is for such readers that books of social commentary are written. I ask their forbearance for having written this one without waiting until I had lived in the United States for decades instead of years, and hope they will agree that ideas, like kettles, are generally best seized while still on the boil.

CONTENTS

1 ⁎ The Other Side

"I am willing to love all mankind,
except an American."
—SAMUEL JOHNSON

We think, over there in Britain, that we know you well enough. We have always been on good terms with you, after all. The only time we really fought you was in 1776 (we don't count 1812), and you can hardly be blamed for that; it might never have happened without foolish old George III. Of course you wanted your independence; you came of good sturdy British stock. You are our cousins. You speak our language, more or less; our blood is mingled in yours; we all share a common heritage. . . .

So it goes. We think we know you well enough, and we are quite wrong. We hardly know you at all. We know, in fact, rather more about the French or the Germans than we do about the Americans. Go to France, if you are British, and when you come home people will inquire politely whether you enjoyed yourself, whether you happened to go to that particular little restaurant in the Boulevard St. Germain. But go to the United States of America, and every greeting when you return will be a variant of the same question: "What's it like? What's it *really* like?"

What is it like, to come to America as a stranger? It has a different taste, a different color, a different smell. It is all very

1

surprising. No Englishman, no matter how much he may have read, seen or heard about America before he goes there, is ever quite prepared for the great fog of bewilderment that will eventually engulf him on the other side of the Atlantic. For he has crossed that ocean, probably, with the illusion that because of all this cousin-blood-and-language business, he is not really going to a foreign country. He feels that America will probably be a brash young edition of Britain: bigger, faster, richer, noisier, adorned with all the odd excrescences one has learned about from television, but not different in kind. His first impressions may not do a great deal to contradict this, if he stays only for a matter of days or weeks at a time. But the longer he lives in the United States, the more clearly he begins to realize that the differences from his own country go very much deeper than the surface, and that he is in a foreign land—not hostile, unsympathetic or unwelcoming, but foreign nonetheless.

The illusion of a shared blood and heritage is one of the first to go, when he finds that the racial composition of the American nation has changed considerably since the men of the *Mayflower* landed. Fewer than 30 per cent of the people of the modern United States have British ancestors, and most of those ancestors are so far buried in the past as to have no influence whatsoever on their descendants' temperaments or minds. Of 24,000,000 first-generation Americans today, only 2,000,000 were born of British parents. Of a total of more than 9,000,000 foreign-born Americans, only some 830,000 were born in the British Isles. Thus the whole total of the U.S.A.'s foreign stock, made up of 34,000,000 living Americans, contains less than 3,000,000 of British origin. The remaining 156,000,000 citizens of the United States have no real temperamental connection with Britain at all; it takes only one generation to make a family American. Are you all our cousins? Hardly.

And soon enough, the visiting Englishman's other illusions go the same way. In their place, there comes the gradual realization not only that automatic Anglo-American understanding is a mirage—but that a great deal of automatic misunderstanding exists instead, caused by the various influences and misconceptions which compose, at least for the purposes of this book, the Golden Curtain.

Part of this misunderstanding is caused by elements in the American mind, the American way of life. But part of it too is the Englishman's fault. He has for too long taken it for granted that membership in the English-speaking world makes Britain and the United States necessarily members of the same family: he has forgotten the length of time during which the different branches of that family have been growing in different directions. Often, Americans have forgotten this too. Unless you, the American, have lived in Britain for some years and acquired grounds for comparison, you may not know how great the divergence has become—or why. The solution, here, is to take you briefly back across the Atlantic to the land from which the *Mayflower* came. In spite of all those green fields and thatched cottages, it really has changed a little since then.

*   *   *   *   *

Any English Saturday: autumn, in the afternoon. It is perhaps the most introverted moment of the week for any nation. From Newcastle to Portsmouth mufflered men and boys, and some shrill women, are swelling the four-lettered roar of football crowds; twice as many are watching them on the fourteen-inch screens of fireside television sets, waiting for meat-paste sandwiches and cups of tea. In Central London the double-decker buses have thinned to a scarlet trickle; the mist is beginning to gather round the plane trees, and the aunts and schoolchildren are settled in their matinées.

Down in the garage of a national newspaper office, facing a cobbled alley, the newspaper vans wait; neat yellow-and-blue vans, rubber-winged for bouncing off passing vehicles at speed. The presses will not start to run for five hours yet. One driver, in sharp pork-pie hat and pearl tie-pin, is taking a book on the re-

sults of the two-fifteen horse-race at Aintree; another is offering
round some handsome sets of children's paints at half the retail
price.

"Where'd you get them, then? They hot?"

"Nark it, mate. You want one, or not? Ten bob a box . . ."

The unions have been asked to start the paper's run half an
hour early, to outwit a seized-up machine in the wrapping room;
in a corner, the father of the chapel and five others are estimat-
ing with earnest suspicion what inducements the management
will have to offer them. Underground, two benches wait beside
one of the great presses: on these, all night, five machine-men
will sit playing cards—there is no work for them to do, but because of the extra half-hour's run the machine-room union will
force their employment. They will all be "casuals." At this moment they are knocking back a pint or two in one of the Fleet
Street pubs, waiting to find out which paper will need them that
night.

Isolated by earphones, the copy-takers upstairs in their glass
cubicles are tapping out stories from reporters, correspondents,
"stringers" all over Britain and the Continent. The teleprinters
from the agencies have been stuttering out news since the small
hours of the morning; the staff men have already sent in most of
their long reports from Paris, Rome, Bonn, Berlin, Moscow, New
York, Washington, Madrid, Geneva, Hong Kong. One of the
London reporters is telephoning from a self-service restaurant in
Birmingham, where he has lunched, thumbing through his notebook, on fish fried in doughy, fat-sodden batter, a pile of pale,
limp chips, and a vast cup of hot sweet tea. His story covers the
by-election in which this division of the Midlands capital will
vote on Monday.

". . . and the posters in car-windows and coffee-bars seem to
justify his high spirits. Stop. Para. But if the Tory is confident,
Labour are unshaken. They have held this seat since 1945. And
the candidate, Jim Phillips, 34-year-old schoolmaster born and
bred in Birmingham, has been gathering waving bands of house-

wives as he tours back-streets seated precariously on the roof of his loudspeaker van . . ."

The reporter sneezes. "Bloody Brum," he says in savage parenthesis. "Got my first cold a good two months early."

Reporter Two is talking to the news editor from a telephone kiosk in Whitehall. He is a young reporter; three years ago he was still reading philosophy, politics and economics at Oxford. Behind him, the sidewalk is covered as far as the eye can see with dogged sitting supporters of the Campaign for Nuclear Disarmament. Resigned navy-blue monoliths of the Metropolitan Police stroll up and down beside them, trying not to appear to enjoy the sound of the sitters' guitars. Reporter Two has been greeted from the pavement by four acquaintances already, and is beginning to feel uneasily that by rights he should be sitting there with them. He says enthusiastically into the telephone: "It's terrific, biggest one yet, and you should see old Bertie Russell there, tough as you like . . . how much space can I have?"

"Here, go easy," says the news editor, alarmed. "You aren't writing for Peace News. Hundred and fifty words, and keep it tight."

Reporter Two sighs, and exchanges his conscience for his notebook.

From the office, Reporters Three and Four have walked the quarter-mile past the enclosed green lawns and towering chestnuts of Gray's Inn, and the great gray Saturday-deserted façade of the Admiralty, to eat lunch at an Italian-speaking coffee bar: *polpettini alla marsala* and espresso coffee, one dollar. The shops on either side are closed: the florist's window crammed with set-pieces of dusty artificial flowers, and the tailor's serried with ties and blazer-badges ranging from the Scots Guards to Trinity College Dublin. On the corner of the street an ancient shambling man with a wisping gray beard, his overcoat belted with string, is mumbling his way to nowhere. Reporter Three makes off for the Ritz, where an African prime minister is giving a high-spirited press conference on the faded red carpet, under the weary chandeliers. Reporter Four goes back to a telephone, to check road accident figures; to ask Transport House why a minister, on a lunchtime platform, has not kept to the text of a speech issued the day before; to drink intermittent cups of murky tea and to watch the gray English sky fade into darkness through the window.

Gradually the newspaper pace mounts: a bishop makes a speech attacking a pop singer; a spectacular car crash kills six men in mist on the M1 expressway; a Russian trawler begins behaving strangely near the Shetland Isles; shots are fired by Turks at Greeks in Cyprus; by Cubans at Cubans in Havana; the flow of copy from subeditors to printers swells and rustles, and the editor and his deputies shape the front page.

"Lead on Brandon's presidential stuff, of course . . . nine A.M. in Washington, we'll have more later . . . then Margach on the Labour split . . . the picture of de Gaulle across four, and *that* deep . . . my God, the man gets fatter every year . . ."

The front news pages of a British national newspaper can give the impression that London lies at the hub of all the world. This paper will sell one and a quarter million copies in the morning, from Land's End to John o' Groats, and will be read by perhaps 10 per cent of the entire British population. The bundles of its airmail edition which arrive in Boston, U.S.A., on the 2:30 P.M. plane will be gone by four. The contributor who has written this week's main feature article will within the next three weeks receive letters from readers in New York, San Francisco, Rome, Melbourne, Toronto, Madrid, Karachi and a remote part of Burma. The business section is fat and prosperous with advertising; the "careers" pages dangle juicy jobs before British university graduates; the pages of theater, film, book and music reviews are confident and allusive. Clearly this is a paper written by civilized writers for civilized and comfortable readers; it will cast an absorbed hush over the teapots and bacon and eggs in the morning. Like London, it has its finger on the pulse of the world.

But London is not the world; London is not even Britain. The bustle of the newspaper office rises, as the deep rumble of the presses begins underground; for a few hours the journalists have the hypnotic illusion of being at the center of things. Then gradually the pace slackens, the last main edition goes to bed, and Reporter Three makes the last conventional telephone calls: "Scotland Yard? Back hall inspector, please . . . evening, *Sunday Times* here, anything for us? . . . Okay, thank you. . . . Fire Brigade? Duty officer, please. . . . *Sunday Times* here, anything doing?"

A six-appliance job down at Bermondsey, says the fireman laconically: ground floor of a warehouse, no one hurt. Small stuff.

"Okay, thank you. Have a quiet night. . . ."

Work is over. The streets are quiet, on the midnight ride to Paddington Station, though there are still wandering figures on the edge of Soho, and in the glare of Piccadilly Circus where the neon flickers and glows: COCA COLA . . . SCHWEPPES . . . and the sad little clarion call of the Institute of Directors: EITHER EXPORTS GO UP . . . OR BRITAIN GOES DOWN. . . .

Reporter Three goes down the dusty gray length of Platform One at Paddington; beneath the war memorial to railwaymen, the high bronze Tommy charging with tin hat and bayonet into space over the unwitting heads of sleepy passengers and trolley-mounted porters. "Mind y' backs, please, *mind* y' backs. . . ." Beneath the great vaulted glass-and-iron roof, memorial to Victorian England, arrogant and ugly and impractical splendor; memorial to Isambard Kingdom Brunel, even the architects have smaller names today. . . . And the return ticket to Wales, 215 miles and back, costs six pounds nine shillings and an extra pound for a sleeping berth. Altogether, about twenty-one dollars.

The big diesel engines throb and roar at the buffers, in the nationalized terminus of British Railways (Western Region); but the older and tougher of the engine-drivers, who sit up in their high glass-walled cabs now with no movement except their hands and feet on the controls, still have a nostalgia for the old bucking flaming sweaty days of the Great Western Railway: when the billowing steam and smoke plastered darkness over Brunel's glass Paddington roof, and the man judging the steam-pressure within his engine's boiler, as a horseman feels at the bit, referred to every locomotive as "she." Nostalgia is tucked in every corner throughout England, like sand in the clothes of children come unwillingly inland from the holiday seaside.

The newspapers travel westward on this train as well; they are stacked high on trolleys, in bundles tied with hairy white string. But not many people go with them. The sleeping-car steward, a cozy Welshman, is boiling a kettle in his microscopic cabin. "Evening . . . ah, Miss Cooper, haven't seen you recently on this train. Ticket? Ta . . . wake you up at six, isn't it, about Shrewsbury, with a nice cup of tea." His voice drops, conspiratorially. "Like a cup now, would you, before you go to bed? I'll bring it along. . . ."

British Railways pot of good strong tea, two cups in it; British Railways cellophane packet of four Rich Tea biscuits, all for fifteen cents; and the train rocks and groans and clatters all the way to Wales, through the long long miles of London's suburban wasteland of semi-detached streets, neat gray roofs in endless rows glistening under the mist. And after the night and Shrewsbury and the second pot of tea, the sun is rising into red streaks of cloud over stubbled undulating fields jointed by the neat British hedges that have been following the contours of the land for centuries, unchanged; and the wedge-shaped sweep of the Long Mynd marks the beginning of the mountains of Wales.

At Gobowen, only two passengers leave the train, to cross the asphalt platform to the three empty coaches that will—within half an hour, or more, or less—be given an engine to turn them into the connecting slow train to Machynlleth. ("Mackinelleth," visiting Englishmen stumble and mispronounce it; for within the British Isles the Celts and the Gaels are still secret, a mere two hundred miles from London, inside the world of accent and old language.) And at Gobowen the one ambling porter is not talking about the mountains, but about the future of the railways.

"Mad it is, to close down all the little branch lines. And the stations—they are keeping us here, but Ruabon has gone, and Oswestry, and Llangollen, not that it will make much difference really to the work, because the boys do not go on to the railway now, oh no, not the way they used to. But what will people do, to get about in these little places? The buses are not so good, and you can't tell me they will be making them any better. Oh they will all buy cars, you mark my words, and in ten years the roads will be worse jammed than they have ever been . . ."

The second little train chugs and chuffs then through the brown and purple and fir-green mountains towards the sea, with its two passengers and twenty milk crates and several bundles of London Sunday newspapers. Past remote sheep farms where English is spoken only rarely, past the remnants of slate-quarrying communities, past a power station or two, towards the coast where the sons and daughters of fishermen do no fishing now, but keep guest-houses and garages and small hotels for the holiday trade, and live off their summer earnings when the empty winter comes. There are a hundred parts of the small British Isles that are like this: where the London papers with their news of Washington and Moscow, and the television aerials bringing the world to every chimney-stack make no impact on a sleeping amiable way of life that appears never to change its complacency or slow pace. The trumpets are very faint here. "Either exports go up . . . or Britain goes down . . ."

The growing gulf between London and the rest of the country is only one of the reasons why the predominant emotion felt by the young, living in Britain today, is impatience. It is not only a matter of the export trade, either, though in the matter of relating our markets to those of Western Europe as a whole the lamentable to-ings and fro-ings of both major political parties, motivated in series by almost everything except foresight, blew away the opportunities of the Common Market long before the *grand éclat* of President de Gaulle.

It is a matter, far too often, of feeling that one is trapped in a country in which nothing happens any more; which ties its children so close with bonds of birth, education, affection and a kind of intellectual comfort that they are seldom quite driven to escape, but which will not give them room to stretch fully at home. Britain, like that other absolute paternal care, will not leave us, but prevents us everywhere—more infuriatingly sometimes than if it were a totalitarian state.

"The old privileged values of aristocracy, public schools and Oxbridge which still dominate government today," wrote Anthony Sampson in 1962 in *Anatomy of Britain,* "have failed to provide the stimulus, the purposive policies and the keen eye on the future which Britain is looking for, and must have. The old ethos was moulded by the success of an invincible imperial machine. Its style was to make big things seem small, exciting things boring, new things familiar: but in the unconfident context of today this bland depreciation—and the assumed superiority that goes with it—merely succeeds in dispelling enthusiasms, blunting curiosity and dulling experiment. The groove-outlook, the club-amateur outlook, the pragmatic outlook are all totally out of keeping with an age which suffers, unlike the Victorians', from an oppressive lack of innovation and zeal . . ."

For every indication of movement and liveliness of mind in Britain today, you can find in serried ranks behind it the immovable platitudes of conservatism. Seven new universities are founded, after ten years in which the existing thirty have been pleading for money enough to expand even to three-quarters the size of the target of 750,000 places which an implacable government has set them. Two years after the new seven's foundation stones are laid, the government's Robbins Report indicates that the seven should have been at least fifteen. And all the time other institutions of higher education—the teachers' training colleges, the colleges of advanced technology, the art schools—exist often in a state of financial starvation which allows one of the country's few surviving areas of supremacy slowly to decay. Britain has the highest standards of education in the world—but the lowest paid teachers, and worst equipped schools.

It is typical of the national tendency to sit complacently back on the couch of nineteenth-century accomplishment. There are instances of modern accomplishment, of course. But each one begins to creak and slow down remarkably soon after its initial impetus has died; no sense of urgency seems ever to last for long. Certainly since 1939 there has been, as the American journalist Drew Middleton admiringly observed in *The British* seven years ago, "a quiet revolution by a quiet people." But the exultant shouts of social change fade too soon; the quiet revolution has become inaudible.

Consider, for instance, one aspect of the welfare state, our most idealistic national acquisition since the war: the hospitals which function now as part of the National Health Service. In 1961, my newspaper set me to report on the average condition of British hospitals. The Ministry of Health had been deluging the press with publicity for its splendid new Princess Margaret Hospital at Swindon, Berkshire, yet more and more young British doctors were emigrating to Canada and the U.S.A.—claiming that they sought primarily not more money but better hospital conditions. In January 1961, the Minister of Health, then Mr. Enoch Powell, had announced a ten-year plan to spend £500 million on replacing old hospitals, yet this met only "guarded approval" from the British Medical Association, and uninhibited fury from many of its members; two years earlier an official B.M.A. report had stated firmly that £750 million was the minimum needed. Sir Harry Platt, president of the B.M.A., had announced flatly: "We are practicing twentieth-century medicine in nineteenth-century hospitals."

There was also the remarkable fact that between 1948 (when the National Health Service began) and 1957, the population of Britain had risen from 48,500,000 to 50 million—but the number of staffed hospital beds had fallen, from 544,000 to 477,000.

All this was enough to instil curiosity, though not much more, about British hospitals. At first, mine was the reaction of the average Englishman: a lot of doctors seemed to be making a fuss, but then they were always making a fuss about some aspect of socialised medicine. Possibly hospitals were overcrowded, especially maternity hospitals; but this was only to be expected in a country where everyone who wanted and needed hospital treatment was entitled to a free bed. And most hospitals looked unbeautiful from outside; but was any more wrong with them than that?

With these bright British illusions, I then spent several months undergoing the most protracted shock of my life. Wherever new wings had been built on to old hospitals in Britain, as in the new £2,000,000 block at Guy's Hospital, all was bright glass and cheerful hygiene. The new hospital at Swindon was certainly well laid-out—though even there doctors had complaints of obsolescence, as in its already over-crowded out-patients department. But of the 3,000 hospitals in Britain, 1,800 proved to be obsolete, inadequately planned and hopelessly overcrowded; built before the Boer War, when the demands of Victorian medicine were very different from those of the National Health Service. In all of these, doctors and nurses were battling against appalling odds; living and working under conditions which most people in Britain would not expect to see outside a slum.

There is no point in listing here all the horrific, wasteful or just plain frustrating details; a more alarming fact was that by the time the investigation was complete, one could not only see how all these things had evolved, but begin to fear that they could never properly be put right. Even now that some government money was at last to be freed for hospital reform, the processes of spending it appeared to have been made unbelievably slow; although urged forward by imploring shouts from all sides, they remained cumbersome, deliberate, and always infinitely cautious. For months I listened to bleak tokens of the future: doctors complaining of the ineffectiveness of Regional Hospital Board officials; Regional Board men bewailing the slowness of the Ministry of Health; Ministry men complaining of planning checks by the Treasury; architects and builders attacking overall government interference. If the state of the hospitals produced an image of Britain, it was one of a great ponderous outdated machine grinding its way stertorously forward: never quite breaking down, always fed with some saving fuel at the last moment, but too inflexible to be stopped momentarily for replacement of some vital part. It produced the same kind of teeth-grinding reaction as other aspects of British life: education, the Church of England, the trades unions, the Army, and the more reactionary sections of British business. All these things keep many of those within them bedded in frustration—and their greatest strength, as I realized from an incident which followed the hospital investigation, lies in the beautiful, idiotic subtlety of their resistance to change.

The hospital articles, full of outraged detail, were duly published in *The Sunday Times* of London in November 1961; republished by a provincial daily paper, quoted in debate in the House of Lords. They brought in a shoal of letters, almost all in agreement, from angry articulate doctors and hospital administrators (those from the latter asking nervously to be signed only "Hospital Administrator"). Since the articles had formed an attack on the government, and specifically on the Ministry of Health, the paper and I then began seeking a chance to put our main points to the Minister of Health for official comment—a practice one finds quite often welcomed by ministers (or, more probably, their permanent staffs) who feel confident enough of their own case to want it publicized. But this time the Ministry of Health appeared not to welcome the idea at all. Every week, the news editor telephoned its principal press secretary to ask for an interview; every week, the principal press secretary said placatingly, "Well, we haven't forgotten you, but the Minister's very busy, you know. . . ." Eventually we gave up, and I became involved in the next scheduled series of articles—on higher education in Britain. Three months after the appearance of the hospital series, when I was so deep in statistics on halls of residence and undergraduate-tutor ratios that I had almost forgotten hospitals existed, the same principal press secretary telephoned one morning and said eagerly, "You know, of course, that the Minister's White Paper on hospital building is published this morning—if you can be round here in two hours he'll give you that interview you were asking for."

Once you are caught in the grindings of the British bureaucratic machine, there is no point in bursting into paroxysms of rage. The ministry man who is concerned to protect his minister from the inquisitions of impudent journalists will be bland, courteous and immovable, only letting his minister out into the cold when he is sure the coat he is wearing is weather-proof. And the coat provided by the White Paper proved exceedingly weather-proof. It contained nothing new; it was simply a detailed breakdown of the plan to spend £500 million on hospital building in ten years—a total which had been announced long before the *Sunday Times* series appeared. But its greatest strength, as the press secretary well knew, lay in the fact that it is impossible for any journalist, or anybody else, to digest five hundred close-printed pages of statistics in the space of two hours. To parry any question thrown at him, the Minister had only to quote, in the certainty that his audience hadn't analyzed the source of his quotations. So he did. Was the Minister concerned about the 34 per cent of junior hospital posts filled by doctors from abroad? "Ah . . . in the White Paper, paragraph thirty-three, we say that the number of general practitioners here had increased to 19,928 by 1960. . . . Now, very few doctors from the

Commonwealth are in general practice. So one shouldn't lose sight of the fact that we are steadily staffing up the National Health Service."

Was the Minister concerned at what his own spokesman admitted was a shortage of architects? We should see from the White Paper that he had taken into account the shortage of architects. Was he concerned at the number of hospital administrators who complained of builders not wanting hospital contracts? He hoped builders would be attracted by the volume of work involved. As we should see from the White Paper. *"L'appétit vient en mangeant,* you know. Ha-ha."* At the end of it all I apologized for not having a closer grasp of the details of the White Paper, privately cursing the effective machinations of the press secretary.

The Minister propped his feet up on his desk, and smiled. "That's quite all right," he said silkily. "We're quits. You haven't read my White Paper—I haven't read your articles. I never read the Sunday newspapers. Any of them." He then showed me down into the House of Commons yard, affably demonstrating how a minister of the Crown is entitled to have a taxi whistled up for his guests by a member of the Metropolitan Police. And I drove away dismally convinced once more of the impossibility, in Britain, of ever getting one over on the machine: the mandarins, the masters, the permanent men and their permanent underlings. It wasn't so much the Minister, it was the system behind him. "Of all the world's bureaucracies," wrote Anthony Sampson, "the British civil servants are perhaps the most compact and self-contained. Their values and opinions are little affected by the values of the press and the public. They have become hardened to ridicule and resentment, and, like the Old Contemptibles, turn ridicule to pride. . . . There are long conversations about 'HMG' and 'SOS' being exercised, seized, having it in mind, being agitated or embarrassed. The recurring word is 'embarrassment'—a word which signalises the dreaded intrusion of the outside world."

And intrusion, as a result, is made almost impossible. Instead, the strength lies in the quiet ability to embarrass the rest of the world—or at least the rest of Britain, the British being perhaps the only ones left in this bustling world who are capable still of so foolish an emotion. Once, when I was a very young reporter in London, I had to deliver a letter to the Queen Mother. This is not a task which occurs every day, and I hadn't the slightest idea, wandering through the maze of alleys around St. James's Palace, which doorbell I should ring. It was a gray day, and there was no one in sight—until I noticed, with great relief, a soldier in a sentry box. I went up and asked him the way. The soldier said nothing. He was even younger than I was, and he stood rigidly to attention. I stared at him: could he be deaf? "Could you just tell me whether I go left or right?" The soldier gazed straight ahead, in the deserted street, and said not a word. It was as if I didn't exist. I felt very foolish and small; and my first and strongest impulse, even when I had remembered that soldiers on sentry duty are not supposed to speak, was to kick him, very hard. He seemed to be a symbol of so much else.

But you can't kick a whole nation, especially if you are part of it yourself. You simply have to live with it: cursing softly, and making the best of things.

In this maddening self-sufficiency—the complacency of the ostrich—there lies the root of the curious mistrust with which most of the British regard the United States of America. On the whole, we are not quite sure about Americans. They didn't join us in World War Two until they had to, dammit; they just sat over there sending those vulgar food parcels and looking after rich Englishmen's children. And when they did come in, with their tanks and Flying Fortresses and outrageously comfortable looking uniforms, they chewed gum and didn't know how to march or salute; some called you ma'am and some called you honey, and many took away poor unsuspecting young English girls afterwards to be G.I. brides. After the war, the first tourists came, with fat wallets and faces and loud voices and clothes; who was to know, in wincing Stratford upon Avon or Hampton Court, that these weren't typical Americans?

Since then the picture conjured up by the word "American" in the mind of John Englishman has developed a little further, but not much. Schoolchildren are taught next to nothing about the country; the two basic categories of history in the General Certificate of Education syllabus are English and European, and study of America tends to end with the Declaration of Independence—with a cursory description of the Civil War tacked on afterwards, in parenthesis. Americans, as far as the English school curriculum is concerned, are still a lot of rebellious colonists.

Yet at the same time these children have one vivid impression of modern America thrust at them constantly; the more misleading because they have nothing against which to measure it. Daniel Boorstin, Professor of American History at the University of Chicago, gives a wryly accurate picture in his book *The Image:*

> The most important single influence (in producing an image of America) in parts of the world which have heard of the United States has been the prevalence of American movies. I encountered this myself in a trip to South Asia in 1960. For example, in Bangalore in southern India, we had an admirable United States Information Agency library with a wide selection of books. It was being visited by perhaps 250 people a day. Of these, a considerable number were coming in to escape the dust, or because they had no other place to do their schoolwork. Some came to learn about the United States or other Western cultures. At the same time a half dozen motion picture houses in the city customarily showed American movies. Here the language barrier almost disappeared. The people reading in the USIA library were a handful. Any one of the movie houses offered images of America to many more people and at a far greater rate than that at which the library was offering them ideas about America.

As in Bangalore, so in those seething states which treat U.S. libraries only as useful bomb-targets; and so, less alarmingly, in Britain. A similar library of books and periodicals covering every aspect of American life and thought lies in the U.S. Embassy in Grosvenor Square; but most of its visitors are expatriate Americans. The natives are affected far more by the imported American films and "canned" television shows which pour through the country an eagerly assimilated stream of ephemera. Millions of English minds half-consciously form their impression of America from the talk-big-act-tough attitude and the monochrome morality of the Western, and see these reflected in Berlin and Guantánamo, Dallas and Mississippi, and the Polaris submarines sitting quiet and sinister in the Holy Loch. In comedies and melodramas alike they see modern America as a uniformly prosperous, middle class kaleidoscope of fitted kitchens and central heating, martinis and monstrous cars, spoiled teenagers and ulcer-ridden businessmen. It seems an upholstered world, and it seems to be echoed in the comparatively bulky pay packets of American servicemen stationed in Britain, and the lush abundance available to their shopping wives in PXs. During the war and the bleak, austerity-bound years after it, many people in Britain must have been envious—however unwittingly—of the bright-buttered life of America. Now that we ourselves creep nearer to that kind of prosperity, the envy has perhaps become a curous kind of resentment, as we find that every new aspect of our way of life is something that has already been in existence for years in the U.S.A. Some are simply the obvious appurtenances of a society with more money to spend: washing machines, television sets, refrigerators, electric razors, electric mixers, electric toothbrushes. But the supermarkets and the high-pressure advertising, the ornate packaging, the proliferation of American influence and capital in industries like drugs, motor-cars, soap powders, cereals, cosmetics—all these are like the accent and style of the English pop-singer: mid-Atlantic, an unnatural grafting of one civilization on to another.

"The dollars are moving in behind the ideas," wrote Lord Francis-Williams darkly in *The American Invasion* in 1962. "Britain, and much of Europe besides, is being made over." It may not be quite as bad as that; but many of the British, in their hitherto tight little island, find the image they are given of America sufficiently alarming to deplore its influence—without waiting to find out whether or not the image is a true one. Everywhere, among what might be called the British intelligentsia, small anti-American prejudices creep and grow. American scholarship is condemned as prolix, overearnest and trivial. All but the most expensive American clothes are said to be badly made; seams come apart, buttons fall off, wisps of extraneous thread dangle from hems like cobwebs. American pianos are all terrible. The bodywork of American cars crumples if you look at it (though no one is quite foolhardy enough to extend the attack to American cars' engines). American furniture, advertising, salesmanship and martinis are vulgar. The only literate Americans this century has produced are William Faulkner (though even then one has to forget that dreadful Nobel Prize speech, so embarrassing), Mary McCarthy and James Baldwin. T. S. Eliot couldn't really have been an American; look what happened to Isherwood, Auden, and Aldous Huxley when they went to live there. America is Philistine, materialist and anti-art; the only worthwhile American composers are those influenced by the Orient, the only worthwhile American painters, apart from the immigrant-based school in New York, those who depart to live in Europe. The only genuine American art form is jazz, produced by an oppressed minority. Most Americans are bores; nice people, quite often, but boring nonetheless. A first degree from an American university is worthless; an American Ph.D. degree in any non-scientific subject is laughable.

So it goes. Each prejudice has a small grain of truth somewhere in its foundations, but each is derived only from the image; from a misleading picture of America which, through the complacent arrogance of the British, becomes more misleading in

Britain than anywhere else. It is a picture which, once formed, is self-perpetuating; when the British go to the United States they tend to come back and write or talk only about those aspects which people expect to hear and sneer about: women's clubs, Las Vegas, Manhattan Island, Disneyland, political conventions, Texas and Boston. A few examples of Americana carry, in London particularly, a distinct kind of tough prestige: black Ford Thunderbirds, button-down collar shirts, the Peanuts comic strip, Parker fountain pens, Jack Daniels Black Label bourbon, gramophone records of new Broadway musicals, the possession of friends with an apartment overlooking Central Park. Eminences such as Lord Snow of Leicester are much given to wistful public praise of high-powered scientific establishments like M.I.T. and Cal Tech., and glossy magazines like *Queen* and *Town* clearly admire *Esquire* and the old persona of the *New Yorker*. But except among advertising men and the younger members of the Institute of Directors, it is generally thought less interesting to have visited the United States than to have visited Africa or South America. And those Englishmen who have never visited America, however sophisticated and intelligent they be, show a marked eagerness to believe in the general awfulness of the accepted American image. When I wrote some articles in *The Sunday Times* about my first trip to the U.S., I had an enthusiastic letter from one of my least conservative friends: a novelist, translator and general littérateur with a double first from Cambridge. The articles had been in places critical, but nowhere violently adverse; and this was not a man I would have expected to make quick judgments at second-hand. But: "I loved your American pieces," he wrote. "I always think it can't be as frightful as people say it is; and then I read something like your articles, or Julian Mitchell's novel, and realise that my God the place is even worse than one expects. . . ."

Than one *expects*. Let no Englishman be so naïve as to praise the American way of life to his countrymen. They've never seen it, but they already know how terrible it is.

Thus when the young Englishman visits the United States for the first time, what he finds differs spectacularly not only from everything he has ever seen at home, but from everything he was led to expect. Suddenly the pressure is released, and astonishment bursts out in an effervescent flood. "I must tell you what I feel about the U. S. A.," wrote another friend to me, on his fifth day in America; a hitherto cool, rational journalist whom I would have expected to raise analytical eyebrows in all directions: "I think it is like falling in love again. . . ."

The disrespect and the delight both come, of course, from the same root: ignorance. The British are not the only ones who are ignorant about the United States; you can find much the same combination of reactions among the French, the Germans, the Italians and almost everybody else. Although all these countries know one another fairly well, they labor under a curious series of misconceptions about the U.S.A.—even while they are themselves adopting, as their standards of living rise, many habits and ideas which are essentially American.

It would be very easy to blame this whole phenomenon on distance. Of course the peoples of the world lack first-hand knowledge of America and Americans; the United States is several thousand miles away from everybody except the Canadians and South Americans, and even in the era of jet transport only relatively few people are able to cross those miles. By the same token Americans are equally ill-informed about Europe; ask the average American businessman to identify Georges Pompidou, George Brown and Georg Solti, and you will receive some confused replies. We are all out of day-to-day touch with one another; we communicate only through newspapers and the mail.

But distance is not the only culprit. It is not the fault of the Atlantic that Europeans receive this apocalyptic shock when they first visit the U.S.A.—nor, altogether, is it the fault of the Europeans themselves. It is, far more than you may ever have supposed, the fault of the United States.

For America is without doubt the most self-sufficient country in the world. The American can find everything that he needs at home: history, prosperity, beauty, contentment; the security of power, the freedom of spaciousness, the excitement of adventure. For more than a century now, he has not needed to look outside his own shores, and in many cases his own state, for any purpose except those of supporting his country's cause with arms or money, visiting the antique quaintness of the Old World, or welcoming those who want to escape from the Old World to become Americans. In general, he knows that home is best, and he envies no man except another American. And although this is a fine healthy condition to be in, it has a strangely stultifying effect on international relations. Americans have a well-justified reputation abroad for being friendly, outgoing persons; and so they are, when you see them at home. Friendly, outgoing—and self-sufficient, to an extent which draws a tight band of incomprehension around the shores of the U.S.A.

This barrier, of incomprehension on the one side and misunderstanding on the other, is what I have chosen to call the Golden Curtain: a barrier which is scarcely even known to exist. The Iron Curtain between the East and the West may seem more solid, but a danger is halved when recognized. The European can at least see the Iron Curtain; can recognize, that is, the difference between its two sides. And although the world he sees on the other side may be shocking or depressing, it is not strange; it can be described in terms he has himself known. He knows what it is like to live under a regime which one may resent or fear; or to endure deprivation stoically because one believes one's country can in that way accomplish what it thinks to be right. He has lived through the bleak tedium of years of necessary austerity. Political ideologies apart, the European and the Russian have probably more everyday terms of reference in common than can ever bridge the Atlantic. (I don't labor this point; it is of course as depressing to talk to a sheltered Russian as to a sheltered American. The one asks you how many children still work down

British mines; the other inquires kindly whether you have ever seen television at home.)

But the world behind the Golden Curtain resembles nothing the European has experienced before. He has no real idea that the great mid-Atlantic divide really exists at all. Why should he? It is easy enough to grasp the false image of America given by the popular media. And in much the same way, many Americans who leave America for any length of time find themselves so appalled by the picture everyone abroad seems to have of their homeland that they can hardly wait to return to the reality—and to forget these disturbing experiences within what seems, whether they call it a New Frontier or a Great Society, to be a haven of secure content. A terrifying number of the occupants of the United States of America are not aware in any true sense that any other part of the world exists. They are trapped by their own self-image, just as the vast majority of citizens of the Soviet Union and China are trapped by propaganda and introversion: these three great nations, heirs to the power of the world, masters of the world's survival, are appallingly alike in their insulation and self-esteem.

But America may be in the greatest peril. The Iron Curtain is visible, from both sides; the Communists officially recognized its existence when they built the Berlin Wall. Though the Chinese have built no new wall recently, the Bamboo Curtain is also obvious enough. But nobody can see the Golden Curtain. Everyone thinks he knows about the Americans, and the Americans think they know about the world; and both sides are wrong. This book is about the reasons why.

2 ⁂ Behind The Curtain

> *"For the visiting European, a trip through*
> *the United States has, almost inevitably,*
> *the character of an exposé, and the American,*
> *on his side, is tempted by love of his country*
> *to lock the inquiring tourist in his hotel room*
> *and throw away the key. His contention that*
> *the visible and material America is not the real*
> *or only one is more difficult to sustain*
> *than was the presumption of the 'other' Germany*
> *behind the Nazi steel."*
>
> —MARY MCCARTHY,
> *"America the Beautiful,"*
> in On the Contrary

The moment of departure is the moment of doubt. However certain you have been, however deep an impression the travelers' tales and the expatriate natives have made, you know in the moment before leaving that you have not the smallest idea what you will find when you arrive, over there on the other side. The pity is that you never know this until that second, and that afterwards you forget it again.

There is, like as not, fog hanging gray over London Airport. In the departure lounge that is a no-man's-land between Britain and Abroad, the travelers prattle in groups, or sit nervous alone, most of them clutching little oblong carrier-bags of duty-free whiskey or gin. "Farg," says one American to another American, in tones of satisfied disgust. When you go to live in America, you will spend hours indignantly rebuffing those who merrily associate London only with life lived in a thick yellow pea-soup: really, you will plead, it isn't like that at all. Yet every second time you go back, the fog will be there: lying below the aircraft like a lagging of thick raw wool, or misting the airport buildings to a ghostly gray. It's difficult to avoid a sense of symbolism when the great Boeing 707, silver torpedo-engines swaying gracefully beneath the long swept-back wings, consumes time and space and silence in one sudden huge gulp, and roars up from the fog-hazed land into a deep blue sunlit sky.

Six hours later, caviare and champagne later, kangaroo-tail soup and chicken later, the sun has gone down over banks of cirrostratus that ripple like a thin snow, and the blue sky has become a vast orange hemisphere upturned on a glowing red line. Below, in the dark floor of the sky, those lines of prickling lights are America; blinking and winking and not the same, somehow, as the lights of Britain from the air. The bright patches have more color, and the starry necklaces of the roads seem curiously to flow—for they are made up not of the static studded streetlamps that crisscross Britain at night, but of moving headlamps shining from moving cars. Thus the first that you see of America is movement, a sense of improbability; and although the first Transatlantic ground under your feet is solid and ordinary enough, the unreality begins at once to take command. Perhaps it is because your eyes see the clocks here standing at 9:00 P.M., and force your body to forget that by English time it is two in the morning; perhaps it is simply weariness. Whatever the reason, in the beginning all the rules of normality seem to have disappeared, in the echoing customs-hall where passengers stand beside baggage-chutes with their own wire-netting trolleys on sturdy wheels (you will see these later in every supermarket, but now you have never seen them before). Once you pass through immigration and customs, the fist visible native Americans are three enormous striding policemen in leggings, with revolver-butts swinging on their hips. While your eyes remain fascinated on the revolvers, your hand reaches out to the glass door of the main entrance hall (the hall that must henceforth be to you a lobby, as lifts must be elevators, and a flat an apartment, and the autumn the fall). But the door opens of itself before your fingers reach the glass: and inside, facing you, are two idly chatting nuns, a tall thin brooding man in a Stetson, a fat father in a checked shirt with three terrible children who have sat down squalling on the marble floor; and as theme to the mixture, rising over the squalls, a weird monotonous chanting from a line of teenage girls who are marching round and round a high gallery overhead, each of them dressed as Little Bo-peep. A manic un-reality begins to creep over all the world around, and the weary mind tries wildly to fit every unfamiliar detail into the nearest and most obvious slot. Go into the airport restaurant for a cup of coffee, and find the waitress slapping napkin, coaster and glass of iced water in front of you, whether you will want them or not, before you can blink—well, of course; all Americans drink iced water all the time. Everyone said so. Go into a tobacconist's kiosk for matches, not because you need them but because you want to spend your first few American cents, and the man pushes over a book of matches and waves the money away—well, of course, Americans give things away free all the time. Everyone said so.

This is the way the images have grown; this is the way that at first they seem to perpetuate themselves. Things must be classi-fied, as a defense. The evening wears on in America, and the dawn comes up in Britain—a place that has become, suddenly, no more real than the dim remembrance of the actual world that hovers round a man dreaming (and a place that will never seem the same again—as, after a vivid dream one is not again the same as before, being shaken not merely by the vividness of the dream, but by the fact that one's own sober brain could have believed it real). Everything at first seems to shout out lavishness. The first thing that you eat, in this unreal world, is a hamburger, a giant hamburger with strange sweet-tasting seductive relishes inside, and it is called a Mighty Mo. The first hotel room that you are given is subtly different from any hotel room you have ever been given before, though all those in which you stay afterwards, in this country, will be more or less the same as this: a large bed, venetian blinds with twenty-four intertangled cords, a television set that will receive five channels of the twelve marked on its dial, but none of them distinctly; one sheet and one blanket on the bed, an insinuation (sometimes a blast) of heat from the radiators paneled into the wall, a constant humming from the brown box on the windowsill that is the air-conditioning. A telephone, with the letter "O" and the numeral "o" marked in separate holes so that all the numbers you dial for the first three weeks you will dial wrong; a box of paper tissues, that before long will make you think handkerchiefs the most remarkably insanitary survival in the Western world; a small tiled separate bathroom (something to be specially requested in Britain, but a commonplace in the U.S.A.) where you will spray water ineptly everywhere in an effort to find which knob turns on the shower, and gaze astonished at the cellophane-wrapped toothglasses and the proud strip of paper stretched across the lavatory seat announcing with impressive obscurity: "This seat is SANITIZED for your protection. . . ."

It is the unfamiliarity of small things that makes the biggest impact at first: always, in any strange country or town. And the small things in America are, although the country is so huge and diverse, the things that tend to be waiting for you wherever in the country you may go (thus to become soon to you, as to the American, so ordinary as to escape notice altogether). They divide themselves with remarkable naturalness into two: they are the cosseters, and the signs of freedom. They are the first rustles of the Golden Curtain.

Most of the cosseters are urban; they are the details designed to make life pleasanter, to sugar the pill, to rub the corners away. Most grow from some commercial motive; most end as a commercial habit, of variously sinister proportions. There is the music, for instance: the neo-pop, neo-classical mish-mash of Broadway medleys and cut-down Tchaikowsky, all arranged to the same characterless idiom of soupy strings and muffled brass, which grows over all the radio networks like some unconqerable spreading weed, and filters taped through the air of hotel lobbies, supermarkets, department stores, taxicabs, aeroplanes approaching or leaving the ground, airports, workshops, offices and restaurants. It fills the small streets of shopping centers, sometimes even booming out from loudspeakers on strategically placed poles over all their vast parking lots. It jangled, relentlessly Christmasy, over the two acres of market garden where my husband and I went to buy our Christmas tree. And once I had lived in a Midwestern hotel for three weeks, going up and down to a room on the eleventh floor, before I realized that the same Midcult melody was washing over my consciousness several times a day from the walls of the elevators. It is not long before this sound is heard without any effort or awareness at all. At that point, its success begins: as with the music played to battery hens to increase their rate of laying eggs; or, presumably on the same principle, the music played to housewives in supermarkets, which is said to produce a variety of mild hypnosis under whose influence the impulse-buying rate rises noticeably. Few Americans really realize the extent to which they imbibe this gentle drug; but very many people grow so accustomed to it that they automatically switch on the radio, or even the television, when they wake up in the morning and when they come home at night: never fully listening, but never turning the knob off again until they leave the house or go to bed. Even then there may be a portable radio or television set in the bedroom; one Californian couple I met (California being what it is) had a television built into their bedroom ceiling. As nature abhors a vacuum, so many Americans abhor silence. It is as if they have come to rely on their formless music—soothing, reassuring, undemanding, endless—as a necessary prop to life: an anodyne, a tranquillizer. It is remarkably like the description given me by an Episcopalian bishop of one widespread American attitude towards God.

Of the other cosseters, many are *things,* aimed at increasing material comfort: the central heating, the air conditioning, the frozen biscuits. They of course are largely responsible for the image of affluence which shouts loudest of all among the first superficial impressions; when a deep freeze, a waste-disposer, a dishwasher, a second car are symbols of wealth in one's own country —as they are in Britain—they must inevitably seem the same in another. It is only when his first impressions have begun to settle and clear that the Englishman, confused by an apparent uniformity of accent into believing America really free of social stratification, realizes that these are symbols of universal *vie de luxe* only in the sense that English municipal housing would seem so to the Indian or Chinese laborer. Wealth, like speed, is relative. The point about the so-called symbols of affluence in America is their ability to smooth the corners of life, and so, perhaps, of national personality: it is easier to drive the car with automatic transmission (alas for the road accident figures) than the car with conventional gear-shift. It is easier to drive any car than to take a train, bus or bicycle, or to walk on one's own two feet; to use a packaged biscuit mix than to mix the ingredients oneself; to buy by installments than to save for a total payment; to "charge it," than to pay cash. There are not a great many shops in London, let alone in Britain, where a salesman will automatically ask: "Will this be on account, madam?" But in America, it is a rare store in which he does not ask, as easily as blinking: "Charge or cash?" And it is a rare middle-income American couple who do not possess between them charge-cards providing an open sesame to several stores, a telephone company, at least one type of gasoline and, if the husband is connected in any way with the world of business, two or three restaurants, a hotel chain and an airline. The plastic folder with slots for a dozen charge-cards is a safe Christmas present in the U.S.A.

The true complexity of the cosseters shows itself to the foreigner only when he has lived in the U.S. for some time. They prove the masters, in the end, of that fairly common phenomenon in America, the homesick European wife. A young immigrant couple arrives, and the husband soon settles happily into a job offering far better pay and prospects than anything he would have found at home; he comes easily to terms with America, and it is not long before he is thinking ahead to the time when he can take out citizenship papers. At this point, a year or two after arrival, he begins to have trouble with his wife, who is still not reconciled to the loss of her family, friends and home surroundings; she is constantly criticizing American schools, parents and children, she appears to have developed a deep nostalgic affection for socialized medicine, and she waits like a fretful child for the arrival of the mailman each day, observing plaintively as she does so that "at home" the post used always to arrive at eight in the morning, not at lunchtime. There is no help for it: sooner or later the new immigrant takes her back to Britain (or France, or Germany, or Switzerland) for a fortnight's holiday, hoping gloomily that the sight of her parents will either reconcile her to absence or decide her to stay with them. And nine times out of ten, the result is totally predictable. America prevails; the victory goes to the cosseters.

"It was marvelous at first, seeing the family and hearing English voices all round you." She was an English girl from a modest home in Croydon; her husband was now employed by an engineering firm in Pittsburgh. "It was like coming down to earth after years up in an aeroplane. I actually cried when I saw my first double-decker bus. And my brother's kids seemed so bright, and I heard the BBC again, and all the hoardings on the streets looked really attractive and—well, in good taste." She grinned, and wrinkled her nose: the phrase no longer came naturally. "But after about a week, well, I dunno, I began to feel sort of restless. My parents' and my brother's houses seemed terribly small, much smaller than I'd remembered. And so cold. It was November, of course, but it was much colder than it had been when we left Pittsburgh. I'd forgotten the business of all of you huddling round a fire in one room to keep warm, and having to steel yourself to get out of bed in the morning because the air feels like the Arctic. I hadn't thought of us as having got all that much better off in the States, but the more we all talked, the more I realized how many things I'd come to take for granted, that we'd never have had if we'd stayed in Britain. My kitchen, and being able to have the washer and drier down in the basement, and the size of our Chevrolet—and d'you know, I worked it out, we spend three times as much on food every week here as my sister-in-law in Surrey, and she's got two kids—*and* that isn't just a matter of prices being higher in the States. You live better here, that's all there is to it. And that's what brought me back again. What you miss about England is things like Kew Gardens in the spring, and being able to pop down to the shop on the corner for a chat—but, well, you can remember those, can't you? It's a lot more difficult to have to remember central heating every time you get down on your knees to light a fire."

Thus the restless immigrant wives come back, to relax more or less into satisfaction with their surroundings, and to become, in the end, Americans. And the sense of being in the midst of plenty, of being partakers of a better life than the rest of the world, laps them around as it does the native Americans themselves: the complacency which is raised so often as a banner in "the fight against Communism"—the conviction that, given the choice, nobody in his right mind could conceivably prefer any other pattern of living to that available in America. Once, at a university staff party in Ohio, I heard a professor of history seriously put forward the view that if all restrictions were lifted on the borders of the Soviet bloc, and all information freely exchanged, every single inhabitant of Eastern Europe would begin planning to make tracks for the U.S.A. "What is there," he demanded, "that would make any of them want to stay behind?" Nobody offered any suggestions; heads nodded, with sad complacent sighs. Of course everyone from over there would want to share their enviable lot if he had the chance. It involved, after all, not merely the comfortable cosseting of material things, but Freedom.

And the sense of freedom, indeed, is the second of the two irresistible whoops with which America greets new arrivals. Nobody can sense it quite so acutely as the stranger, and he himself will sense it only while he remains strange: once he has settled down, it will curiously dissipate. For the freedom in the air of America is, especially for the British, a matter of contrasts. It shows itself first in mere speech: few Americans have an experienced enough ear to tell one kind of English accent from another, and suddenly therefore the Englishman is liberated from the label he has worn all his life at home. He is not yet saddled with the American social shibboleths; he knows only that his own no longer apply, and he is suddenly free of the various handicaps that go with the accents of Oxford or Bethnal Green, Pinner or Bradford. Nobody cares about the precise nuance of the way he pronounces the words "go" or "try" or "way"—they are aware only that he sounds English. This too can be disconcerting, of course. On my first visit to the United States I went into a Washington drugstore and asked for some toothpaste. A strange glazed expression came over the face of the girl behind the counter, and she called to another assistant: "Joe! Come here a minute." A large, amiable-looking man ambled over to us and the girl turned back to me: "What was it you wanted, honey?"

"I just said, please could I have some toothpaste."

The girl gave Joe the proud smile of one exhibiting a prize. "Isn't it beaudiful? I just love that English accent." They both stood chatting warmly for some minutes, and eventually they fetched my toothpaste. I have tried to imagine some complementary incident happening in England, but it is difficult; except in warm, cozy areas like some parts of Yorkshire or the East End of London, the English are much too constricted by politeness to comment on anything so personal as a foreigner's accent —to his face, at least.

Not so the Americans. It is another reason for the impression of freedom, the sense that here, anybody can do anything. It is like the difference between, for another instance, the structure of taxicabs in London and in New York. In London (where every cab is still built to a height which, by rule of the Hackney Carriage Act of 1843, enables a man to sit upright inside wearing a top hat) a glass partition still firmly marks the division of status between driver and passenger, so that a driver feeling inclined for friendly conversation must either bellow or dislocate his neck. In New York—and for that matter every other American city— the cab is of course simply a car. Most drivers are thus able to throw in with the ride a free discourse on politics, the weather, international affairs and other drivers, to the delight of tourists and visiting journalists, and are quite likely to join uninvited in any animated conversation which happens to be going on in the back seat. Why not? This is America, land of opportunity, where every man is as good as the next—in theory, anyway, and in the Constitution—and where imagination, ambition and "drive" are enough to overcome almost any other handicap (except, perhaps, the color of one's skin). A single generation can build a bridge over any social or financial gulf: within a week in America you can meet a prominent managing director whose father was a glass-blower, a professor who is the son of a farm laborer, a prosperous lawyer whose childhood was spent barefoot in a poor Jewish quarter of Chicago. The image of the poor boy who ends up in the chairman's seat is a commonplace which has no equivalent in Britain; it can produce an extraordinary sense of refreshment, of lighthearted freedom, of room to stretch and grow, in someone from a country where ability is only just beginning to replace time as the only passport to accepted success. There are too many Galsworthys in England still; you can hear the crackle of their rising eyebrows in the phrases "Grammar-school undergraduate" . . . "rough diamond" . . . "self-made man." The really deep admiration there is reserved not for the Henry Ford or the Charles Clore but for figures who have permanence behind them, and can call forth warmer phrases like "traditional loyalties

. . . the old guard . . . the right ideas." After longer observation one suspects that this sense of inherited merit permeates most Americans too, at least in the East; their fascination with the British Royal Family is the same impulse that lends status to their own "aristocratic" families like the Kennedys, the Cabots and the Lodges. But at first, degree seems absent. "Men are there seen," wrote de Tocqueville, "on a greater equality in point of fortune and intellect, or, in other words, more equal in their strength, than in any other country of the world, or in any age of which history has preserved the remembrance." In the first traumatic plunge into America, you hear the echoes of his wonder still.

And of course, the place is so big. Nothing can forestall that curious childish astonishment with which the newcomer first tries to comprehend the vastness of the United States: when he looks down from an aircraft thirty thousand feet above the Rocky Mountains to see nothing but range after range of snow-silted peaks in every direction; when he drives over the Nevada Desert, and knows himself enlapped by a relentless unbroken horizon of dusty, rocky, scrub-patched wilderness; when he boards an express train in San Francisco to cross from Pacific south to Atlantic north, and leaves it in New York after three days and two nights of speed—after crossing this one country in a journey roughly as long as that from London to Baghdad. It is at about this stage that the Englishman begins to realize the full enormity of the fact that the whole of the United Kingdom would fit comfortably inside the state of Colorado, and would take up about a third of the area of Texas; and that although America has a population only between three and four times that of Britain, it has thirty-two times as much space. He has always vaguely known the figures, and the relative sizes of the countries on the map, but actually to feel what they mean is a sensation like moving from a one-room apartment into Buckingham Palace.

So there comes, very quickly after this, the impact of mobility: the most accurate part of the popular image of America—

and the most misleading. Europeans tend often to assume that Americans worship mobility, travel, speed, simply for their own sake: that there is some kink of instability in the whole nation, emerging in the dominance of the motor-car and the aeroplane. Not so: it is far more complicated than that.

A country as small as Britain can conveniently link all its main centers by a well developed railway network; Birmingham in the middle is after all only 110 miles from London in the south, and 201 from Newcastle in the north. And for businessmen—that vague generic term which is in any country a fair description of most working travelers—this kind of travel is enough. The regular B.E.A. Viscount flights between London, Manchester and Glasgow have become an accepted institution now, but still the first-class compartments on morning and evening trains are full of briefcase-carriers stoutly claiming that they prefer a direct city-to-city rail journey. And many of them always will. Since an airport must always be about fifteen miles from its city center, there will never be any point in flying from London to Bristol while the Bristolian express from Paddington can cover the 116 miles in a hundred minutes.

But America, and the American businessman, cannot escape the tyranny of the country's size. St. Louis, in the middle, is 1,193 miles from Boston in the north and 1,925 from Los Angeles in the south. And as for east-west travel: the 154 miles between Cardiff and London can hardly match the 3,063 between Seattle and New York. If the United States are to be properly united, as a functioning unit, air travel has to be as easily taken for granted as telephones or television. And so indeed it is; reaching a zenith in those multiplying short-hop "shuttle" flights for which the passenger pulls a card from an automatic machine in the airport lobby, fills it in with his name and address, hands it in at the gate as he boards the plane, and pays his fare to the stewardess in mid-air as if he were on a bus. In fact, he probably takes flights like these far more often then he ever boards a bus.

But far fewer passengers fly the equally short distance from the Eastcoast cities up to Montreal or Quebec. Far fewer businessmen commute monthly between New York and London or Paris than do between New York and Los Angeles, or San Francisco and Washington. The Golden Curtain is in the way. Americans think big in terms of distance and speed inside their own country because they have to; there's no other way to exist. But the man who lives in the big house, tramping over enormous floors all day, does not necessarily want to cross over to the little house across the street.

This, however, you do not see at first. You see only an immense freedom and openness of outlook in the ease with which people use aeroplanes. You see the same in the lavish scale of the railways, and the roads. Whatever the changing nature of their economics, the American railroads have an enormous archaic romance about them, like something out of Mark Twain, that seems to mark the survival of the old pioneer outlook; the image of the wagon train setting off along the California Trail from Missouri, or of the riverboats making their leisurely way down the Mississippi. The railroads are a part of the first freedom, the time when anyone could go anywhere, pretty well, because there was so much of America that was still unclaimed and unexploited. The romance survives in the big long-distance trains, almost the only ones that make money now: the giant locomotives that hoot long and deep and mournful, like ocean liners, and the cars high-stepped and silvery outside and grubby within—except on crack expresses like the California Zephyr, which are like long snaking hotels. The romance is in the sight of the names, magic as sailors' plunder when you are deep in the murk of a city like Chicago or Detroit: Southern Pacific, Santa Fe, Union Pacific, Baltimore and Ohio; in the way the tracks roll casually beside, across, or even down the center of main streets in small towns, and the way the great trains stop in the middle of hundreds of miles of prairie at a point that has hardly even a platform, and that probably has not changed very greatly since the first settlers came there some two hundred years ago. It is on the railroads that the stranger begins to feel, inside the invigoration of the sense of freedom, the first glimmers of what the land behind the Golden Curtain is going to be like when it shows its real—and very new and very old and infinitely complicated—face.

It is as if you have got to know someone's features very accurately from looking at pictures of him in the newspapers, and then you come to meet him, and recognize him at once—"Of course! You look just as I expected!"—and are so taken by the appearance that it is a long time and a shock before you realize that the personality behind the face has not a great deal to do with the features at all. It is like that most of all with the motor-car, and with the roads.

Round and through the cities, the kings and queens of the American way of life run: the long six-lane transcontinental highways, cutting relentlessly straight through prairie and mountain and rolling farming land, given deliberate curves sometimes as reinforcement for the ominous signs on bridges overhead: "STAY AWAKE" . . . "STAY ALIVE." Looking down from the air, wherever you pass over great stretches of forest, or of wooded hills, you find them dissected by long smooth lines: sometimes the wide swathes cut for a ski slope or a fire-break, and sometimes the thinner pencil holding a power line; but most often the long cleaving stroke of a road, obeying the contours only when a cutting cannot be blasted out, or a tunnel driven through.

They are seductive, these roads. You drive towards them down the smaller access road, curling round in a cloverleaf circle and merging gradually, gradually, into the main stream of the highway (or thruway, freeway or expressway, because they are given different names in different places and no one seems to think one term more accurate than the rest). As you pause at first by the red round STOP sign, on the edge of the roaring road, it is like nosing a dinghy out from harbor into a wide perilous tide-race beyond. For an instant it seems impossible that you can ever get into it, without being shattered by speed. But in the average American car you have one hundred and forty horse-power be-

neath your foot, and suddenly with only a small decisive movement you are part of the tide-race. Soon you are hardly aware,
flicking an indicator and changing lanes to pass one of the vast
thunderous locomotive-length diesel trucks, that your speedom-
eter needle is creeping past eighty miles per hour. If you miss one
exit to a nearby town, or to one of the always identical chain restaurants (twenty-eight different kinds of ice-cream, Golden-Fried
Jumbo-Size Gulf Butterfly Shrimp, salad with everything) it
seems only slightly tiresome to have to drive the twenty or thirty
miles to the next. Speed obviates distance: the highways let the
Americans dominate their country's size. More than railroads,
airlines or any other single institution, they make a framework
for the growth of a pattern of living. Once a fast road exists,
every kind of development that is permitted will follow; the billboards and neon signs and restaurants and motels spring up in a
gaudy cluttering jumble along any highway that is not controlled
into tree-lined peace. Along Route 128, outside Boston, giant rec-
tangular factories lie isolated among acres of parking lot; they
are miles from any housing areas, and ill-served by public transport, but that's no matter—the workers' cars can spin easily down
the road from a radius of thirty miles around. And the workers
themselves no longer need to live in, or even near, the town.
They are freed from the pull of urban gravity by the motor-car
—and the roads.

Thus suburbia has grown. It is not suburbia as the English
know the term; not the image of street after red-brick street of
identical semi-detached houses, each enclosed in its neat fenced
plot of garden. There are pejorative overtones about the word in
America, certainly, but they are sinister in a different kind of
way. The first and most astonishing thing about the suburbs, as
you drive newly arrived through the United States, is that they
do not appear to be there. No mirror-image rows; none of the
brick-and-tile wastes of British suburban streets. Instead, one
finds attractive, idiosyncratic houses built mainly of wood, with
double doors, porches and patios; each set among its own few

trees, with only grass keeping it from the road and the house next door. The sense of freedom, of space and openness, is back again, very strong. Here, very little is fenced in. There is no need; few people pass on the roads. Only cars.

(But in one suburb, on the road from the airport in a Northern city that could have been any other Northern city, I did see children playing on the sidewalk outside the peeling doors of battered graceful houses; and one prosperous-looking velvet-collared man said to another, sitting in the airport limousine: "There were nice houses here, until They took them over. Always the same, whenever They move into a district. It goes down." And because this was the enlightened North, there seemed at first no obvious meaning in the deliberate words to my new-arrived ears; until I realized that every man and woman on the street, and every child playing, was a Negro.

Much later, a Negro journalist said to me cheerfully: "D'you realize what's happening? The whites perhaps don't know it, but they're leaving the cities to us. Everywhere they move farther out, and when they've gone we move nearer downtown.")

When there is space, and a good road, the suburban communities begin to grow. Soon, some enterprising developer will build a shopping center, and the department stores and banks and supermarkets in the center of the town will all open branches there. They have no choice; nothing will draw the everyday shoppers back to the town center again. The giant screen of a drive-in movie theater will then rise nearby, and "specialty" restaurants like pancake houses and waffle shops appear beside the roads—always surrounded by the all-important acreage of parking lot. All these things are scattered through an area of several square miles. And before long, the suburbanite, who was at first freed by his car from the need to live close to the town and to his work, has become his car's prisoner. He cannot lead a normal life without it. His suburb, which owes its whole structure to the availability of the motor-car, went through no phase of development during which its inhabitants possessed nothing but their own two feet; as a result its public transport system is often poor and sometimes nonexistent. There begins then the tyranny of the two-car system, which for the family who can afford it is by no means so much of a faintly improper self-indulgence as it seems to be to the untraveled Englishman. When the suburban husband drives to work (as he is bound to do, because this is the way the suburbs grew up in the first place) the suburban wife is left without transport of her own between about eight-thirty in the morning and five-thirty at night. She seldom has a bus service within easy reach, and the supermarket is probably half-an-hour's walk away, if it is within walking distance at all. One young couple I know, for instance, live in a newly built house on a hilltop which is part of a growing Massachusetts suburban area; last Christmas the husband gave the wife her own car. "Sounds a great gift, doesn't it?" she said. "But honestly, we were going mad with only the one. Bob's firm is about eleven miles away down Route 128—the only way to get there is by car. But the car is also the only way for me to get to the stores. So every morning I'd drive him into work so that I could have transport during the day—and that meant getting both kids up as well and taking them, because they were too small to leave on their own. Then I'd have to take them again when I drove out to pick him up at night, and in the winter. . . ." She waved an expressive hand in silence. "The fun begins again, of course," said her husband cheerfully, "when one of the cars goes on the blink."

These last few pages of description sound, I dare say, a little naïve; a description of the obvious. What's so remarkable, to an American, about roads, cars and the newer suburbia? They are an ordinary part of life, not worth mentioning. Yet this is the point of mentioning them. It is precisely those innocuous things you take most for granted which can have the most influence on your attitudes and habits of mind.

Consider, for instance, the equivalent patterns in Britain, which have an equal effect upon us and our attitudes. There are today a number of expressways (called motorways) in Britain, carved with reluctant ruthlessness through cities and countryside to link the major centers; but the basic network of the country's roads is very old—in some cases two thousand years old. The broad highway along which trucks rumble from London to the southwest is still for the most part the Bath Road; still the route along which the stagecoaches clattered, the carts creaked, and the Roman legions marched. From it, as from all the rest, the side-roads wriggle and twine to join village and village, town and town, in the same casual pattern taken by the footpaths in the days before automobiles or even horses were common. In our small island, we cannot afford the space to reshape all these roads, however inconvenient to motorists they may sometimes be; and so we cannot mold our lives round fast long-distance road travel to the extent that you can. Our own pattern of bold direct routes arrived only when the Victorian railroad engineers drove their iron tracks (still called, in their confident phrase, "the permanent way") through the countryside, and even these do not have the same social effect as your roads. There can be no impulsive hopping into a car to drive five miles to a supermarket when the five miles involves half-an-hour on twisting roads, or a half-mile walk to a railroad station; the English housewife sticks instead to her small local store. And this same constriction produces the difference in the suburbs themselves. Ours did not grow, like yours, as the automobile grew; and they do not depend on the automobile now. Most of them are crowded, rather characterless places, and they begin outside every large town, once the central offices, shops, factories and public buildings thin out: street upon street of neat terraced or semi-detached brick houses, each with its own small tidy plot of garden behind a small tidy hedge or fence, and its TV aerial on the chimney. Most have a pub, and a few shops, within walking distance, with cinemas and bigger stores a short bus ride away; the car parked in the street or small garage tends to be a family car, used more for weekend outings than for daily chores, and often the wife cannot drive.

The people who live in these suburbs, commuting each day into city or factory estate by train or bus, do not often look far beyond the limits of their own lives. Home—journey—work—

journey—home . . . the middle and lower income groups of the people of Britain are a conservative lot, even though they may vote for the Labour party at election time—for there is nothing very revolutionary about Labour policies these days, nothing that can alter the ordinary man's way of life. Yet somehow that ordinary man is not conscious, in the way that you tend to be in the United States, of *having* any definable way of life. He jogs along. He is, like his roads, a kind of ancient accident; it is both his weakness and his strength. His pride in his country, and in his unremarkable surroundings—which function, but with no exciting aura of efficiency—is an inscrutable thing.

> Smile at us, pay us, pass us; but do not quite forget:
> For we are the people of England, that never have spoken yet . . . .

But the people of the United States have spoken, and continue to speak, very loud and clear; at first through the words of the Declaration of Independence, and now, more clearly than ever, through the manner in which they live. America, as has been observed a considerable number of times before, is a place of contrasts, and for every one of your first impressions you can find, if you stay there long enough, a complete opposite. But the first impressions of what Mary McCarthy called "the visible and material America" have this to be said for them: they make so strong an impact that from the very beginning the stranger can see how close a hold this fiercely individualistic way of life must have upon those born into it.

It isn't just a matter of the availability of seductive creature comforts; it's the sheer force of character the place has. Naturally the American must be preoccupied with his own surroundings, since their voice is so much stronger than any heard from outside; this is one obvious reason why he might seem voluntarily insulated from the rest of the world. But you do not find the real evidence of his insulation until you take a hard look not only at his surroundings, but at the reasons why they appear as they do.

3 ⁑ The Value of Riches

*"When the Europeans first came among them, the natives
of North America were ignorant of the value of riches,
and indifferent to the enjoyments that civilized man
procures for himself by their means. . . ."*

—DE TOCQUEVILLE,
Democracy in America

It is a large brown room with padded leather walls and thirteen
electric outlets, and it has the whole of the American way of life
inside.

On the bleached orange door, under a heavy bolt and chain,
hangs a cardboard notice reading: "I'm a Sleepyhead today! So
please move as quietly as you can." There is a picture of a little
man with a large yawn, in a bathrobe. On the other side of the
notice, the little man is leaping out of bed. "I've got an early date,"
his caption cries. "So, maid, please hustle and make up my room
as speedily as you can." The padded leather is attached to the walls
with rows of brass studs. More brass studs outline darker leather
panels set into cupboard doors. On a rough estimate there are
six thousand brass studs in this room.

But this is an American hotel: over-generous, as if it were trying to convince itself of something. Light blazes from seven different sources in the room, but little creeps in through the venetian
blinds even at midday; the central heating indoors remains at
seventy-five degrees, although the day is forty degrees colder outside.

43

The television set lurking like a giant grey eye behind the door relentlessly babbles advertisement ("Get Kissy, the toy that can really *show* affection!") through waves of excellent news and cartoons, terrible quiz shows, and educational lectures that would splendidly educate if only they didn't all begin exactly at the moment when the telephone gently shrills and a cool voice comes: "Your seven A.M. call, good morning . . . all rightie, you're welcome . . ."

Most of the other hotel residents are already up by then. Like the little man on the notice, they have an early date—at work, to which they will swish through the straight, crowded streets in one of the long cars from the prairie-like parking lot eight floors below.

They have made their breakfast in the self-contained rooms on this residential floor of the hotel: orange juice from the refrigerator that hums under the sink set into one wall: eggs cooked on the electric hotplate; coffee from the electric percolator. They have left their washing-up for one of the coloured maids, and half of them have forgotten to turn off their lights. But nobody minds. The prosperity of America, the constant pressure to scrap last year's model, or last month's, simply because it is no longer brand-new—all this leads to an extravagance that Americans themselves scarcely notice at all.

This room expects extravagance. In the nine cupboards and seventeen drawers, sixty-five pounds of air luggage makes only a pitiful gesture of gratitude. You can answer the challenge partly by stubbing cigarette-ends in all the five ashtrays, which is not difficult in a land where cigarettes cost about two shillings for twenty. But some of the offerings that accumulate every day defy consumption: the twelve folders of matches in mounting heaps beside the ashtrays; the bathroom, supplied now—for one person—with four bath towels, five face-cloths, six hand-towels and seven bars of soap. There is no way out. Life is padded, like the walls.

Only at night, alone in this remarkable hotel room, does one feel the pattern of life all around seem to flicker like the needle on a lie-detector. The venetian blinds glow, reddened by neon signs ten feet high across the street; the mutter of a late-night television programme undulates from the room next-door. But one letter is blacked out on the neon sign, to leave it reading 'Liquor S ore', and the television is disturbed by the rough honking of a locomotive out in the dark.

The refrigerator throbs and rattles in sudden decisive jerks, and the air-conditioning clucks like an unquiet hen all night. One cupboard, beneath its leather padding and showy, useless brass studs, creaks and creaks without a pause. I think it is that organised little man, trying to get out.*

Thus one European, writing back to a public at home upon first coming among the natives of North America—some hundred and thirty years after de Tocqueville, whose observation at the head of this chapter makes ironic reading now. To the new arrival today, the natives seem to have grown only too well aware of the value of riches. Courtesy seems to have come to mean lavishness; extravagance to be such a commonplace that the man who clings to a belief in moderation is in danger of being thought either eccentric or mean. When a foreigner looks at the most prosperous country in the world, its prosperity, not surprisingly, is the thing that first impresses him. A great proportion of the immigrants entering the United States today are drawn by the chance of sharing this prosperity; as, on a far smaller scale, it is the chance of a higher wage and a better standard of living which still attracts West Indians and Irishmen to the British Isles. Wealth is a vivid and inevitable part of the image of the U.S.A.

So it is that so many people make the very large mistake of classifying the United States as an affluent society *tout court.* "They base everything on materialist values, of course. . . ." says the lofty outsider surveying Broadway, where the advertisement display is free and the theater seats cost the earth. Perhaps: but this is the very warp of the Golden Curtain. The danger of the

* From an article by the author, "Padding Out Life," *The Sunday Times,* London, December 30, 1962.

American manner of valuing riches is twofold; it acts as a blind-fold both to those outside the country and those within. It leads many Europeans to dismiss the entire population of the United States as a lot of wealthy clods; and it blinds Americans themselves in a most curious way to the conditions, values and beliefs of the rest of the world.

Between the haves and the have-nots anywhere, nations as well as individuals, there is always a bottomless gulf of misunderstanding. The rich and the poor have never been able to speak the same language; they have had too many differing assumptions bred into them from birth. But both Americans and Europeans forget this. Their gulf of misunderstanding is so long established that they misunderstand even the reasons why the gulf exists. Instead of trying to understand precisely how the Americans are rich (in other words, the real implications and influence of wealth in their way of life), the Europeans pounce gleefully on statistics about poverty in the Appalachians which they can use to convince themselves—like ostriches—that the Americans are not really rich at all. And the Americans themselves? In their half of the marsh of misunderstanding, they are so embedded in the consequences of capitalism that they assume everyone else ought to be as well. If a man does not attach the same *kind* of value to riches as they do, their subconscious reasoning runs, it is because he doesn't have enough: let's give him some more. . . .

Thus the system of capitalism itself, the material foundation of the American dream, becomes a Transatlantic barrier simply because no one bothers to examine the assumptions it breeds, both in those who like it and in those who don't. (In fact, of course, its political and economic merits or demerits are not in this context important. It is simply a system by which one particular society lives, a system very little modified as yet by time—unlike that in Britain, where not only the tenets and practice of nineteenth-century capitalism have changed, but the national personality as well.)

Americans themselves tend even to avoid the word "capitalism" in argument, possibly because the Soviet Union uses it so often as a kind of symbol of the Evil Eye:

> For many years this term, which denotes that the men who own the business, or those who are directly or indirectly their agents, have a major responsibility for decision, has been regarded as vaguely obscene. All sorts of euphemisms—free enterprise, individual enterprise, the competitive system, and the price system—are currently used in its place. None of them has the virtue of being more descriptive and none is as succinct.
>
> JOHN KENNETH GALBRAITH, *American Capitalism*

"The men who own the business"—already in the one phrase there is a casual assumption. By his existence in a capitalist system, every American is a real or potential capitalist; and at the center of his universe there must, ipso facto, be the world of business (engagingly defined by the *Oxford English Dictionary* as "a commercial enterprise as a going concern. (mod.)"—after a three-inch historical definition beginning, in a nostalgic echo of past glory, with the word "diligence").

As a result, on an everyday level the world of business and its values have far more significance for the American-in-the-street than their English counterparts have for the Englishman. It is not merely a matter of occupations—though the U.S. Bureau of Statistics classifies these in such a way that some 70 per cent of the country's work force appears to be occupied in the Siamese-twin pursuits of business and industry. It is not even a matter of deliberate judgements made on the relative values to society of, say, banking, brewing and beachcombing. It is simply a matter of exposure.

In Britain, it is possible to live a normal, socially active life in any number of different *milieux*, and to come across no economic issues larger than the mortgage rate charged by building societies, or the increased purchase tax on Scotch. The world of business there is still to a great extent the concern of a self-propagating elite, and the ownership of stock even more so. The latter barriers have admittedly begun to crumble in places under the assault of the unit trusts, formed some five years ago, which make it possible for shares to be corporately owned by thousands of people who would never had dreamed (and still wouldn't) of approaching a stockbroker individually. But stock is still far less widely owned than in America.

The British "businessman," with his even more ambivalent fellow the "company director," exists in a world of his own, as distinctly set apart as is the City from the rest of London. The magnetism of the capital has a certain amount to do with this, of course; the City itself concentrates in one small space far more men and power than does any single American business center, even New York. In America, in fact, *every* major city is a business center; and if it isn't yet, it is trying to be.

For from the start, in the U.S.A., there has been no setting apart of business from the rest of the country's life. Here were no centuries of feudalism, or slow development of a mercantile class despised by aristocracy. Every man who first came, in the tremendous beginnings of the place, had the freedom and responsibility of making his own living from his own land; there was no lord or state to do it for him, and the only lord now is the company or corporation. It is in many ways a far more tightly-knit society than any except that of a totalitarian state. Everything is interwoven, and the warp of the weaving is always business, industry, money—the value of riches. If the intelligent Englishman can live a life divorced from all thought of finance except his own immediate problems, the intelligent American cannot. Economics are all around him. Consider, for instance, the things which the Republican Party claims as the greatest achievements of its Presidents:

> They shaped governmental policy which encouraged the development of the country's vast resources; built up its defenses; created its national banking system; established a currency which circulated throughout the world on a par with gold; made the credit of the country the most stable in the world; formulated economic

policies which made this country the leader among all nations in agriculture, mining and manufacturing—in short, made the United States first among the nations.

Republican Fact-Book, 1948

There is not a single issue mentioned which does not deal with money or its acquisition—with the possible exception of the defense program, and even that is currently one of the largest props of many American firms, with a total of about fifty billion dollars a year being spent, largely within the country, through government defense contracts. Is it idealistic, moral, ethical leadership which is cited as having "made the United States first among the nations"? Not at all. It is "the development of the country's vast resources," etcetera, etcetera. In the same way, it is virtually impossible to conduct a dinner-party discussion in the United States on any topic—with the occasional exception of civil rights—without finding the central theme becoming sooner or later, by some strange osmosis, an economic issue. Foreign policy? "I really can't understand Britain's attitude in making so many trade agreements with the Reds." Medicine? "These goddam dentists—ten bucks a visit, and not a penny from Blue Cross–Blue Shield unless you go into the hospital. . . ." The arts? "Those musicians at the Met, now what gives them the idea they can get a *60 per cent* increase in pay?"

The law? I once asked an extremely pleasant and prosperous Manhattan lawyer for a breakdown of the divisions of his profession. "Well," he said, "there are the political lawyers, who hang round the right clubhouses and get to be judges if they play their cards well. Then the ambulance-chasers—the negligence lawyers, making their money from the thousands you can get in damages from insurance. The petty bourgeoisie, poddling along modestly like your small-town solicitors: the captive lawyers, who join one firm and become its house counsel and even one day its president. And there are the really successful lawyers who've worked their way up to getting the larger firms as clients, earning twenty-five thousand and up on company law." It all seemed to have a great deal to do with business, insurance and politics, and very little connection with the prevention of crime, and I said so. He spread his hands. "Criminal law?" he said fastidiously. "That's a grubby business, you know."

As for politics: they are, even without the Republican Party affirmation above, inevitably involved with economic concepts to an extent unequaled in any other country. "For most Americans," says Professor Galbraith, "free competition, so called, has for long been a political rather than an economic concept." And to take the point further: free competition is also, by the nature of the Constitution, not merely an economic or a political but also a social concept. This is what is hidden so effectively and disastrously by the Golden Curtain. Free competition, in the American vocabulary, is the same as individual freedom; the most natural and obvious expression of the ideal. Anything which seems to encroach upon its operation tends to be regarded with dread; I was startled, when I first went to the United States, by the number of Americans who seem to consider not merely Soviet Communism, but socialism in general, an intrinsically evil thing. Intellectually a product of postwar Britain, I had no proper idea of the extent to which not only industry but everything else in America is run on the lines of free competition, as if it were a business enterprise. Here, it does not seem strange to you that colleges, hospitals, charities should compete with one another for funds and efficiency, even to the extent sometimes of calling in a management consultant; or that a headmaster, a judge or the director of a museum can be as concerned about his "image" as if he were the president of a company, and can go about improving it in much the same way.

To you in America, this is not unnatural; it is the way things must necessarily be. It is not only a way of life, but a language and a way of thinking. In a country whose automobile industry employs more than a million men and women, it is not surprising that some sixty-nine million motor-cars should be in regular use, and that the children of every car-owning family should not only acquire a driving license within months of reaching the necessary birthday, but should then borrow a car at every conceivable opportunity to drive distances which before they would have walked. It happens; it is part of life. The things which seem remarkable, deplorable or just plain incomprehensible to a visitor from the other side of the Golden Curtain are not so to the man who lives in the United States, unless he is one of the professional worriers called sociologists. He takes them for granted. They *fit*.

"The value of riches . . . and the enjoyments that civilised man procures for himself by their means. . . ." The first things man procures for himself, naturally, will be those which satisfy his bodily needs; and when these are refined beyond the point of absolute necessity they become to some extent, I suppose, enjoyments. So the most obvious enjoyments which the American procures for himself are the cosseters and the freedom-givers of the previous chapter: the more spacious house, the second motor-car, the dishwasher, the things that the people of any country begin to acquire as their standard of living goes up. But he does not then go on to the acquisition of the next kind of enjoyment, whatever one thinks that should be. There is no natural progression from the value of riches to the value of other things, equally tangible, which have nothing to do with riches at all. This is where the Golden Curtain hangs down bang in the middle of American life. For the system, the free competitive system which makes the first enjoyments possible, is a demanding servant. Perhaps it is not a servant at all, or at any rate only one like Henry James's Quint, haunting the once-served maliciously until he masters them. For capitalism will not be forgotten. It cannot afford to be. It is not a game played for its own sake; it is the system upon which the way of life of 190 million Americans is based, and without it the country would collapse. It must perpetuate itself. Its great central spine is the law of supply and demand, and this must always be kept functioning. Suppose that every American now engaged upon the pursuit of happiness should suddenly down tools and announce: "Right—I have become happy. I am content with everything I have in life. I need nothing else." What would happen? America, of course, would stop. There would be nothing left for the system to accomplish. So every American must continue the long pursuit; he must never be allowed (or allow himself) to feel that the conditions for absolute happiness have arrived. Demand must exceed supply; and if it should become sated, then a new demand must be created to take its place.

The most obvious illustrations of this constant theme are to be found, of course, in the world of manufacturing and selling "consumer goods." Sometimes I think the word "consumer" itself —fast carried across the Atlantic to Europe—must have been coined by one of the lords of retail, to give the public a subconscious image of itself as a gaping great greedy mouth that will never be filled. We do not merely buy or use, eat or drink; we consume—a word hitherto reserved for passions or whales. There is infinity in it. And certainly the average American buoys up his society by consuming at an immense rate. However bitterly he may complain of the behavior and standards of manufacturers, however earnestly he may read the revelatory warnings of Mr. Vance Packard and other watchdogs of the commercial scene, he is inescapably caught in the spiral of supply and demand. Getting and spending are not forced on him by a lot of wicked scheming commercial ogres; they have become, by now, self-stimulating activities. If a capitalist society is to thrive, markets must constantly bubble and change; a process which would continue now even if the watchdogs were able to abolish all sinister artificial stimuli like the planned obsolescence of automobiles. The American will always value riches primarily as a means of buying objects and services; if he did not, he would cease properly to be American. This is his national climate.

It is also, unfortunately, the kind of climate which has thickened the Golden Curtain from the other side. In the mind of one

who has never been to the United States, the image and implications of the country's day-to-day economic life present a far
nastier picture than they do to even the severest American critic.
Sometimes it is almost as difficult to make the American system
sound attractive to this untraveled foreigner—unless he happens
to be poor and unprivileged at home, and sees the United States
as Golconda—as it is to give an American a picture of socialism
which he will admit sounds even tolerable. On either side of the
Atlantic, assumptions, overtones, habits of thought differ; even
facts, those impregnable units of truth, can become perilously
misleading when their relation to one another differs according
to which country you are in. So Europe's image of the American
domestic economy is that of a joyous cacophony of fierce salesmanship and shrieking advertising, credit buying and standardi-
zation, of voracious consumers grabbing at novelty—a picture
brilliant with horror, but lacking in humanity. On our side of
the Golden Curtain, there is nothing to give us any idea of what
these capitalist surroundings mean to the Americans themselves.

And do you really know what they mean to you, or to your
children?

Consider, first of all, a comparison. In Britain, we have billboards enough beside the roads, and neon enough in the city
centers—at least since 1949, when we had recovered sufficiently
from the aftermath of war for the lights to go up again. For
Britons of my generation, who had grown up with the war and
seen no lights but those of the bombing, this was a revelation; it
took years of life in illuminated London before I could go
through Piccadilly Circus at night without a faint *frisson* of wonder at the great blaze of neon advertisement (much of it, as a matter of fact, belonging to firms with their head offices in the
U.S.A.). But today, not all the advertising in Britain will prepare
the British visitor for what he finds on the other side of the Atlantic. The billboards are so much bigger, the neon signs so
much more frequent; facing fiercer competition, every kind of
visual advertisement must strain more desperately for novelty. So

the giant steam-iron on its poster in Times Square puffs real steam through its huge base, past the moving words and figures of other hoardings that emulate drive-in screens; the white clouds writhe for a moment and then dissipate over the scurrying heads, and over the windows of the discount stores calling Reduction! Savings! Bargain! from scrawled carboard notices round their glittering shoddy goods. And high above them all, words painted in letters two storys deep announce like the Last Trump: LOEW'S THEATERS BRING HAPPINESS TO MILLIONS! GET YOUR SHARE!

And so an endless sequence of small neon signs (Barber . . . Coffee . . . Liquor . . . Drugs . . .) jut like frozen flags along any shopping street, large or small, in any city from Boston to Los Angeles, and on city approaches like those three or four scruffy miles of road leading in to New Haven, Connecticut, from the north, motels and diners and catchpenny cafés line either side in a thick litter of tarnished metal and misspelt signs. The same spelling is everywhere, the endless deliberate gimmickry designed to catch attention, even outraged attention: Donuts . . . Kwik Service . . . Open Every Nite. . . .

It is the kind of method and intention which reaches its climax along the Strip in Las Vegas, the incredible bright city shimmering through the dark like a lost jewel, magical in the distance as you drive the hundreds of miles through the Mojave Desert from that other visual desert, Los Angeles. It lies ahead like an oasis, the gambling city; and the great flood of brilliance that engulfs you when you arrive has at first a kind of lovable hideousness, like the Albert Memorial in London. But see the Strip in daylight, the lurid dollar-hungry mile of hotels and casinos and restaurants rearing high overhead on the very edge of the desert, and everything is suddenly tawdry; the advertisements stand stripped of every quality except their single naked purpose, that of getting people inside to spend money. Thunderbird . . . Sands . . . Riviera . . . Golden Nugget . . . under the clear-blue-white sky of Nevada, enormous Las Vegas becomes all at once a very small place, dwarfed by the mountains even though the mountains are low on the horizon; and the only thing that most sane people want to do is to drive out across the dusty scrub and mesquite, away from this place that is exerting every wild effort to suck them in.

Yet they come back to the lure again, at night; to jerk at the slot machines, and to sit wide-eyed over the tables at roulette and black jack. Despised, Las Vegas nonetheless flourishes, because it is part of the fabric of life. The city and its prosperity are a mirror for all America's lure-inside advertising; the American can dismiss it with "Ah, they're all crooks there," but all over his country's road system there lie the molecules of this same city: the motels and billboards and ice-cream-cone-shaped coffee-shops, calling for the passing motorist's wandering eye. Remarkably few Americans would like to live in Las Vegas; yet there it is, with its 83,000 population which has trebled in ten years. Remarkably few Americans can be heard praising the roadside litter of advertisement which decks the United States—many will instead praise any new piece of legislation that forbids it—yet there it is too. The fact is, of course, that remarkably few Americans even notice it any more; in self-defense you have all become deaf, so that the advertisements, like spoiled children, must bid for your attention with louder and louder shouts.

The shouts are loudest of all, obviously, on radio and television. The impact that these make on an English newcomer is again a matter of contrast; and it is a contrast worth considering, if only for the sake of casting a sidelight on phenomena that seem normal to you at home. In Britain, we have no advertising at all on our radio (except for one or two local "pirate" stations privately operated from ships moored off the coast, and a pop music program beamed across the Channel from Luxembourg). Our four radio channels, which range from very pop to very highbrow, and two of our nine television channels, are operated by the British Broadcasting Corporation, a public corporation set up by Royal Charter, run by a Parliament-appointed board, and financed by the annual fifteen-dollar license fee paid by anyone who owns a television set. (This includes radio; anyone who owns no television, but one or more radio sets, pays five dollars a year.) We have fifteen commercial television companies, covering different areas on seven channels, with their proportion of advertising time controlled by the charter of the Independent Television Authority—which was set up when a Conservative Government, amid many objections, allowed commercial television into the country in 1963.

Out of this pattern come the contrasts. The BBC, which tends to be known by the British as "Auntie," breeds radio announcers whose restraint is so much unlike the hopped-up bounce of their American counterparts as to sound like a comic symbol of the differences in national character. And even commercial television is more relaxed, being allowed only about half the quantity of advertisement put out in the U.S.A. The effect of this, in general, is healthy. American radio, most Americans would sorrowfully agree, has degenerated almost everywhere now into a continuous and not very discriminating purveyor of music, news and commercials; and even the voluntarily-supported FM stations tend to be limited by lack of funds to a higher-brow version of the same kind of pattern: a sequence of classical music, news, and superior commercials from things like record stores and art museums. True, they often put on discussion programs and talks of their own devising, and good educational material, but when a really ambitious feature program or play appears on the program schedule it often turns out to have been bought from the BBC.

For radio in Britain, in its sheltered, subsidized world, has been able to develop into a genuine artistic medium with its own characteristics and potential; in the course of a week its four channels can provide an exhaustive range of information and entertainment impossible in the U.S.A. It is strong enough to attract and produce the best: Peter Sellers began his career as a BBC radio impressionist; Dylan Thomas wrote much of his work for the BBC; Harold Pinter's plays were first given a hearing on the air; and no performer from John Gielgud to Tommy Steele will turn down an interesting offer from BBC radio—even today, when television has put the older medium into partial eclipse.

Within television, the difference shows in the same way. Commercial television in Britain tends, like your own, to keep the standards of light entertainment low in order to attract majority audiences for its advertisers (and indeed buys many package shows, from Westerns to *Peyton Place,* from the United States networks). The BBC attracts much criticism for doing the same thing, in order to avoid becoming only a minority-serving institution, and it too buys programs from America which no American would be very proud to claim as typical. But even so, on all channels, the proportion of live drama, documentaries, outside broadcasts of current events, and small offbeat feature programs is staggering to anyone raised on television in the U.S.A.—where for many people the Huntley-Brinkley report is the only worthwhile spot in an average day. When British television makes mistakes, they tend to be due to errors of human judgment, rather than to the limitations of the system. The British playwright writing for BBC television, for instance, is limited only by a length of perhaps one and a half hours, and by the critical judgment of editor and producer. If he writes a bad play, it is because he is a bad television playwright, or is at any rate going through a bad patch. But in the United States, there are many pressures on a writer which have nothing to do with writing. Rod Serling, the American television playwright who wrote the excellent *Requiem for a Heavyweight* and is responsible for the "Twilight Zone" series, once told me wistfully that he longed for the day when he would feel himself ready, like Paddy Chayefsky, to turn away from television writing to the theater. "You've no idea," he said mournfully, "of the strain involved in writing a play that must keep up its dramatic tension while being interrupted every ten minutes by some frivolous irrelevance. The shape must always be the same, you must cut out so many things you would like to do. . . . And as for what the sponsors do to you—"

Everyone has since learned a little about what the sponsors can do from *Only You, Dick Daring.* Inevitably, in American television, commerce diminishes art. And even when a good program reaches the screen, it can be affected by what might be called subliminal derogation.

In 1964, almost every part of the United States received one particularly well made set of television programs: a series of hour-long portraits of literature in Britain, Nigeria, Greece and others. The program on Britain boomed gloriously over green fields in Sir Ralph Richardson's mournful vowels; Nigeria's modern theater was seen growing remarkably from ancient tribal themes; Greece was magnificently bloodied by Minotis and Paxinou. Yet somehow the identity of each program was, in the end, lost. They were all thoroughly and resplendently advertised, in well-produced booklets sent through the post, or large spaces in the *New York Times* and similar papers, using that large-gray-Roman-type-in-lots-of-white-space restraint which announces "Quality" in newspaper advertising. But always they were advertised as Esso World Theater. The three five-minute commercials which punctuated each program were miniscule documentary films, very educational, showing petroleum refining or similar activities in the country concerned: all about Esso. The entire project had a strong flavor not of literature, but of oil.

This was, of course, unavoidable. It always will be. America has a system of commercial television in which almost every program must be "bought" by a sponsor or group of sponsors: only solemn major events like the funerals of President Kennedy and —over some networks—Sir Winston Churchill are presented without advertising. Sometimes network and sponsor will collaborate on a program from the beginning—as with Esso World Theater. But the sponsor's money and motive are necessarily all-important; without them the system could not exist. If you want literature translated into television, there must be a commercial company which thinks it worth financing; and obviously no company is going to finance prestige minority programs unless it can make quite sure that its name is firmly attached to the prestige. So, in this case, the U. S. television networks acquired a set of better programs than they had shown for a long time, but only at a price: that of leaving a final impression, in the mind of the viewer, that Shakespeare, Chaucer and Euripides are, though important, not really quite so important as Esso Oil.

We tend to forget, we who live on the other side of the Atlantic, that the American does not see these things objectively, in opposition to a world which lacks them. For him, they have always been there. To a great extent he has resignedly learned to blot them out, as if he held in this head one of those devices which allow you, by pressing a button, to blot out the sound of a television advertisement. I believe, as the next chapter points out, that he has suffered a great deal of harm by the juxtaposition of Esso and Euripides; but I may be wrong. It may be that the average intelligent American is hardly affected at all by his bombardment of advertising, but is, as a good disciple of Vance Packard and the Consumers' Union, able to brush aside the persistent irritations of commerce as if they were so many flies. It's possible. From where we are, we can't tell. The Golden Curtain is in the way.

But never forget, if instead you live in America, that these persistent irritations are not flies; they are the leaves of your Tree Igdrasil, a necessary part of your living society, and without them the U.S.A. would not exist. You can't pretend they are not there; you must always remember that while they keep your body alive, they can come perilously close to killing your mind, and while you encourage the one ability you must control the other—or at least provide a comparison to act as antidote. The most demanding way of providing a comparison is to look at Europe; the least demanding is to retreat to some part of your own country so wild or secluded that the irritations are missing. (It is the least demanding because a great many other things are missing as well.) And indeed, you do this very often; though since your motives for doing so are not always clear, it is not possible to tell whether you gain any objectivity from your retreat: whether you are standing critically back like a painter, or trying desperately to run away like a leashed dog.

There is no running away from one more personal kind of advertising pressure in the U.S., unless you want to cut yourself off completely from the outside world. When the telephone rings, the voice at the other end may be that of a friend; or, more probably, one of your children's friends. But about once every week it is the voice of a stranger, greeting you with a throb of that word more misused than any other in the United States— sincerity. "Good *morning*, Mrs. Grant, this is your Filene's store." There is an infinitesimal pause between the greeting and the sales-talk, but not one which dares wait for an answer. "We have a special offer to make to you, one that's limited to only a few selected customers of the store in your area. Now that spring is coming, I know you must be thinking about renewing your slip-covers. . . ."

I am a foreigner, and I tend to hear these people out and then, no doubt childishly, to decline their offer in the most affected English voice I can muster. My husband, who is American, puts the telephone firmly down as soon as they are fully launched. Perhaps this shows, again, the inoculation of the native; the American's growing imperviousness to the pressures exerted on him. Those who live with it take (*pace* Mr. Packard) this relatively harmless intrusion of privacy for granted; they are not disturbed by the shadow-play, the falsifying of human communication. There is so much minor falsity of this kind all around them that they dismiss it as a move in the commercial game: not as hypocrisy, but as another unavoidable irritation. It simply adds to the number of things that they have ceased to see or hear—even when they are doing or saying these things themselves. When I paid my bill at the first American hotel I ever stayed in, the clerk smiled warmly and said: "Come back and see us again soon." As a wide-eyed and rather lonely traveler, I found this immensely cheering. "Well thank you very much," I began on a wave of bonhomie, "I probably shall actually, I have to come back to Washington in . . ." I stopped only when I caught sight of the clerk's face; it bore, suddenly, a mixture of astonishment and horror, as if I had begun to strip in the middle of the lobby. Perhaps I had, in one sense, by revealing a habit of valuing human contacts; now, of course, I hear the glassy-eyed, insincere "Come back soon" so often from waitresses, shop assistants, hairdressers, hotel clerks and bellhops that I too have taken it for granted as a meaningless phrase, like "How are you?" or "How do you do?" or "Take it easy, now." How are you? Who cares?

The other kind of immediate advertising, the communication that pretends to be personal, is that bugbear of all American mailmen, "direct mail." Every day the average householder sifts through his handful of envelopes, removes the advertisements, sighs, drops them in the wastepaper basket and settles down to open his real letters. But the advertisers, undeterred, continue the deluge; while one firm in any one field uses direct mail methods, the others must nervously follow suit, to keep up.

The man who does read "personal" advertising is subjected, in his morning mail, to every kind of approach from the swift bludgeon to the ultra-soft soap. His attitude to all of them will be suspicious—"Where's the catch?"—but even so he probably falls for about three or four offers a year. He is perhaps prevented from building a completely impervious wall of indifference by the fact that the same advertising methods, and to a distressing extent the same phraseology, have been adopted by most of the United States' major charities.

The trouble with all these forms of advertising is not simply their ubiquity, but the fact that their standards, in general, are alarmingly low. To put their message across, they take various forms of communication from the arts—words, pictures, music— and unfailingly degrade them. For every intelligent, well de-

signed billboard (like the picture of a Volkswagen labeled simply "Mother's Little Helper") there are fifty ill-drawn, gaudy
pictures of a gigantic pretty girl eating somebody's potato chips,
or a vast cleft-chinned young man smoking somebody else's cigarettes. For every engaging television commercial, usually of the
kind that is sending itself up, there are a hundred tasteless vi-
gnettes of the girl who has no dates because she doesn't use X's
deodorant, or of the woman who saves her failing marriage by
switching to Y's instant coffee. So it goes on. For every catchy
advertising jingle there are a hundred blasts of dismal noise; for
every piece of well written advertising copy, a thousand pieces of
semi-literate junk. ("This most unique offer comes to you . . .")
Their overall motive, of course, is that of selling; of persuasion,
of overcoming resistance, of influencing desires. They have no
other reason for existence. And though they may measure up
well to this one self-imposed standard, they almost always fall far,
far below the intrinsic standards of the communications media
they use. What do any other standards matter, if your own is
enough to persuade people to part with their cash?

". . . ignorant of the value of riches, and indifferent to the
enjoyments that civilized man procures for himself by their
means. . . ." Two things come out of the particular kind of
value which is placed on riches in the United States today. Very
few Americans can escape the assumption, on which their free
enterprise society is based, that money is one of the most desirable things in life as a source both of pleasure and of power.
("Sure," most will say cheerfully, "I like earning thirty thousand
bucks a year. How else could I afford the boat/summer place/six
kids/payments on the house?") They know clearly what it can
do; they know how much they enjoy most of the things it can do.
They will ask you themselves, with an amiable grin, how many
Presidents of the United States you can name who reached that
office without the help of a family fortune, or someone else's
family fortune. They are accustomed to the stuff. Out of this

there grows perhaps their best-known national characteristic: a kind of compulsive generosity which often stops only just this side of neurosis.

Those Americans who came to Europe during or immediately after the Second World War were inevitably so much richer than anyone else that they were universally branded as vulgar splash-abouts. The image grew up of the pudgy man with loud tie, large cigar and broad-brimmed hat, his long grinning car shadowy in the background and his hand in his pocket spilling out the dollar bills with which he would over-tip in all directions while trying to buy everything in sight. Those Americans who still live in Europe on American salaries continue to arouse resentment, by behaving in what is to them a perfectly normal fashion, but which by native standards can seem ostentatious. Londoners hunting houses or apartments mutter uncharitable oaths about the hordes of American officials who put up the prices simply by being able to afford them; and in 1960 the young American writer Clancy Sigal, putting together a report on "The American G.I. in Britain" for the magazine *Encounter*, came upon the landlord of a pub in Lakenheath, Suffolk, observing bitterly: "Yanks? Plain as the nose on your face. They corrupt our girls with their money; it's nothing else but that. Well, I say any girl who likes it can keep it." (So indeed a great many of them do, since as Mr. Sigal points out later on, every year 3,000 American G.I.s stationed in Britain marry English girls.) Lord Francis-Williams, in *The American Invasion,* made a resounding case for the argument that American capital is pumping into Europe like a particularly sinister kind of blood; and members of emergent small nations can often be heard remarking cynically that America seems to think that foreign aid is the sole price of friendship, whatever her own motive for giving the aid. Many Americans do in fact think so: "Ingratitude!" they cry indignantly, as some African prime minister prepares to receive a state visitor from the Soviet Union or China. "After all those millions of dollars we sent them last year . . . !" Then they try to put pressure on Congress to cut that particular nation's aid program down, since "it isn't worth it": as if allegiance were a commodity to be bought on the world market, like gold or platinum. It is all a legacy of the system's implicit lesson: money, spent or given generously, can be the way to power, respect and even love.

No one of course could ever claim that there is any malice in this way of thinking, or even any cynicism. The American does tend to hide sentimentality behind an appearance of cynicism, as the Englishman tends to hide nervousness behind an appearance of arrogance, but the true cynic is rare in the United States. This is perhaps one reason why the average American, thinking and acting according to his country's ways, finds it difficult to understand the extent to which a foreigner's assumptions and values may differ from his own; and still more difficult to understand why foreigners may not accept his own as readily as he does himself. He can see only the good and useful things that come out of his view of the value of riches; it is only the wondering stranger who is made uneasy by what seem darker overtones. Anyone who has ever traveled for long through the United States as a visitor from abroad, for instance, knows all about the extraordinary hospitality showered from all sides on the stranger: the lavish meals, the special parties, the letters of introduction to relatives on the other side of the continent, the offers to drive one across several states. When I worked for some months on an American newspaper, with my by-line labeled as that of a foreign "exchange" journalist, hardly a day passed without some complete stranger telephoning and offering lunch, dinner or a day with his or her family. The total, even when one eliminated those ladies whose ulterior motive was to acquire a lecturer for their Modern Affairs Circle, was astonishing and highly agreeable. And yet, and yet . . . Churlish though it may seem to question generosity, that rare and valuable quality, there was all the same something troubling about the cumulative effect of it all; as if there were somewhere an element of emotional one-up-manship in everyone concerned. There is no knowing when the first intimations of distress at this idea occur in the visiting stranger; they come, I think, like gradually growing twinges of indigestion during a long and gourmandizing Christmas holiday. For one British friend of mine who spent six months in an American city they came at a precise moment, through one tiny incident. He had been made particularly welcome by one American couple; they had invited him often to their home, taken him to numbers of places he wanted to see, and generally given him a warm, relaxed time as an adopted member of the family. When Christmas came, he bought them a present, feeling this gave him a chance to say at least a small affectionate thank you for their exceedingly bountiful generosity. They were deeply touched—and immediately rushed out, the day after Christmas, and bought *him* a present in return. "It sounds stupid, but I was frightfully upset," he said mournfully afterwards. "I know they meant it in the nicest way, but suddenly it seemed as though they couldn't bear the relationship to be equal even in intention—they had to be on top. Either that, or they felt that since I'd spent some money they couldn't express their own appreciation without doing something that involved doing the same. Somehow it diminished us all."

And this of course is the danger; the thing that may not be happening at all in the United States, and yet is a dreadfully natural consequence of the economic structure of its way of life. If the value of riches is allowed to creep out from its place in daily life, like an insidious cloud of protoplasm, and invade personal and national relationships, those relationships will be curiously diminished in value without the United States ever quite realizing why.

That is the first development.

The second is something in which every subsequent chapter of this book inevitably has its roots. To state again its central theme: clearly, the modern American is well aware of the first layer of the value of riches, the commodities and services and luxuries that money will buy, and in self-preservation the economic spirit of his country makes sure that he is kept always conscious of these. (And, again, these more than anything else create a false impression of America in the eyes of the world: an incomplete sketch, with the prosperity itself drawn far more vividly than the details of the living people who support and are supported by it.)

But what of the other values of riches, the other "enjoyments that civilized man procures for himself by their means"? What is it that makes the assumptions of the Englishman, in ordinary general conversation, so much more similar to those of the Frenchman, the Austrian, the Dane—themselves all widely different—than to those of the American? What are the relative values that the United States attaches to philosophy and football, theater and theology, painting and poetry, science and music and education and social welfare and politics and religion . . . ? Are they the same as those anywhere else?

There is not one single thing in the image that emerges from behind the Golden Curtain that can give the answers to these questions; even an emerging American can't explain them, unless he has seen enough of other standards to be able to judge his own. The would-be objective stranger must ferret around in the real America for answers, probably making himself—or herself—very unpopular in the process. For the fact is that these other values, though visible, have not yet fully evolved. They are not at all like those elsewhere, but nor have they yet reached their final form—which is sometimes, when you look at them as they now are, a comforting thought. It is less comforting to reflect that if the Golden Curtain is allowed to remain as firm an insulator as it has already become, no values other than that of riches may ever grow to their proper height at all.

4 ⁂ A Culture in the Making

> "Culture, *absol. The training and refinement of mind, tastes, and manners; the condition of being thus trained and refined; the intellectual side of civilisation.*"
>
> *Oxford English Dictionary*

> "*I reckon I got to light out for the Territory ahead of the rest, because Aunt Sally she's going to adopt me and sivilize me, and I can't stand it. I been there before.*"
>
> —MARK TWAIN,
> *Huckleberry Finn*

"Let us restrain ourselves," said Mr. Eliot in 1948, "from using the word 'culture' as a comprehensive term. For thus we slip into the assumption that culture can be planned. Culture can never be wholly conscious—there is always more to it than we are conscious of; and it cannot be planned because it is also the unconscious background of all our planning."

True. True, that is, in those countries whose culture, in the blanket anthropological sense, was fully evolved before this unhappy word ever began to deteriorate in meaning. In Britain, it is now intellectually non-U: a joke-word, to be spoken with a neo-Cockney accent that makes it something like "cowcha." (In my day on *The Sunday Times* we used to call that section of the paper devoted to reviews of the arts "the culture pages"; and the in-joke was so completely accepted that we even did without the accent.) Such contempt for a perfectly respectable word grows, of course, from the usual unconscious arrogance of taking things for granted. For the British, the creative arts, the performing arts, all ideas and "movements" and ways of thinking, form part of a complex evolutionary pattern that has embraced the whole of Europe and the Middle East for three or four thousand years: so interwoven with religion and myth that the intellectual landscape is as familiar and available as the grass and the trees. This is the "unconscious background" of which T. S. Eliot wrote; although it has on occasion fossilized itself perilously into sets of traditional rules, it forms a landscape that will always be fertile, fed always by great rivers flowing naturally out of the past.

But the American landscape is not the same. These rivers do not flow across the Atlantic. Once there were others inside the continent itself, but they have almost all been dammed and lost. The unconscious background is not there, in the New World; and the sense of its absence, to any European who lives in the U.S.A. for long, is inescapable. This is one reason why the word "culture" *is* used in America, without contempt or self-consciousness. Because the Americans are also aware that something is missing, and because they have been able in almost every other field of endeavor to catch up with and pass the rest of the world, they seem in many ways to be trying to take the short cut against which Eliot warned: the planning of a culture, the manufacture of a feeling for the arts and "the intellectual side of civilization." Perhaps it is because of the fear, voiced by many anxious intellectual Americans, that the other side of life is growing too strong too fast: that the greater part of the American Way of Life is producing a sterile atmosphere in which a properly balanced culture will never be able to evolve. At any rate the result is that one hears "culture" spoken of as a kind of abstract package, like "leisure" or "entertainment."

Many Europeans still have a simple and lofty view of their contemporaries on the other side of the Golden Curtain. To them America appears as a kind of void, in which a few remarkable individuals accomplish great or good things in the arts in a state of separation, with no debt or relationship to their surrounding society at all. Willem de Kooning, now the dean of the New York painters, emigrated to the United States from Holland in 1926 with a classic version of this idea:

> We never heard in Holland that there were artists in America. There was still the feeling that this was where an individual could get places and become well off, if he worked hard; while art, naturally, was in Europe. When I had been here for about six months or a year, I found that there were a lot of artists here too. . . .

Most of Europe today has heard rather more about the artists in America; the "Pop Art" school and others are influencing young painters and critics on the other side of the Atlantic to such an extent that most of them now feel New York to be indisputably the capital of the world of avant garde painting. But the feeling with which de Kooning crossed the Atlantic still persists in every other field: you can make money in America, but the arts are in Europe. Naturally.

But what's natural about it? Man is a thinking animal in America, as anywhere else. Americans are born with the same proportions of talents as men in other countries. Clearly any deficiencies in the "cultural scene" are not a simple matter of natural resources, in the way that one country has rich coal deposits and another has none. And indeed they are not; but it takes an American to point out the first reason why. I had lived in the United States for about a year, gloomily wondering why, as a writer, I should be finding the air of this great open country so difficult to breathe, when I came upon James Baldwin's description of the American writer who visits Europe. "It is as though he suddenly came out of a dark tunnel and found himself beneath the open sky. . . ." Only then did I begin properly to understand the particular kind of schizophrenia that must develop in any contemplation of the United States; for Baldwin's

image is, of course, the complete reverse of the sensation commonly experienced by those crossing the Atlantic. Freedom ex-
plodes around one's ears when arriving in America, not leaving.
And so it does; but this freedom has more limitations than the
outsider can at first perceive:

> The American writer, in Europe, is released, first of all, from the
> necessity of apologizing for himself. It is not until he *is* released
> from the habit of flexing his muscles and proving that he is just
> a "regular guy" that he realizes how crippling this habit has been.
> It is not necessary for him, there, to pretend to be something he
> is not, for the artist does not encounter in Europe the same
> suspicion he encounters here. Whatever the Europeans may
> actually think of artists, they have killed enough of them off by
> now to know that they are as real—and as persistent—as rain,
> snow, taxes or businessmen.
>
> Of course, the reason for Europe's comparative clarity concern-
> ing the different functions of men in society is that European
> society has always been divided into classes in a way that Ameri-
> can society never has been. A European writer considers himself
> to be part of an old and honorable tradition—of intellectual
> activity, of letters—and his choice of a vocation does not cause
> him any uneasy wonder as to whether or not it will cost him all
> his friends. But this tradition does not exist in America.
>
> On the contrary, we have a very deep-seated distrust of real
> intellectual effort (probably because we suspect that it will de-
> stroy, as I hope it does, that myth of America to which we cling
> so desperately). An American writer fights his way to one of the
> lowest rungs on the American social ladder by means of pure
> bull-headedness and an indescribable series of odd jobs. He prob-
> ably *has* been a "regular fellow" for much of his adult life,
> and it is not easy for him to step out of that luke-warm bath. . . .

Now this terrifying passage—which comes from James Baldwin's *Nobody Knows My Name,* and which should be read aloud
annually in all American high schools—contains a clear diagnosis
of what is holding back the cultural development of America, or

at least of one symptom of it: the crass scale of values which encloses an artist within a mass of tiny, insidious, hostile pressures,
and which is not in the least mitigated by the national profusion
of prizes, fellowships, grants from benevolent foundations and
businesses (who between them are said to have given 75 million
dollars to "cultural causes" during 1963) and university plums
with titles like Poet-in-Residence. Mr. Baldwin has himself been
awarded at various times a Guggenheim Literary Fellowship, a
National Institute of Arts and Letters Fellowship, and a Ford
Foundation Grant-in-Aid. A good thing too: it never has been,
and probably never will be, an easy thing for an artist to earn his
living without compromising his particular art, and every kind of
patronage helps. Unfortunately, in a society without unconscious
cultural standards, even congratulatory labels have their drawbacks. "Unless I can get to a major competition and win it," a
young American concert pianist said to me despondently once, "I
haven't a hope of establishing myself here. When Van Cliburn
won the Tchaikowsky competition in Moscow, everyone in the
States went wild about him—yet they'd taken no real notice of
his concerts before that, which had been just as good. They
hadn't even noticed that he'd already won most of our own com-
petitions at home. The American public doesn't make artistic
judgments. It waits for some real big signpost telling it which
way to lean."

If inexperience and timidity were the only failings of the
American public in this context, there would be nothing wrong
with the artistic climate that could not be put right by time and
education—the right kind of education. But among the many
American writers and critics who have, in varying degrees of
anguish, anatomized the characteristics of America's burgeoning
culture, there are an uneasy number who feel that the country's
greatest intellectual peril comes from the middle of the road:
from the gigantic creeping morass of the popular second-rate,
which is so much more demanding than the fourth-rate that nobody notices—until too late—how easily it pulls down first-rate

standards into oblivion and decay. One of the principal source-documents for this kind of concern has been for the last twenty years or so Dwight Macdonald's splendid essay "Masscult and Midcult," published most recently in 1962 in his book *Against the American Grain*. Macdonald's own standards, like Eliot's, are resolutely anti-egalitarian:

> Today, in the United States, the demands of the audience, which has changed from a small body of connoisseurs into a large body of ignoramuses, have become the chief criteria of success . . . . If there were a clearly defined cultural élite here, then the masses could have their *Kitsch* and the classes could have their High Culture, with everybody happy. But a significant part of our population is chronically confronted with a choice between looking at TV or old masters, between reading Tolstoy or a detective story; i.e., the pattern of their cultural lives is "open" to the point of being porous. For a lucky few, this openness of choice is stimulating. But for most, it is confusing, and leads at best to that middlebrow compromise called Midcult.

Macdonald's condemnation of the flourishing ambiguity of Midcult is based on the charge that "it pretends to respect the standards of High Culture while in fact it waters them down and vulgarizes them." When he comes to play the classification game, he demolishes a number of pillars of American life in a manner which would pain and startle any "regular guy." He analyzes, devastatingly, four works which he chooses as typical Midcult products: Ernest Hemingway's *The Old Man and the Sea*, Thornton Wilder's *Our Town,* Archibald MacLeish's *J.B.* and Stephen Vincent Benét's *John Brown's Body*. He then takes joyous swipes at the *Saturday Evening Post,* Steinbeck, Marquand, the Revised Standard Version of the Bible, Oscar Hammerstein, the Book-of-the-Month Club, Vance Packard, *Time* and *Life* ("the Lucepapers"). The portrait which emerges is like that of an enormous BBC Home Service; and when Mr. Macdonald has finished classifying America there does not seem to be very much left except the Little Magazines, the *New Yorker* ("a Midcult magazine but one with a difference") and Mary McCarthy. If any literary rebels do manage to fight their way out of the web of Midcult, he sees their work tending towards eccentricity "because it lacks contact with the past and doesn't get support from a broad enough intelligentsia in the present." And in the end, his only hope for America's cultural future—if she is to have more than the occasional rogue genius brave enough to go it alone—lies in urging this intelligentsia to become properly self-conscious: "insisting on higher standards and setting itself off—joyously, implacably—from most of its fellow-citizens, not only from the Masscult depths but also from the agreeable ooze of the Midcult swamp." We are back again at Mr. Baldwin's picture, in which the American writer must by pure bull-headedness get himself out of the lukewarm bath of being a "regular fellow." What with dark tunnels, lukewarm baths and swamps, the artist in America seems to have as many images of frustration to describe his lot as the graduate of Harvard Business School finds in the world of English business. Perhaps the two worlds share some of the same faults.

I quote Messrs. Baldwin and Macdonald at such length because they, as Americans, put their respective fingers so accurately on many of the things which I, as a foreigner, find still most alarmingly apparent in America. But if they, and others like them, are so articulate in pointing out peril, why does the overall situation not noticeably improve? There are a lot of obvious general answers to that question, of course, but perhaps the most relevant lies in a picture of the kind of ears on which these warnings fall.

On November 29, 1962, I was working in one of the twenty-four cities in the United States which that evening received on closed-circuit television a kind of a high-level variety program entitled "An American Pageant of the Arts," designed to raise money for the projected National Cultural Center in Washington. (This has since been renamed, mercifully, the John F. Kennedy Center for the Performing Arts.) It was an elaborate occasion. Fur-wrapped, bare-backed, dinner-jacketed and candle-lit, two or three hundred people began the evening by eating a dinner at one of the city's largest hotels, at a cost of fifty dollars a plate. The city orchestra played while the waitresses scuttled efficiently round with duck and champagne; a local soprano sang; an actress named Miss Signe Hasso made a little speech in which she paid tribute to "the marvelous culture of this country." Against each plate a small gold card was propped. "You will receive a unique gift as a remembrance of this evening," it read. "A free copy of the pre-publication edition of a magnificent new hard-backed book entitled CREATIVE AMERICA. Already heralded as a landmark in publishing, CREATIVE AMERICA includes ninety-six pages of pictures by the staff of Magnum—powerful photos, many in full color, depicting sources of inspiration, accomplishment, and learning, all focussing on America's leading artists. The text includes articles by President Kennedy, Louis Kronenberger, James Baldwin, Mark Van Doren, and Joseph Wood Krutch; poems by Robert Frost and John Ciardi; messages from former Presidents Eisenhower and Truman. . . ."

Having wined and dined, the crowds were carried off in buses to the city concert-hall inside the local Museum of Art, whose imposing neo-classical interior was already filling with others, less wealthy or less generous, clutching tickets labeled: "Closed Circuit Telecast: Admission $10.00 (tax deductible)." For three hours, there they sat, watching a giant screen on which the late President and Mrs. Kennedy (in Washington) and former President and Mrs. Eisenhower (in Baltimore) could be seen at dinners just like the one they themselves had just left; watching, just like them, the "American Pageant of the Arts" which then unfolded on the screen, with Leonard Bernstein compèring a series of eminent turns ranging from Pablo Casals to Danny Kaye. The conversation to be heard in the foyer afterwards had little connection with the arts or the program; it was more the variety of: "Jennie managed to pull Bob along, did you see?" . . . "There was shrimp cocktail standing on the President's table, I hope they'd had dinner" . . . "I don't see the Smiths, do you, I think they ought to have come. . . ." Naturally, inevitably, it was primarily a social occasion, falling into the same category as a benefit performance of *Oklahoma!* or a charity ball. A certain proportion of the audience had a genuine interest in the arts; those with the most genuine interest of all had probably paid for their tickets and not bothered to turn up. The rest were the kind of people who, for goodnatured, public-spirited or pretentious reasons, will always support this kind of thing. The couple sitting behind me at the telecast seemed fairly typical. "Who's he?" demanded the husband, when Bernstein appeared on the screen. "He wrote *West Side Story,* sweetie," said the wife.

The next morning I sat down at my typewriter in the office of the local daily newspaper (which was, I should add, an excellent and liberal-minded organ which gave me great freedom), and wrote a gently ironic description of the evening's festivities. It began, as I remember: "You can't eat culture, but it will be difficult after this not to associate the National Cultural Center with food and drink." It was a mild piece, never really achieving wit, let alone satire, and I left it on the Editor's desk expecting him to drop it—perhaps with a gentle smile—straight on the spike.

Ten minutes later I was summoned urgently to a conference of the Editor and two departmental editors. They were sitting gloomily round a table staring at a copy of my mild little article, and Departmental Editor One seemed quite worked up.

"We can't possibly print it!" he was crying.

"O, I don't know," said the Editor ruminatively.

"No no," said Departmental Editor One.

"I'd never give space to a thing like this," said Departmental Editor Two.

They both glared fiercely at the Editor. The general effect was most disconcerting.

"Well, can't you just leave it out?" I said. "It isn't a particularly good piece, I do see."

The Editor said, somewhat ambiguously, "That's not what's bothering them."

The other two were leafing through the article, and clicking their tongues. "Look at this!" said Departmental Editor One. " 'They were a contented audience, they clapped the culture as if they'd been sitting at the President's own table.' . . . You can't. . . . People won't. . . . There'll be a lot of trouble."

"But why?"

Departmental Editor One said: "It's *funny*." He uttered the word with distaste, as if it were obscene. "People will be offended. There are some things you just can't be *funny* about."

God. Old ladies. The Pope. Disfigurement. The Crucifixion. But *the arts* . . . ?

Marveling, I took away the article and rewrote it. The new version dropped all ironic description and became a straightforward plea for self-examination. It was no longer even an article about the United States, but about people in general. Let us be certain, it suggested, that when we profess concern for the arts our motives are genuine, for if they are not, the arts will surely suffer. "On both sides of the Atlantic," I wrote, "the word 'culture' is in danger of becoming a meaningless label for a kind of spiritual spinach." I took great care to ask questions that showed I was referring to Britain just as much as to America. How many of the English who flocked to see the Royal Academy's imperiled, much-publicized da Vinci cartoon at the National Gallery in 1962 bothered to look at the rest of the pictures at the same time? How many of those who had called so loudly for a National Theater would quietly support their own local repertory company? And in America, how many of those who paid fifty dollars to be seen dining in the cause of the National Cultural Center would have paid the same amount anonymously, if there had been no social occasion involved? "Of course," the article rather pompously observed, "there is much genuine devotion to the arts in Britain and the U.S.A. But there is also a great deal which is less than genuine. We should take time out for a little self-examination, if our great new cultural symbols are not to become great mausoleums with nothing going on inside."

This now seemed harmless enough stuff: a fairly commonplace admonition, not funny, not likely to offend anyone. But in thinking that, I underestimated the thickness of the Golden Curtain, and the defensiveness of those who will hear no wrong of any part of the American Way. On the day the article was published, I found a laconic little note on my desk from another departmental editor. "The culture vultures will get you," he wrote, "if you don't watch out." He was quite right.

The rude letters began arriving the next day. Most of them went to the Editor, as such letters do; one of those which came to me demanded simply: "Why don't you go home?" They were written principally by people who had been at the National Cultural Center dinner; they formed a uniform roar of hurt pride, and not one of them concerned itself with anything but local activities. How dared I suggest that they, in that city, should examine their motives? Didn't they pay good money to keep their orchestra alive? Didn't they support an art museum that gave classes to thousands of schoolchildren? In great detail and with great persistence, they all thus missed the point. Clearly the managing editor and the executive editor had been quite right; people would have been very offended if I had tried to be funny about Culture. One letter, from the manager of the local orchestra, was written under the irate impression that I *was* trying to be funny, even this time. He wished to take serious exception to the article, he said: certainly the people who attended the National Cultural Center telecast were those who supported the performing arts in the city. (I hadn't said they weren't: I had asked why they supported them.) The manager went on:

> Their personal development in the community's cultural life is simply demonstrated by their attendance at all such cultural functions. It is demonstrated again by the tremendous support given both economically and through volunteer work hours contributed to these organizations. . . .

The enrichment in the lives of millions of people provided by the arts should spare us all from such facetious attacks. It would do Miss Cooper no harm to refer to one of the great cultural works of all times before writing a *New Yorker* style parody circa 1933: the *Oxford English Dictionary.*

I was not sure what I was supposed to be parodying, having been unborn in 1933, but I reflected sorrowfully that if, as it appeared, the article had brought response only from people disinclined towards general discussion of the arts and their value, or indeed anything except fulsome praise of the local scene, then it was not surprising to find one of them describing a dictionary as a great cultural work. It was not surprising to find no professional theater, opera or ballet within a radius of fifty miles of this particular city; not surprising to find the two considerable creative artists living there given far less public recognition as valuable members of the community than the prominent committee-ladies seen organizing Culture in pictures on the paper's Society Page. It was not even surprising, two or three years later, suddenly to see again the name and face of the orchestra manager, writer of the indignant letter. He was smiling out of a cigarette advertisement, in the company of an "executive secretary" and a farmer. "Chesterfield People," read the legend above their heads. "They like a mild smoke, but just don't like filters. (How about you?)"

Communities like this one compose Mr. Baldwin's dark tunnel, Mr. Macdonald's lukewarm bath. They are self-righteous without self-examination. Culture is their sacred cow; it must not be criticized, and nor must their worship of it. Yet their culture is not alive; it is an adopted thing, and incompletely adopted at that. Its two bulwarks tend to be pictures painted in alien civilizations, and music composed by dead alien composers; and often it does not acquire enough insight even from the study of these to give value to the work of living native painters, or the music of living native, or even alien, composers. Its most solid claim is that it usefully educates the young in the acceptance of artistic values; certainly this was true in the city where I first worked, whose part-professional orchestra took pains to arrange school concerts and private teaching, and whose well-stocked art museum had a fulltime staff of twenty people giving classes for some 2,500 children a year, and courses for amateur adults and students from the local university. The same is true too of most of the country's two or three hundred professional orchestras, four or five thousand art museums. But it is questionable all the same whether abbreviated "courses" in any of the arts, administered like a kind of spiritual pill, can ever touch anyone's basic sense of values. If you are educating a child into awareness of the grace and beauty woven into his way of life, it must be difficult, in America, to persuade him that there is more true relevance in the simple shape of a pot made two thousand years ago in Rome than there is in the clutter of neon and billboards and drooping ugly wires that will be all around him as he walks the streets of his own home town. And when you come to America from outside, and begin to see how much money and lip-service are devoted to collecting the one, it is even more difficult to understand how people can tolerate the ubiquity of the other. I suppose it is the same as with the universal canned music which they no longer hear: the universal urban ugliness is something which they no longer see. Yet this is one of the few phenomena that can be described as "native American"; this is something that had its beginnings, and still has its most complex development, in the United States; and as such it is a genuine part of the lower reaches of American culture, again in the anthropological sense. Since it has no accepted label, however, nobody pays it much attention—which is one reason why it never improves. Instead, the average American community is concerned with acquiring its chunks of Culture from abroad, rather as it imports jars of marmalade and bottles of Scotch; with setting these up to be admired, and taking care that it is seen admiring them. Even the proliferating orchestras, as one American composer remarked to me, seem often to be treated by those who finance them as so many particularly chic record-players: a medium for imported Culture, in the shape of Beethoven symphonies and so on, rather than things worth improving for their own sake.

The average community has a vague, uneasy sense that there is something lacking in its own appreciation, and so it takes care that its children shall be taught to admire the imported chunks more knowledgeably. But it has not yet perceived that the thing that is wrong is not the treatment of Culture, but the lack of an all-pervading culture; that admiration is no good unless it creates a climate friendly to creation; that children are more apt to learn well from example than from precept; and that it is useless to import Rembrandt, Mozart, Shakespeare and the odd French château unless the values, standards, ideas and attitudes that make up "the intellectual side of civilization" have been allowed to develop into a kind of unselfconscious atmosphere in which the arts, and all people connected with them, can not only grow but stretch. As it is, one of the most extraordinary things that one learns, behind the Golden Curtain, is that in this great spacious freedom-worshiping country, the proper growth of a living culture is most astonishingly cramped.

Then why?

The fundamental reasons are both obvious and paradoxical: obvious perhaps less to Americans themselves than to an outsider —in the brief space during which he can live in America and still resist the pressures of subjectivity. They are paradoxical because the very qualities which hamper the intellectual side of civilization in America are those which form in every other way its greatest strength. We are back again at freedom: the elbow-room, the opportunities, the excitement of space. America began with freedom, with the escape from the frustrations and inequalities of the Old World; but even in doing so she became immediately in one sense a confined Old World herself—confined to certain kinds of occupation. It is not yet one hundred and ninety years since the Declaration of Independence was signed, and inevitably the over-riding concern of those years has been the ensuring of comfortable survival, first of the family and then of the nation. The process followed a swift, straightforward development, so that the necessity of the plough and the shotgun became that of the computer and the anti-missile missile; and it left little time, energy or emotion for bothering to keep up with other nations in pursuits which were not materially useful. As a result, the patterns of growth on either side of the Atlantic have gone on showing the shape that was already apparent in de Tocqueville's day:

> . . . at the very time when the Americans were naturally inclined to require nothing of science but its special applications to the useful arts and the means of rendering life comfortable, learned and literary Europe was engaged in exploring the common sources of truth and in improving at the same time all that can minister to the pleasures or satisfy the wants of man . . . .

So now, when America has progressed so far that she can sit back and consider her development, she finds one side of her civilization superbly advanced, the other painfully old-fashioned. She is lopsided. Her highly individual nation has not grown naturally, as other nations do—absorbing an influence here, a movement there, from near neighbors—but for more than half its life has imported ready-made those things for whose natural evolution there was no time or energy to spare. "They were enabled," explained de Tocqueville paternally, "to enjoy the treasures of the intellect without laboring to amass them." And the premature decadence of the fine arts is not the only result: areas like religion and education are also regarded, in the United States, less as bedrock eternals than as sturdy bulwarks of the ideal of family and national health. They grew from imported seedlings, not from seeds. Most of the nations of Europe evolved, by historical and geographical accident; but the United States of America is man-made, and it will take very much longer than a hundred and ninety years for the unsteady pattern of that making to grow into a natural equilibrium.

Thus, in effect: you can't expect the people of the United States to value the arts in the way that older nations do, as a necessary and natural foundation for living: they haven't had long enough to learn. They have been busy with other things. That historical freedom which came with a bang when they first arrived in their country pushed them immediately into a rut from which few of them have yet been able to escape. For this lack of time, the only remedy is the passing of time.

There is too that other hindering freedom: the giant size of the U.S.A. In the context of the arts, Europeans can very easily forget the overwhelming effect of this, talking of a cultural entity called "America" as if all Americans must necessarily share the same tastes and ideas and habits of mind. But how can they? Many different cultures and shades of artistic effort are embraced within the distances between London and Baghdad, between the English Channel and the Sahara Desert; and it is these same distances which stretch between the coasts of America, east to west, north to south. Geography would work against a unified "cultural scene" in America even if history did not. Had the country been evolving gradually for three thousand years, instead of rapidly for three hundred, it would contain not one national culture but a number of highly idiosyncratic regional cultures—a very much intensified version of the differences in climate and ideology that exist there now between the east and the west, the north and the south, the coasts and the hinterland. It is easy to see where America's modern tribe-lines would have been drawn, and easy to realize that they never will be drawn; for the development of regional cultures demands isolation, and the educated American is far too mobile to grow unshakeable roots now. It remains to be seen whether he has become mobile enough for the country to coalesce, one day, into a new and flexible kind of cultural whole.

Certainly it is no such thing yet. As an intellectual or cultivated élite, with leisure, has always proved the most vital ingredient in the diet of the arts (as audience, patrons, critics), so a country acquiring its own definable artistic personality has always seemed to require a focus: a London or Paris or Milan

which will attract the best and set up the resultant high standards as a yardstick for the rest of the nation. But how can America have such a focus, being so big, and containing so many local
loyalties not strong enough to promote regionalism but strong
enough to hinder unity?

There are many large American cities which must seem, to
their loyal inhabitants, to contain the elements of such a focus.
"Oh come on," say these inhabitants, when one is less than enthusiastic about the cultural climate of the U.S.A., "in X we have
really a very good orchestra . . . and the Met touring company
comes once a year . . . and the Junior League does a lot for the
arts. . . ." But although they love and admire their own city,
they can judge it only by the standards they have acquired by
living there; and those standards, ninety-nine times out of a hundred, are simply not good enough. The second-rate, in any one of
the arts, is harmless enough when it can be measured against the
real thing; but the real thing is too seldom found, and there is no
substitute for it in warmly praising the second-rater for the sincerity and effort he has put into becoming second-rate. Where is
the city that differs from these: the city whose cultural aspect any
American would be proud to exhibit to the rest of the world and
say: "This is the best we can do"?

Consider some of the contenders. There is Washington, for
instance. The noise made about a "culture invasion" when the
Kennedys arrived there, with French chef, White House concerts
and Harvard men, seemed curious to people in London and New
York; to them the President and his wife appeared merely as persons of civilized and reasonably sophisticated tastes, with enough
money to indulge them. One look at the nation's capital, however, makes it understandable that Jacqueline Kennedy should
have developed a certain sense of mission. Washington does have
some good pictures: a collection of moderns at the enchanting
little Phillips Gallery; a Whistler collection at the Freer; and a
solid representative span of the centuries at the National Gallery.
Its symphony orchestra is mediocre, its concert hall awful; but

there is an agreeable chamber orchestra attached to the National Gallery, run by the ebullient American composer and conductor Richard Bales, and a good weekly recital at the Phillips. Its theater is minimal, consisting of a large theater for touring musicals, and a small, beautiful theater-in-the-round, the Arena Stage, whose director and repertory company spent twelve years battling their way up through a minute cinema and an ancient brewery before finally blossoming with a grant of $800,000 (which came not from city, state, or federal government, but from private donations and the Ford Foundation). There are three "summer theaters," which can hardly bear much weight in the business of finding a focal city; ten cinemas, no resident professional opera or ballet. There is, in short, enough to make the place agreeable to live in; but it would be farcical to suggest that Washington has the resources—even with the founding of the Kennedy Center for the Performing Arts—to evolve into any kind of national concentration point for the arts. The only things that come remotely near the necessary standard are the pictures and the *Washington Post,* which is one of the three best newspapers in the country. And the untimely departure of the Kennedy family leaves the city of government even less likely to grow into a cultural capital than it was before.

Then there is San Francisco, magical city of street-precipices and gull-clouded wharves, clanging cable-cars and creeping Pacific mists, with the steel-lace of the briges and the gleam of the sea calling you down between the hodge-podge of slanting roofs that crowd every hill. This is the city with which every European falls in love, feeling after his long loud trek across the continent that he has in some curious way come home; this is the city in which every other American will tell you he would one day like to live, though he never will. This is the only really bewitching city in the United States; the city which did not deserve the racket of the Republican convention in 1964. Here you will do and see things that you do not, somehow, find yourself doing or seeing anywhere else: watching the dawn light the Golden Gate from Telegraph Hill; surveying the suit of armor, the skull, the red plush and all the other splendidly ostentatious junk in Melvin Belli's improbable law office; drinking Irish coffee in a wharfside bar among beards and stringy hair; dodging among the firecrackers and dragons and paper lanterns of New Year in Chinatown; wandering on foot among the flower-stalls and Volkswagens and skittering lunchtime office girls without ever feeling that you should be about to leap into a car. One morning I was lost in San Francisco, standing in a sidestreet peering at a map, when a little man stopped beside me and said very courteously: "Excuse me for troubling you, miss. But I think you need to know your way in my city, and I very much need a quarter for a glass of wine. Perhaps we could help one another?" I looked at him; his breath stank of cheap wine, but he was not drunk; the shabby clothes were neat, and his face was grave, with the alcoholic's faint air of desperation but no obsequiousness. So he gave me my directions, and I gave him a half-dollar, and he lifted his hat with a curious dignity and went his way; and there seemed more to it than just a nifty touch by a wino. In Washington I had been appalled when a small Negro boy stopped me in a street and asked for a nickel to get something to eat; could this be prosperous America, in which a child had to beg? But in San Francisco, one can take good and bad more placidly, without astonishment. Indefinably it is more urbane, more sophisticated, better-informed than most other American cities; it takes things for granted that they have never learned; and it has, in this sense, a culture which they lack.

All the same, it is not the hub of a national wheel. It is a local center, and an excellent one. A magnificent museum of modern art; one of the only three professional opera companies in America, one of the eighteen professional ballet companies outside New York. An agreeable array of the telling sidelines of the arts, ranging from clubs like the "hungry i" to the leisurely well-stocked bookshops. An orchestra which is not so good; no newspaper of the first rank. But one very lively theater, the

Actors' Workshop, which has been on the verge of bankruptcy once or twice but now flourishes after acquiring a two-year grant of $98,500 from the Ford Foundation and $10,000 a year from the city. (They also give the opera $70,000 a year, and the orchestra $65,000.) The city's motives are not altogether altruistic; the money comes from a fund for promoting tourism. Pseudo-culture has its place in San Francisco too; "The opera," said one actor scathingly, "is patronized very flamboyantly by people who've inherited boxes from their parents and want to be seen sitting in them." Nevertheless, there the theater is, with a fulltime staff of thirty-three, with good repertory actors, and with a founder-director of uncompromising views (albeit one who has since been lured away to New York City to co-direct the Lincoln Center repertory theater).

> Part of my philosophy is rooted in the fact that American audiences aren't educated. So during school terms I take the five best actors in the company who aren't currently in a play, and put them—all in black, just to give a semblance of costume—into a forty-five minute cavalcade of comedy, pieces from Aristophanes, Molière, Shaw, Ionesco. Then we offer this as a public service to any high school in Northern California who wants it. Sometimes we play twice a day. The kids get really elated by the program. And at off-peak performances here, like matinées, we let them in for a dollar a head, and they come in bus-loads. That way, we're beginning to develop the theater-goers of the future—and it's top-notchers they're seeing, not amateurs. I deplore bad theater . . . .

A city in which a professional man of the theater could say rude things about the amateur stage without worrying about setting Society on its ear is an adult city, deserving of respect. And San Francisco has the air of a place that has been quietly growing to maturity in its own way, at its own speed, without much dependence on anything that was happening elsewhere in the U.S.A. It is an old city, and polyglot, and already it has a slightly seedy air, as if its glorious self-reliance were beginning to run down; but there is a refreshment to be felt from the moment that one drives in from the airport past those alternately green and roof-cluttered hills. San Francisco has an indefinable grace—but it is, unfortunately, a grace that cannot be disseminated across the rest of the United States. This city cannot be the throbbing heart of the country's cultural standards and life; for although it is in itself an ideal microcosm, its magnetism is of the wrong kind. Playwrights and players, composers and musicians, and all the rest, need a spiritual and material market-place containing the ruthlessness of rejection, as well as appreciation and taste. And San Francisco is above all a tolerant place; the ruthlessness on her coast is all further south, in Los Angeles. The young artist does not announce to his family: "I'm going to San Francisco" as he might in England breathlessly say: "I'm going to London." It is more as though he said: "I'm going to the South Seas."

There is taste in Boston too, though perhaps not quite as much as most Americans think. History hovers here as it does in Europe, from the London-like calm of Beacon Street's tall brick houses to the top of the Bunker Hill monument; and time and genealogy are valued by the "proper Bostonian" families, though their ascendancy is diminishing now. For all its less decorative aspects—the slums, the "muggings," the constant grubby roar of pneumatic drills as expressways or office-blocks are built—Boston is, like San Francisco, a gentle city. Learning is in its air, as well as reconstruction; from the great teaching hospitals downtown, to the ivy and glass towers of Harvard and M.I.T. across the Charles River in Boston's Siamese twin, Cambridge. And the heart of the place is not a geometrical criss-cross of undistinquished streets, but a broad green common scattered with elms and chestnut trees, whose new leaves mark, in April, the turning of the iron New England winter into a London spring.

Boston has arguably the best symphony orchestra in the United States; the Boston Symphony, like the New York Philharmonic, can stand comparison with any orchestra in the world. The Museum of Fine Arts and the Gardner Museum are splendid art galleries. There is perhaps something disquieting about the sight of thirty-two Monets strung out in a row at the former, as there is with all those Rembrandts and Rubens at the Hermitage in Leningrad; as if one were eating so much at once that the palate became numb. But there is also an uncommon sense of a national artistic background in the sight of rooms and rooms of American silver and furniture from the eighteenth and nineteenth centuries (though this too, alas, can cause despondent reflections when one turns to Sears Roebuck and the big popular furniture stores. There still are the colonial American designs, skilfully mass-produced in modern veneers; but of the good modern American design which should have grown out of them there is, outside the expensive small stores, very little sign).

Turn then to theater, opera and ballet, and the picture in gentle Boston changes. Although there is a splendid concert-hall, there is no resident ballet; and the only approximation to a resident opera company is the Boston Opera Group, which has a highly dynamic director, and stages several excellent productions each year with guests like Joan Sutherland and Geraint Evans, but is not comparable with the Met. There are three theaters, of which one, the Charles Playhouse, contains a brave repertory company, founded in 1957, good enough to flourish with Beckett, Ionesco and Genet. The other two are the home of Broadway try-outs and touring companies. In this respect, as in the parallel between the Boston Symphony Orchestra and the Hallé, Boston is the Manchester of America. It is an accepted stopping point on the international tour-circuit of the United States, so that it will get a Menuhin recital, or a week of the Kirov Ballet, or three days of the band of the Black Watch, if any of these is "doing" the continent. It has recently acquired a much needed new auditorium inside the Prudential Center skyscraper. The pre-runs of new plays and—far more often—new musicals on their hopeful way to Broadway can sometimes agreeably broaden Boston's theatrical diet; the member of an intellectual élite would, however, have some difficulty in finding out beforehand precisely what the new play is like, since the critical standards set by reviewers in the Boston papers are, like the standard of the papers themselves, a long way short of those in London or New York. His only hope is to buy the *Christian Science Monitor*, Boston's nearest equivalent—continuing the Manchester parallel—of the *Guardian;* but if he buys no other newspaper at the same time he may find his picture of the world taking on a faint and curious tinge of the religious organization by which that otherwise admirable journal is run. ("We don't specify that our staff shall be Christian Scientists," said its excellent editor to me once, deadpan, "but most of them are.")

Like the rest, then, Boston must fall short of being a cultural standard-setter for the United States. It is good to live in, but it exerts no national influence in any of the arts. It is a civilized city of art dealers and antique shops, and the odd bookshop here and there; it trains some of America's best future musicians at the New England Conservatory of Music. But it is a New England focus; its lines of force stretch only through the northeastern corner of the United States. It is not the Mecca that every civilization has seemed to need since civilizations began.

There are a dozen, two dozen other major cities; the list could go on in a long diminishing train. There is Chicago, with its symphony orchestra and marvelous modern French paintings; its jazz clubs and coffee bars and expensive antique shops, and all the other things that make up the other side of the coin from the gangster-image of the Windy City. There is Los Angeles, with its magnificent new concert-hall, with Forest Lawn and Disneyland, freeways and smog, flamboyant restaurants and grubby seashores, and all the tinsel and dream-glamour of the mini-culture of Hollywood given their future memorial in the Watts Towers, those weird inter-twirling spires of steel and junk and broken glass, quietly built over thirty years by the Italian immigrant Simon Rodia. There is Detroit, St. Louis, Houston, Philadelphia, Cleveland, Salt Lake City; in these and other cities one may live and not starve from a lack of those involved in the arts. But not

one of them has any great awareness of what is being thought or
said in the other; nobody from one of these cities would gladly
flee to one of the others as if to a fount of wisdom and excitement
and ideas. Not one of these is king of the rest; they are all, in the
end, provincial centers, separated by too many hundreds or thousands of miles from one another and from the rest of the world.
The hunt for Mecca has to end, inevitably, in New York.

There is no point in detailing the "cultural attractions" of
New York City; the list would become tedious—which is, of
course, an obvious sign of the vitality of the place. It is the only
city in America, as far as the arts are concerned, which can be
mentioned in the same breath with the capitals of Europe. There
is nothing anywhere else in America to equal the Metropolitan
Opera, or Balanchine's New York City Ballet; no other city
which could support several small orchestras as well as the New
York Philharmonic; no other city with a twentieth of New York's
theater. Greenwich Village may contain a sizeable amount of in-
verted Culture-worship, but it is about twice as alive as Hamp-
stead or Chelsea, not least because it contains so many of the plays
which have been forced to flee even from the idea of Broadway
by the appalling cost of putting anything on its stages. New York
has all the appurtenances, good and bad, of a civilized capital;
the supper clubs with the off-beat jazz pianist or the small neo-
satirical revue; the private galleries, the books, the antiques, the
foreign-film cinemas, the art schools, the music schools, the drama
schools, the nuts that are called kooks, and so on and so on; and
as well—perhaps it is almost a necessity, since every other "civilized capital" has its equivalent—the dark side. Here too are the
beaten or rebellious poor, usually immigrant or Negro; the
crime; the vicious, ambitious competition; the stoniness of Wall
Street and Madison Avenue mentalities; and the failures. These
last may not seem very relevant to discussion of a culture; yet
they are. They are side-signs of the necessary ruthlessness of the
place that is to set standards, the signs which San Francisco lacks;

for no center can become a Mecca for the excellent unless it is capable cruelly of rejecting the mediocre and the weak.

And so it is to New York that many of the hopefuls in the arts go to find the home of the best; that magical, misted Manhattan skyline is evocative of more than money, as are the grubby golden pavements of London. The European reacts strongly to life in New York, feeling either love or loathing, as he does to the fierce personalities of most other capital cities in the world. All roads in Britain lead to London; all roads in the United States of America lead to New York City.

And yet, and yet—do they really? Is New York highly civilized, or merely highly sophisticated? Does she draw those who seek the best, or those who seek the greatest success? Does she exert any strong unifying influence on the "intellecual side of civilization" behind the Golden Curtain? I rather doubt it. None is very obvious. Perhaps she would never grow to complete capital status unless government were to go there to join commerce and the arts. The only examples of her effect that I can recall finding elsewhere in America are the sorrowful plaints of a New Yorker transplanted by his firm to Ohio, and longing desperately to go back ("The theaters," he mourned. "The restaurants, the music. And most of all the people. . . .")—and the fact that the Actors' Workshop in San Francisco was established by two expatriate New Yorkers, Herbert Blau and Jules Irving (who later returned to the fold when invited back by the Lincoln Center). The citizens of Charleston and Seattle, New Orleans and Dallas, do not look to New York City for the best of their cultural life in the way that the people of Bristol or Liverpool or Brighton look—grudgingly, but realistically—to London. Geography is against it; the distances are too great. History is against it; why should these people look to New York for cultural standards, when for two hundred years they have never been accustomed to look to her for anything at all, except possibly their employer's head office and the Stock Exchanges?

So there is no really effective cultural focus in America, capable of changing the assumptions and values of people in every other state of the union, and perhaps there never can be. Perhaps in any case I have the wrong idea, and none is needed; and instead there lurks somewhere in the country the seed of an alternative method of creating a friendlier climate for the arts. Perhaps this lies, as Dwight Macdonald suggested, in the self-conscious development of an intellectual élite. But although the United States of course has its men and women of the arts, its scholars and thinkers, those who create and those who appreciate, they do not seem at present to conjoin in ways which can make this absent climate. Their communication is of a private kind; they are insulated from the rest of the nation, as such people generally are in every country of the world. They live and work in small groups in many American cities, or in isolated retreats; many of them are to be found in villages or small towns within concert-going distance of New York, Boston or San Francisco, or research-going distance of Harvard, Berkeley or Yale—primarily, that is, in Massachusetts, Connecticut and California. God forbid that they should all be slung together in one great cultural community. But as it is, they do not manage to affect the overall development of American civilization; to check the advance of Midcult, or the pretentious sterilization of High Culture. They remain oases in a kind of desert, with the irrigation channels not yet built: and it is not their job, after all, to worry about building such channels. Their job is simply to do their own work, which itself is difficult enough.

This is the dilemma of the stranger: to feel a great uneasiness about the cultural climate of America, when comparing it with that of the country from which he came, and not to be able to see anything that will put the uneasiness at rest. It is very easy, of course, on this subject more than any other, for a European to irritate Americans beyond measure. We English, French, Italians and the rest have done nothing to deserve the comparatively sophisticated cultures of our countries; we simply happened to be born into civilizations which had already been developing for upwards of a thousand years, in close relationship with one another. What right have we to come finding fault with the cultural characteristics of the U.S.A.?

We have this right: that through the sheer size, prosperity and youthful vigor of their birthplace, the strongest of those American characteristics have begun to spread their influence rapidly over the entire world; and that unfortunately the strongest characteristics are also those which happen to be valueless, even destructive. The multi-national Renaissance of seventeenth-century Europe was a kind of glorious flowering which happened at its own speed, through a happy combination of social conditions and talent; but the Renaissance of Rubbish for which the United States has unintentionally been responsible during the twentieth century is no such thing. It is a forced development, without real roots; something which owes more to the ease with which hundreds of prints of a movie can be distributed throughout the world than to any burning original talent behind the movie itself. Although it thrives through the excellence of modern communications, it does not seek to communicate. The so-called popular culture which embraces both Mr. Macdonald's Masscult and Midcult, and which is born out of the social efflorescence which J. B. Priestley labeled "Admass," has very little to do with the real "intellectual side of civilization"—and can, in fact, eat away at it like a form of dry rot.

We have, as foreigners, this right to point out how the pseudo-culture is blighting the growth of a real culture in the U.S.A.: that this same pseudo-culture, vigorous as a weed, may very well at its present rate choke out the live cultures of our own lands. How much genuine musical talent and appreciation is trapped half-grown by the soporific treacle of Broadway musicals, or the undemanding hiccups of rock'n'roll? How much feeling for words and drama is suffocated among the thin-kerneled corn of movies, television and big bad novels? The real blight of a deep-rooted feeling for culture in the United States is not lack

of time, or excess of distance, but the strength of mediocrity—
and the fact that mediocrity itself breeds a kind of defensive self-
satisfaction that is one of the most effective components of the
Golden Curtain.

If you do not yourself share this self-satisfaction, you will
know what I am talking about. If you do share it, you will by
now be seething with resentment at my apparent ignorance of
the rapid modern development of the arts in the U.S.A. But before you begin to write me an angry letter about the vast
amounts of money now spent on building cultural centers, or the
great boom in children's music lessons, pause a moment to consider some of the condemnations you yourself have made of 90
per cent of the stuff which goes to make up your national culture.
It is no good trying to split that culture into a serious, educational side and an entertainment side, and pretending that the
former is the only one that matters. A culture, and the arts which
are its skeleton, cannot be split; though their basic intent is serious it is part of the business of the arts, all of them, to
entertain—so long as they do not sacrifice their integrity in the
process. But how often have you denounced the infantile, ratings-
catching noise which television programs offer as an apology for
music? How often have you regretted spending good money on a
movie which turned out to be made as a trite vehicle for a face or
a body, or turned away from a cinema showing one of those
effusions which are aimed at attracting teenagers, but which deliberately keep their audiences down at the mental level of a re-
tarded child of twelve?

When did you last congratulate yourself on having seen a
satisfying straight play, acted by a cast which could draw good
notices in London, Paris, Moscow or Berlin? How often, in the
last year, have you been offered a concert by an orchestra of international rank? How many operas have you had the chance of
hearing well sung in the last ten years? When did you last watch
a full-length ballet, danced by professionals?

I could, of course, put these same questions to anyone living in one of the remoter parts of Britain, or of any European country, and be given some depressing answers. But these are the countries which have acquired, after slow centuries of development, the definable artistic focus which acts as a showcase for the highest standards. That focus itself is not necessarily easily accessible to more than a minority of the nation; its riches are not widely distributed (though they are perhaps more easily available to the outposts than are the lesser riches of New York City to the cowboy in Nevada or the farmer in Illinois). The point is that its standards exist, and have gradually become diffused throughout the land. It is not accessibility which is the real strength of the arts in the older countries; the best measure of their cultural maturity is what might be called their intellectual atmosphere. And this, in most cases, is very different indeed from its counterpart in the U.S.A.

How long, then, will it be before that atmosphere changes in the United States? How long, before the American artist ceases to feel that he is living in a dark tunnel, or a lukewarm bath? What is it that must happen to improve his lot—and the lot of those whom he exists to serve?

Clearly the answer does not lie in regionalism, as it might once have done if the people of each region had had time to think of such things. Americans may be insulated, from one another and from the world, but they are not isolated; speed and mobility have made it so easy for the Masscult and Midcult unifiers to spread—television, the Lucepapers, pop records and brand names—that no region now can develop a cultural personality distinctive enough to cut it off from the rest. The fifty states have much autonomy, much fierce state-loyalty (usually in the wrong contexts, as in Mississippi) and many differing habits of living due to climate and historical circumstance; but in matters relating to "the intellectual side of civilization" none of them differs in kind from the rest.

Clearly too the future does not lie dormant in the cultures that flourished in the United States before most of the Americans came. The single-minded Early American machine was as good at extinguishing these as it was at killing off the buffalo. Mohawk Indians work steel-helmeted as steeplejacks in New York City today, and Apaches fight fires in the mountains of the Southwest; the Cherokees have an Olde Indian village for tourists in North Carolina; the Chippewas harvest wild rice in Minnesota; and the Plains Indians live poorly on reservations in Montana. Nobody gives much thought to the first Americans, except as inferior people. Only the Navajo, ninety thousand of them in a Southwestern reservation twice as big as Belgium, or the Pueblo Indians in the valley of the Rio Grande, have anything like live civilizations now.

Culturally, those Indian lands have an air of the might-have-been. None of the Indian tribes anywhere has made much imprint on the American way of life; only their names remain, in places as far removed from one another as the Algonquin Club in Boston and William Faulkner's Yoknapatawpha County—which was, they say, the original Indian name for Oxford, Mississippi. But Santa Fe, in New Mexico (fifty-five miles from Taos, to which D. H. Lawrence went briefly to live), lies on its seven-thousand-feet-up plain between the blue-white sky and the bleak brown dust, like a living monument to another culture that allows the comforts of modern American living to rest on it only like a veneer. All the buildings there have the square solid lines of Indian adobe, or baked mud, of which many of them are still made; and the paintings and sculptures and pots of the artists who live and work there are nearly all natural developments of the Spanish-Indian world that made up the Southwest of America for three hundred years during and after the Renaissance.

And the pueblos of the Rio Grande, set on land that was given in perpetuity to the Indians by the federal government, hardly seem to be part of modern America at all. The endless brown scrub called mesquite stretches round the snow-tipped peaks of the Sangre de Cristo mountains, and the sunsets through the rarefied air are red and purple and green. Nothing will grow up here without irrigation (which is uncommon) though in some parts of the reservations further west oil and uranium have been found, and the Indians drive about in Cadillacs. But this is not really Cadillac country. There are no roads in most of the pueblos; dirty children play barefoot on the hard-baked mud, among the adobe huts and round beehive ovens, and shout "Give us a dime" at the occasional strange car. The pebble-decked adobe churches, nominally Catholic, seem dedicated both to the old gods and the new. But although bustling modern America is slow to give the Navajo good drains or education, it treats the products of their culture with respect. From San Francisco to New York City the work of the Southwest is sold: Navajo, Pueblo, Zuni, Hopi; the gleaming black pots from San Ildefonso, the strange bright chunky designs woven into woolen cloth, the stylized paintings of ceremonial dances, and the beautiful wrought silverwork—rings, brooches, bracelets, neck-clasps (and, these days, cuff-links) of coin silver and rough turquoise from Indian mines. There are a few technical colleges in New Mexico at which the silversmiths have learned to improve their techniques, but their fundamental designs are as old and distinguished as the pueblos—a roof timber in one of which has been found to have been cut in 1370 A.D.

One Pueblo silversmith took me from his workshop into his house, past the children tumbling in the dust and the heap of piñon pine chips. Crude Indian rugs and bright pictures of the Virgin hung on the adobe walls, and in one corner his mother, old and wrinkled as a prune, sat drilling holes in turquoise beads. She had never traveled more than a few miles from the pueblo, but two of her sons had been killed in the Pacific, fighting in the U.S. Army in the Second World War. It was difficult to imagine what picture she had of the values of her world. The silversmith went proudly over to a corner, pulled back one of the brightest rugs and revealed a television set; he had saved up to buy it when electricity came to the pueblo two years before. He turned it on, and a chorus-line from a variety program blared forth, Masscult at full blast, the light glinting out of it on to the silver clasps lying on the table with their secret, runic, graceful designs. It was even more difficult to suppose what the old woman of the pueblo made of that, as she sat there using a hand-drill of the kind her people had been using when the *Mayflower's* timbers were still acorns. But perhaps she made nothing of it at all, for she spoke not a word of English. America has more than one kind of insulation.

It is only the difficulty of reaching them which keeps small worlds like this from being swamped by Masscult, or at best Midcult. Americans are curiously reluctant to learn from others; from the beginning there seems to have been an element of the defensive, even before they had a way of life to defend. When they first came to the east coasts, they behaved—perhaps because so many of them were English—as the English did in India: as stiff-necked colonists, refusing to see anything worthy of adoption in the native cultures they found. They lacked the wisdom of the Romans, the Saxons, the Normans, the Danes; they took the Indians' advice on survival, but in the matter of any art or craft that was not materially useful they had about as much interest as they had in intermarriage. So the old cultures remained separate, as they do now except in places like Santa Fe; or they died.

Even the constant influx of immigrants from outside cultures, European, Mediterranean, Middle-Eastern and Asiatic, has produced no overall long-term influence; except perhaps in the effect of Jewish idioms on the American language, and in the more diffuse effects of Spain and the Orient on the architecture, music and religions of the West Coast. There are only the innumerable different "specialty" restaurants, spreading a tolerance for alien foods; and still, in every sizeable town, the insulated groups—the Polish district, the Jewish quarter, the Swedes, Italians, Irish, and so on—keeping to their old ways of living for two or three generations, but not communicating them much beyond families or districts because no one beyond wants to learn. And in any case, of course, these are not whole cultures that have been imported, but only random parts of them; immigration is a far more fragmentary thing than the migrations of long ago in Europe and Asia, when whole tribes, whole cultures, would plant themselves in a new land. Today, the real values may remain behind. So in modern America, this mixture of people born into different sets of standards, yet not necessarily bringing the full height of those standards with them, has not yet fused into the lively, vibrant, multi-national culture that could, in every district and region, be the only substitute for one formed gradually by time. Midcult and Masscult are here, but the uncompromising standards are not. America is often called a melting-pot; but the different lumps in the pot are a long way from melting together yet.

So here is the United States, which has developed some marvelous ways of using its money but has not yet found a way of using its mind in the way that it could be used. Instead of a lively complex culture it has—beneath a veneer of immense activity—a patchy, static almost-culture, threatened with an early death by any number of influences which pretend to be part of the arts but which really belong to entertainment or intellectual snobbishness. Whether it really begins to grow, and whether it grows in the right direction, depends on several things which have nothing very much to do with the fine arts, or even with the portmanteau concept of Culture. It is the intellectual climate of the country which needs to change; this climate is made by people, and by their prejudices and preoccupations and their readiness to learn. And it is unlikely to develop usefully beyond its present stage unless there is a breakdown in the insulation which at the moment keeps it tightly bound to the completely irrelevant concept of the American Way of Life. America may be a federation of states, but it is also a nation; it may be a nation, but it is also part of the English-speaking world. If only it could forget about the deliberate seeking of Culture, and take rather more real interest in the rest of that world, it would find that by that strange osmosis which is a commonplace in the history of

Europe its own cultural life would become richer and more individual in the process. Objective self-examination is not a characteristic of the average American, which is perhaps why all those
anxious sociologists are publishing his self-examination for him.
But it would not do him any harm to go in for a few reflections
of the kind once made, for instance, by the American thriller-
writer Raymond Chandler in his working notebook. Chandler,
British-born but American-minded, happened here to be writing
of the relationship between the American and English languages;
but everything he says, translated into more general terms, could
equally well be applied to the relationship—or lack of it—
between the intellectual side of civilization in America and that
on the other side of the Golden Curtain. In everything he says he
is honest with himself, neither defensive nor aggressive; he is, in
making his judgments, deliberately and dispassionately mid-
Atlantic. How many other Americans involved or pretending to
be involved in Culture could say the same? And how many of
them would be prepared to discuss the idea that this kind of approach, in the long run, is the only way to develop American
civilization into something better than a dark tunnel or a lukewarm bath?

> . . . American is a mass language only in the same sense that
> its baseball slang is born of baseball players. That is, it is a
> language which is being molded by writers to do delicate things
> and yet be within the grasp of superficially educated people. It
> is not a natural growth, much as its proletarian writers would
> like to think so. But compared with it at its best English has
> reached the Alexandrian stage of formalism and decay . . . .
> . . . The language has no awareness of the continuing stream of
> culture. This may or may not be due to the collapse of classical
> education and it may or may not also happen in English. It is
> certainly due to a lack of the historical sense and to shoddy
> education, because American is an ill-at-ease language, without
> manner or self-control.
> It has too great a fondness for the *faux naif*, by which I

mean the use of a style such as might be spoken by a very limited sort of mind. In the hands of a genius like Hemingway this may be effective . . . . When not used by a genius it is as flat as a Rotarian speech.

The last-noted item is very probably the result of the submerged but still very homespun revolt against English cultural superiority. "We're just as good as they are, even if we don't talk grammar." This attitude is based on complete ignorance of the English people as a mass. Very few of them talk good grammar. Those that do probably speak more correctly than the same type of American, but the homespun Englishman uses as much bad grammar as the American, some of it being as old as *Piers Plowman,* but still bad grammar. But you don't hear English professional men making elementary mistakes in the use of their own language. You do hear that constantly in America . . . .

Since political power still dominates culture, American will dominate English for a long time to come. And American cannot as yet vitalize itself—it just isn't good enough. America is a land of mass production which has only just reached the concept of quality. Why then can it produce great writing, or at any rate writing as great as this age is likely to produce? The answer is, all the best American writing has been done by men who are, or at some time were, cosmopolitans. They found here a certain freedom of expression, a certain richness of vocabulary, a certain wideness of interest. But they had to have European taste to use the material.

5 ⁂ Insulated New World

> *"Does he want to be a giant?"*
> *"He hates the giants, but he is making himself one all the same; he likes their apples!"*
> *"He will be very miserable when finds himself a giant."*
> *"Oh no, he will like it well enough. That is the worst of it."*
> *"Will he hate the Little Ones?"*
> *"He will be like the rest; he will not remember us—most likely will not believe there are Little Ones. He will not care; he will eat his apples. . . ."*
>
> —GEORGE MACDONALD,
> *Lilith*

When Senator Barry Goldwater won the Republican Presidential nomination at San Francisco in July, 1964, both sides of the Atlantic echoed with cries of astonishment and dismay. The alarm was particularly marked in Britain, where most observers had thought it impossible almost up to the last minute that anyone with the Senator's record of blinkered, reactionary statements could ever be taken seriously as a candidate. The size of their mistake—Goldwater's 883 votes to Scranton's 214—is the most remarkable example yet of the insulating effect of the Golden Curtain, that two-way barrier of strong wrong images. Nobody was able to see through it, into America, and to comprehend quite how many Americans are cut off on the other side, blithely and unwittingly insulated from ideological contact with the outside world.

This is the most astounding of all realizations for the visiting European. It creeps slowly into the mind, like a cold mist. Inevitably the first chill strikes when you encounter blank ignorance about your own country: I remember from my own first weeks the businessman who thought Scotland and Wales had their own parliaments; the State Department official obsessed with the idea that the great mass of the British public spent all their free time playing bingo; the high-school sixteen-year-old, visibly struggling to find some scrap of knowledge about England as she shook hands, who could come up with nothing but: "Do you do much fox-hunting?" Often the American who will tell you proudly that his great-grandfather came from Essex will not be able to tell you the name of the current Prime Minister of Britain. His general knowledge tends to be limited to his own country. France, for him, means de Gaulle, Paris and perfume; Italy means pizza and spaghetti; Greece often means nothing at all. If he is over forty, he probably picked up a certain amount of social geography from his travels during the Second World War; if he is about thirty he may in the same way know something of Korea. But otherwise he tends to know far less about the rest of the world than does the average modern European; he has more in common with those nineteenth-century Englishmen who thought the English Channel the outer limit of the civilized world.

All this is puzzling at first. Surely the basic geography and history taught in American schools is no more introverted than that taught anywhere else? (Oh yes it is—much more.) Surely the immigrants bring information with them? (Perhaps—but of a patchy kind.) And what about the nationwide American worship of the Fact, which has led to the enormous rise in sales of "non-fiction" books and encyclopedias, and to the vast circulations of predigested-fact journals like *Time* and *Newsweek?* Do none of these things give a sense of wider horizons beyond the seas?

Apparently not—for understanding requires more than exposure. The alarming thing is not that the American doesn't know much about the world, but that he doesn't care. Few people anywhere are well informed on subjects which do not interest them; and for a great many Americans, nothing that happens beyond the shores of the United States can conceivably be interesting unless it has some connection with U.S. business, U.S. servicemen or the great U.S. enemy, Communism. As a result, the international flavoring in their generous diet of facts is very small. Except for one or two extended surveys like the Huntley-Brinkley report, most radio and television news bulletins pay only token attention to foreign news, and the only newspapers to give it anything remotely resembling the space it gets in the major European papers are the *New York Times,* the *New York Herald Tribune,* the *Washington Post* and the *Christian Science Monitor.* Local, or at the most national, news covers almost every other front page every morning in the U.S.A. And it is natural, for the growing young American, to assume that this is the proper order of things. Let us spread knowledge of America to the rest of the world, through the embassy libraries and the Voice of America, the European editions of American newspapers and the living propaganda of the idealistic young members of the Peace Corps. But let no one suppose that there might be any kind of self-obligation to bring the equivalent knowledge of others into the American home.

Obviously and mercifully, there are exceptions to this. The U.S. government spends millions of dollars every year on bringing in foreigners of various kinds for "exchange" visits, often one-way, and there are many members of small specialist professions in America (ranging from the curators of art galleries to the upper executives of firms with foreign markets) whose work keeps them in close touch with Europe and Europeans. The academic world tends naturally to keep up the old international free-masonry of scholarship, whether it involves an M.I.T. professor commuting between Cambridge, England and Cambridge, Massachusetts, or the liberal arts student at Stanford University

—or any of about seventy-five other colleges—who spends a required year of his undergraduate course studying in Italy, England or France.

There is tourism, too. During 1962, some 990,000 Americans visited Europe (and spent about $660,000,000 there). But then tourism is a commodity of dubious value. Even if the American does not stay at Hilton Hotels wherever he goes, or travel on one of those "package tours" which insulate him so devotedly from everything except the accepted Sights, he seldom gains much from his peregrinations except tired feet, a stack of color slides, a few comic anecdotes of the "Connie-and-that-guy-in-Milan" variety, and a hodge-podge of impressions of beauty, rain and bad plumbing. "What is remarkable, on reflection," says Daniel Boorstin ruefully, "is not that our foreign travel has increased so much. But rather that all this travel has made so little difference in our thinking and feeling. . . . As the obliging foreign producers work harder to give Americans just what they expect, American tourists, in turn, oblige by becoming more and more naïve, to the point of gullibility." Abroad even more than at home, many Americans are extraordinarily good at remaining cut off, in the way that nearly all U.S. service communities abroad are cut off from the surrounding life; good at going everywhere and encountering nothing. They have fun, and good luck to them; but still many of them are as insulated as the ordinary non-Atlantic-crossing American.

And it is above all this ordinary American, who will never be able to afford to leave his country, and may even never leave his home state, who is unaware of the events, ideas or standards of the rest of the world.

To a great extent this perilous innocence is no more than the effect of physical separation. It is not difficult, if you settle down inside one community in the U. S. A., to see the way perspectives become ingrown. Outside the centers of administration, business or the major universities, there comes creeping in very soon a feeling that Europe is infinitely far away, a slow-moving community of small tired men; a kind of dim-lighted irrelevance round the bright tension point of Berlin, with the black sinister mass of the U.S.S.R. looming beyond. What meaning has this kind of place for you, if you are the Indian silversmith on his high pueblo in New Mexico, the steak-weaned ranch-hand in Texas, or the campus-caught assistant professor bound up in the thought of gaining "tenure," in a remote college somewhere in Oregon?

In the big cities, the world is the city, or at most the state; and outside the cities the world is smaller still. The European goes to America holding in his head the vague image of the great arterial expressways that cross the continent, throbbing with streams of driving, go-getting businessmen and salesmen; but he has never been given cause to think about the other Americans, hidden in the sidelong acres to which the expressway is only a remote roaring streak on the horizon: the people in the small communities with names like Middletown and Springfield and Bowling Green.

In one of these in Ohio—Northwood, a place with the kind of roads on which every house is known not by number or label, but by its owners' name—a small, gnarled, brown couple called the Pachelieffs farm twenty acres of land. Their son and daughter have both gone away to the towns, the daughter to teach, the son to run a garage; but their parents stay on the farm they have run for thirty years. It is a small holding typical of those individual lots in northern Ohio which still resist the inroads of land-hungry, corn-growing, mechanized farms—though the suburbs are crawling nearer over the flat fertile land, and the real-estate men will soon be knocking at the door.

Thomas Pachelieff came to the United States from Bulgaria in 1912, and his accent is still thick. He and his American wife are in the process of moving from their weather-scarred wooden farmhouse to a long, low brick house which they have built sixty feet away across their muddy yard. The new house has a kitchen of which they are very proud, with innumerable tufts of wires bristling from its bare plaster walls to embrace, eventually, the ovens and the deep-freeze and all the other everyday electrical cosseters of the country. The Pachelieffs are by no means wealthy, but they follow an American pattern; they have made money and used it, they watch their television set and read their local morning paper—and their world extends no more than fifteen miles away, to the market, which is about to close.

"Mister grows all kinda crazy vegetables." Mrs. Pachelieff, in red shirt and baggy blue jeans, is tough and tiny; she looks indestructible, like something out of the Li'l Abner comic strip. "Endive, peppers, eggplant, parsley root, salsify, dill for pickles . . . last year we raised a lot of leek. And this smooth li'l lettuce, bibb lettuce, we been raising it for ten years. Up to recently there was this élite grocer used to buy it for his customers, some of them'd be people who'd buy *ten dollars worth of wine a week.* . . . Oh, Mister loves the garden work."

She looks out at the bent, cloth-capped figure levering himself down from a tractor on the flat brown fields. "This used to be all sparrowgrass once, clear to the back. We used to raise twenty-five bushel a day. But its real difficult now you can't get the help. Times have changed. Why, years ago everyone round here had a cow for their own family—today there isn't one cow on this whole road. And times is awful hard for vegetables and such. They don't take things to market any more, they take them to a co-op. The market is dead. Mister says he just don't understand it, he says people still have to eat. . . ."

In the making of the American image abroad, people like the Pachelieffs, with their private preoccupations, are given no part. But they are important because there are so many of them; and because they are necessarily insulated people. Thomas Pachelieff was an immigrant, but he was only eighteen years old when he came, and if you ask him about Bulgaria he smiles vaguely and does not have much to say. "I was learning the tailor trade three years in the old country. We came over on a boat. Then I did some factory work, and when I was a young man twenty years old I went to work in a garden for the first time. It was in *this* country," he says with careful emphasis, "that I learned gardening."

He sifts absently through a pile of root vegetables on a cart in his yard, and holds up a bunch of salsify. "See this oyster vegetable, every year I grow it now. I got regular customers. The Poles, they cut the root in chunks, claim it tastes just like sea-oysters. But the Syrian people, they use the tops. . . ." And for a moment there is a strange example of the paradoxical double-insulation of American life: the Bulgarian-American is completely American, and the old life has contributed nothing much to the new except his accent; yet although the Syrian-American and the Polish-American have become just as completely absorbed into the civilization as he, instinctively he still refers to them as Syrians and Poles. The ordinary American, insulated from the rest of the world, is often insulated from other Americans as well.

The remoteness that comes from geographical separation is hardly anyone's fault—though neither does it constitute a virtue, which is why Europeans, with a thousand years of quarrelsome neighbors behind them, tend to be irritated by Americans who trumpet proudly that their country has never started a war. But there comes a point, for the marveling stranger, at which the insulation begins to appear emotional, connected more with people than with types, and one begins to suspect it of growing from some general American attitude to life. This is the first encounter with the national subconscious: the curiously defensive pride in the American way, or the American dream, or any of the other introverted synonyms used so often in the U.S.A. It is the pride that hits the stranger hardest, before he has had a chance to examine the parts of the thing everyone is so proud of.

It is more than local pride, more than patriotism, more than the built-in response to the "Star-Spangled Banner" and the words of the Declaration of Independence. It is a kind of accidental complacency, which is a little less than arrogance and a little more than smugness: and it can sometimes be very alarming indeed. It alarmed me exceedingly, for instance, on the twenty-third of October, 1962. I was in Washington, then, at the most nerve-wracking point in the Cuban crisis. After the White House had been mysteriously incommunicado to everyone for three days, the President had burst the mystery the previous evening by appearing on television with the grim revelation of Soviet missile bases in Cuba, and the Americans' subsequent naval "quarantine" of the island. He said, uncompromisingly: "It shall be the policy of this nation to regard any nuclear missile launched from Cuba against any nation in the Western Hemisphere as an attack by the Soviet Union on the United States, requiring a full retaliatory response on the Soviet Union." It was not a very comforting time to be English; further Soviet ships were steaming towards Cuba, American troops and missiles were massing in preparation for possible invasion, and I could think of nothing but the fact that was painfully obvious to everyone back at home: that the easiest, nearest and most necessary target for Soviet nuclear attack in the event of any spark-off was a small NATO base half the size of California, called Britain.

But it was not just this reflection which made the twenty-third of October a frightening day: it was the reaction of everyone all around. From end to end, Washington—a highly strung city at the best of times—was prickling with the nervous conviction of three-quarters of a million people that an atomic warhead was about to come whistling down on them at any moment from the south; and, worse, with the grim belligerence shown by almost everyone, Republican and Democrat alike, in support of "strong-arm" tactics at any cost. In hotels, in restaurants, in stores, no one seemed to be talking about anything else. It began for me in a bus, where a large, hot-faced man in a sweatshirt drew me and my neighbor, all of us strangers, into compulsive conversation. "We should show that Khrushchev we mean what we say," he boomed, militant and unsmiling: "We should go out and drop bombs on the whole damn lot. Get rid of all those bases, show them we're tough." He really did say "Show them we're tough," and all round him there were approving nods.

Outside the White House the pickets were parading in two kinds of groups, all of them seeming fairly young. One set of placards read "Invade Cuba" and "Less Profile, More Courage": the others "The UN is Our Last Hope" . . . "Brotherhood Not Bombs." I passed two women talking: "I think it's time to call Khrushchev's bluff," said one with much vehemence, and the other looked at her and said simply: "I'm terrified." And then later, in a drugstore, there was a drunk. He sat slumped on his stool at the soda-fountain, wearing a Stetson, and being deliberately rude to the pretty Negro girl behind the counter. He was drunk, but he was also American; and he was saying loudly and remarkably clearly to all the drugstore: "Blast 'em all off the face of the earth, that's what I say. All the foreigners. Just leave the Americans. Blast off all the foreigners." I was beginning to feel very foreign by then; very English indeed.

They were not all like that. I crossed Washington in a taxi, and the driver was a self-possessed Negro woman in bright green earrings and a neat suit. She said almost at once when she heard the accent: "D'you hear our President last night?"

"I heard him."

"Didn't you think he was wonderful?"

"He spoke very well. It won't be so wonderful if we all get blown up."

She made no kind of wrathful retort; she turned round nodding in such violent agreement that the taxi nearly went into the curb, and after that the conversation became a kind of warm Southern monologue.

"Yes, *ma'am*. Me, I'm scared. Such terr'ble times we live in, no one trusting no one else, and that bomb li'ble to go up—

almost by accident they could do it, press the wrong button. But there ain't much for us to do 'bout it, is there? Live one minute to the next, I say. Enjoy life. Me and my husband, we're Cath'lics, we believe whatever's going to happen, it's to happen. But it's serious all right, this time. You hear that little quiver in the President's voice? . . . We got to trust him, I guess. But me, I'm praying."

It seemed somehow a saner reaction than most of the rest; without the unnerving assumption that only what this country thought, what this country wanted to do, should control the fate of the rest of the world. I began to feel a little less like a nervous hamburger about to be crushed between two gigantic approaching hunks of bread. But I was soon reminded where I was. Before long I was being given a lift by a State Department man, who pointed out with a certain sense of drama the shotgun lying in the back of his car. "It's for some friends of mine," he said, wholly serious. "They haven't got one in the house, and they'd feel safer with it, a time like this."

The key to the whole day seemed to come later from the same man. "Of course," he said in passing, quite casually, "now that Washington is the capital of the world. . . ."

There is one saving grace in the terrifying insulation of this kind of American, and that is the way in which the engaging ridiculousness of some fringe of his life always, in the end, interrupts. Cheerfulness will keep breaking in—which has never been the case with properly megalomaniac nations or regimes. On the evening of October twenty-third, the anxious tension over what Russia or America would do next about Cuba was probably at its cracking-point; nerves clanging, people in millions of homes sat glued to their television sets—and, so did I, bitterly reflecting that if I were going to be blown up, I would rather have been blown up in Britain, instead of receiving what James Reston has since called "obliteration without representation." A news bulletin flashed on to the Washington television set, and in the middle of making the tensest of all the announcements about what was to happen next to the world, the announcer stopped. "We'll be back in just a moment," he said, "after this message." And an underwater girl in a swimsuit twirled across the screen, advertising soap.

But then as any good American knows, it is the freedom to advertise soap, to make, sell or buy soap or anything else, to love or hate soap as you please—it is this freedom which must at all costs be defended from any threat of alteration. The Soviet footing in Cuba constituted such a threat, and therefore must be removed—preferably under its own steam, but failing that, by force. It was not a good way to make friends, in America during the Cuba crisis, to suggest that one might consider—just *consider*, just *suppose*—whether the ordinary Soviet citizen might not be forgiven if he sometimes felt similarly alarmed, for the preservation of his own system, by the equal proximity of the NATO missile bases in Turkey and Great Britain. One woman to whom I made this rash suggestion looked at me with immediate suspicion and dislike. "I didn't know," she said coldly, "that you English were pro-Communist."

The witch-hunting days of the late unlamented Senator McCarthy are thirteen years past, and it would not be easy to find anyone outside the John Birch Society who would admit to wishing them back again; but this does not mean that the ordinary American has learned to pronounce the word "Communist" as if he were not talking about Antichrist. Instead, he manages in a most striking way to give the impression that he not only disagrees with the Communist system, but hates and fears it. Say this to him, and he bristles instantly at the word "fear" and begins at once to argue, somewhat irrelevantly, that godammit he isn't afraid of any Red and if they think he is they'd better watch their step, that's all, and so on; and the more ardently he proclaims this, the more an outside observer feels inclined to think he doth protest too much. However they may be defined, the emotions he feels about the Soviet Union and its system are strong and hostile; and when he finds out that you have visited the place, and begins asking questions, it is a melancholy business to watch the suspicion creeping over him if you praise anything dating from the years after 1917.

For one of the most striking things about the insulated American is this: he is utterly convinced that the ultimate aim of the gospel of Communism is the overthrow of the United States of America, and he will not therefore countenance any kind of attitude towards it but hostile watchfulness. If he goes to Russia as a tourist, he comes back deeply relieved by the contrast between the Russian's gloomy way of life and his own; he will still be watchful, but his fears have been allayed. The enemy may have sharp teeth, but he doesn't look any too healthy. . . . Sometimes I think—and I thought it particularly at the time of the Cuban blockade—that this is all yet another example of too little time and too much distance; that because America has not had the European nations' long weary experience of living cheek-by-helmet with former enemies and possible future enemies, she is subject to a kind of virginal hysteria; expecting imminent rape with the sort of conceited alarm that is liable to bring it on even if it weren't intended in the first place.

At all events, there is one particularly distressing thing happening in America today, which nobody gave me any reason to expect to find. It is the rapidly advancing identification of anti-Communism with Americanism; the growing assumption, far more insidious than any of Senator McCarthy's vicious outbursts, that all the ideals and attitudes involved in the American Way of Life should be respected and promulgated not simply because they are worthwhile, but because they can help to prevent the spread of Communism. Capitalism becomes anti-socialism; Christianity becomes anti-atheism; the Bill of Rights is invoked as if it were a kind of blueprint for civil defense. The United States began their existence with a relatively tiny war against a system whose pride conflicted with their own; and the way of life which they now enjoy springs, as monuments and national holidays remind us, from the success the Founding Fathers achieved in that war. But the old relationship between revolutionary war and way of life is beginning curiously to blur. The way of life itself, now, seems to be dissolving into the shape of a weapon to be used in another kind of war against another kind of system's pride: a propaganda war, in which organizations like the patriotism-promoting Freedoms Foundation compete with, say, Russia's Young Communist League in exactly the same terms. "Our country," says the Freedoms Foundation literature, "is in peril because the Communists make it so. The world is in turmoil. Two ideologies are locked in deadly battle for the souls and property of men. On our side are the forces of feedom and liberty led by the United States of America; on the other, the forces of atheistic Communistic enslavement led by Russia, Red China and their satellites. . . . One system, and only one, will survive this struggle. . . ." Turn the names around, and these are the identical accusations made against wicked capitalist America by any system-supporting Russian or Chinese. Does the United States really need such stuff?

Organizations like Freedoms Foundation have no political affiliations in the United States; they take, indeed, great care to avoid any taint of partisanship. Yet it is sometimes difficult not to see, within the country's convoluted political framework, a continuous emotional stream that links the supporters of such groups with the Goldwaterite Republicans, the Southern Democrats, and all other American conservatives. Conservatism, of course, is not an isolated political entity in the U.S.; it is not a credo, but a quality of mind, and as such it stretches across both political parties—a fact which many Europeans failed to realize until civil rights and Barry Goldwater became properly live issues in America and the international press. And the same is true of fervent Americanism and fervent anti-Communism—two of the most common ingredients of insulation. Yet these are not

its only ingredients: they do not make up the single inevitable
recipe. They make, rather, a kind of vague triple influence waving its way in and out of American political and economic life;
those Americans who exert or are affected by the pressures of
insulation are seldom those who are fanatical or obviously preju-
diced in any way. A typical example is former president Eisenhower, a collection of whose utterances over the last twenty
years—each of them in itself mild and unexceptionable—would
make up a handbook for the weaving of the Golden Curtain. As a
Republican, Eisenhower tends naturally to have a more conservative outlook on economic policy than the Democratic Party; but
he is not in general a man of overwhelmingly conservative views.
Yet it was Eisenhower, at the 1964 Republican convention, who
proved a crucial influence in the adoption of the ultra-conserva-
tive Barry Goldwater as presidential candidate. By ostensibly
standing aloof from the battle, and refusing to express any public
preference even when his brother was making the nomination
speech for the more liberal candidate, Governor Scranton, he
proved to be—for Scranton—a classic example of "he who isn't
with me is agin me." Comparing Eisenhower's silence with the
strong anti-Goldwater speeches being made by moderates like
Governor Rockefeller and Senator Keating, the wavering Republican electorate said to themselves: "I know which way he'd vote,
if he didn't feel it wrong for a former President to tell." And
after the convention was over, looking at the pictures of a beaming Eisenhower congratulating a beaming Goldwater, they said
to themselves: "There—you see?"

Thus Dwight D. Eisenhower, meaning only to unite his
party, arrayed himself finally with the forces of insulation; for
Barry Goldwater is without doubt the most insulated American
one could ever find this side of fanaticism. It was not a matter of
weakness of judgment, or of incomplete understanding; Eisenhower's prompt questioning of Goldwater's famous rash statement that "extremism in the defense of liberty is no vice" was
just as promptly satisfied. It was the triumph of introversion, that

leather lariat within which America was consciously enclosed for the whole of the last century, and with which she is in danger of unconsciously strangling herself now. The feeling—which presumably inspired Eisenhower's actions—that "the important thing is what's good for America" can very easily shade over into "the only thing in the world that's important is what's good for America." It is like the nuance of shifting stress by which Americanism becomes identified with anti-Communism. Eisenhower, like very many others, either disregarded or did not see these two changes in emphasis. Standing in the first camp, he looked at the second and saw no mensurable difference; so had no difficulty in giving it his support. But the difference is there; and very perilous it is.

Many Americans, of course, are well aware of the peril. Adlai Stevenson made a speech to the American Bar Association in August, 1964, which put up a deliberate parody of the over-the-line assumptions involved in Goldwaterite foreign policy—and which reads too, therefore, like a parody of the patriotic aims of Freedoms Foundation and the rest. In a world of nuclear weapons, said Mr. Stevenson, the "tacit understanding" between the U.S.A. and the Soviet Union about the need for restraint was "under violent attack."

> The critics claim it is miserable appeasement to accept a world partly under hostile ideological control. The enemy must be made to disgorge people groaning under the heel of exploitation and despotism. He must be threatened right up to the brink of war with the menace of nuclear punishment, and it will be found, then, that his nerves are not up to the strain and he will give way. All this negotiating, all this talk, all these "hot lines" from White House to Kremlin are simply capitulation to the sworn opponent. Such weakness, such slackness, must be rigorously suppressed . . . .

At this point in his speech, with his entire audience assuming the reference to the "tough" foreign policy of Goldwater and other insulated Americans, Mr. Stevenson smiled blandly and said that he had of course been describing the attacks of Chinese Communist critics on the policies of Soviet Russia. Laughter, applause.

> But I should not be surprised if these strident calls have strange
> undertones and overtones of language that we hear nearer at home.
> The two ends of the political spectrum, like the two ends of the
> tuning fork, often vibrate in harmony. Both extremes in inter-
> national politics are lethal . . . .

The furthest extreme of insulation in the United States is represented, of course, not by Senator Goldwater but by some of the organizations, like the John Birch Society, whose support he was forced, for the sake of his own "image," to renounce. At meetings like one called the New England Rally for God, Family and Country, such groups denounce President Johnson's "mild" foreign policy; denounce the Civil Rights Bill; denounce every imaginable kind of outward-looking ideal, and adopt as their final motto: Get the U.S. Out of The U.N. "Crazy people," say all my American friends, with the same kind of bored disgust that the average Englishman always felt for the antics of Sir Oswald Mosley. Yet these crazy people too preach the worship of the American Way, in terms not unlike those of Freedoms Foundation.

It is in this worship that the real roots of insulation lie. Nothing so strong as worship is even necessary; a genuine respect is enough to keep the plant alive. You can still find the God's-own-country complex as you work back through the pattern: from extremism to anti-Communism, from anti-Communism to self-conscious Americanism, from Americanism to normal everyday life. Thus although there is nothing very alarming about the extremists, who take the elements of insulation to such a point of self-caricature that their compatriots find them an object of mirth or scorn, it *is* alarming to the stranger to discover how many of these elements can be present in the normal American mind. They are accidental; they are bred unconsciously by the effect of growing up in an insulated society; but they do exist, and form the main reason why the Golden Curtain has been able to grow up without anyone realizing it was there.

To try to draw a portrait of the ordinary insulated American is of course to court disaster. There is no prototype; there are only various combinations, in various proportions, of certain characteristics. But some of the characteristics can be defined—so long as one remembers that each of them is generally quite harmless on its own, and becomes perilous only when combined with some of the rest. The insulated American tends, for instance, to be a man who is firmly proud of being an American, and not hesitant about saying so. Though he may sometimes envy older nations like the English their unconscious sense of history, he makes the most of his own, and the concept called the American Way of Life—a phrase which he is not afraid to use—was born out of his pride in his own nation's background and beginnings. It is for him an ideal that has been handed down to him by his forbears, and he tends to feel that although the ideal is based on the broad principles of love of God, love of country and love of family, it has come now to incorporate many aspects of life that are linked with the country's modern social and economic structure. Thus he is aware that his recognition of the "way of life" image involves him not only in the past but in supermarkets and the draft, rockets and expressways; in the management class structure, in high-pressure salesmanship, in broad-based education available not as an intellectual exercise but as a constitutional right. If he is employed in public relations, advertising or selling, he feels no lurking private shame over his occupation, but can justify its values to himself. He respects ambition, success, and self-made millionaires. Except in time of national recession, he tends to suspect the poor of idleness. He is often rather serious about himself; cheerful kidding of others is part of the equipment of his sense of humor, but self-mockery is not.

He is not necessarily a Puritan (though many insulated Americans of course are) but he does try to live according to a certain moral code—from motives partly of religious belief, partly of belief in self-control. If he can easily afford liquor, for instance, he is seldom drunk, but does drink rather rapidly during the first determined-to-relax hour of a party—which he will tend to turn, later in the evening, into a kind of innocent orgy, with the spirit of freedom bumping against conformity as it does constantly in the insulated American mind.

He is generally well-informed about his own country. He resents Charles de Gaulle, and anyone who doubts the merits of the war in Vietnam. He would indignantly deny charges of race prejudice, but he is seldom anyone who has given money or help to the cause of civil rights, and he tends to assume unconsciously that Negroes, if not actually inferior to whites, all have simple minds.

He revered Sir Winston Churchill, but has had little contact with modern Europe. He would like to spend a holiday in Japan. He can be rich or poor, Republican or Democrat, young or old, successful or obscure, but he is seldom a first-generation American. He is to be found fairly often in Government posts, notably the U.S. Foreign Service: for if a man is to serve his country abroad, the first requirement is that he shall be safe. And the insulated American, able sincerely and patriotically to argue with equal force in support of such diverse entities as nuclear weapons, Christianity and capital gains, is a good security risk.

Even when glitteringly intelligent, he tends to complacency; the size and strength of his country give him a deep-lying sense of security. He is not intellectually adventurous. If he reads a book, it will be one of the mammoth novels by people like Irving Wallace or James Gould Cozzens or a work of popular sociology by someone like Vance Packard. But however seriously he may discuss the latter, he does not really believe that there could be any major inherent weakness in his own society. At the same time, though, he has a faint subconsious feeling of unease about life in general, and he does not know why. In his heart, I suspect, he feels it is because of Communism; and that the world would be all right if only Russia and Red China would go away.

Now this kind of thing, of course, reads like a gigantic gen-eralization, and is liable profoundly to iritate any American who finds within it one or two phrases which might fit himself, but is certain there is nothing insulated about his own mind. His automatic reaction therefore will be to cry that this is rubbish, there is no such person, these unrelated little observations have no point. But they have. Remember that this is not a generaliza-tion, not a portrait. No indeed, there is no such person (though there might well be, if you search for a while through your ac-quaintance) as the model insulated American. But there *are* many apparently innocuous characteristics, far more than those listed above, which can become disturbing when they reach a na-tional scale; when one finds them occurring again and again, in different permutations, within a particular society of people. "So many million Americans can't be wrong," says the cigarette ad-vertisement. Well, they may or may not be wrong, but they cer-tainly can't be ignored; and nor can a hundred million or so sets of characteristics, all differently patterned, which add up to the word insulation. Many insulated Americans exist, cushioned against the ideas and emotions and hopes and fears of the rest of the world, because a number of ordinary qualities in their na-tures, like the ordinary qualities of their way of life, have become inbred: affected, now, by no influences save those which they themselves produce. Such Americans, institutions and people alike, are very different from what they might be if the Atlantic were only forty miles across.

The most disturbing thing of all, perhaps, is the discovery that the longer one lives in the United States, as immigrant or alien, the less anxious one tends to be about this circumstance. This is America, it's a marvelous place, does anything else really matter? One grows, thus, accustomed to the things that at first caused astonishment and dismay; one makes excuses; one "un-derstands." It comes, of course, from the change in perspective. This is the other side of the fence, where the Giants live. Outside, there are only the Little Ones; and it is possible to forget, and in the end not to believe, that the Little Ones exist at all. Too often, this is the process known as "becoming Americanized."

6 ✲ One Nation Under God

*"There is no country in the world where the
Christian religion retains a greater influence
over the souls of men than in America."*
    —DE TOCQUEVILLE

A handsome young Negro was haranguing the gawping crowd of
men in Pershing Square, under the dusty palm trees that bristle
all over Los Angeles like tired upturned paint brushes. He cried:
"And so, if we all accept the Lord Jesus Christ as our sav-
iour . . ." On the other side of the square an old, old woman
dressed all in white, the withered face strange over the little-girl
clothes, was shouting into the faces of indifferent loungers: "You
people who come out here and sit in the sun, do you think how
much God gives you . . . ?"

The city was hot and airless. I wandered away down the
street and into my hotel. Impressive notices inside advertised a
sun-deck on the roof; perhaps up there, fourteen floors high, a
small breeze would blow. Up I went in the elevator, to find a
landing with some upturned chairs, a drinking fountain which
didn't work, and a furled American flag; and a door, which I
opened gingerly, expecting to find a crowd of people out on a
glossy patio in the sun.

There was no one there. It was very quiet. The roof had an

enclosure with a wooden-slatted floor, and a scattering of about a dozen battered green beach-chairs, half straight-backed, half loungers; two faded beach-umbrellas over tables, and several sandbuckets with dead cigarette-butts stubbed in them to show that at least someone had been there, once, a long time ago. A chin-high barrier ran round the edge of the roof, with window-boxes where nothing grew but two or three stumpy, prickly cactus. The blue-white Los Angeles haze was all over the sky, and the sun went down through it like a furry orange. I looked out at it, past the roofs of higher buildings, past the big sign CALI-FORNIA MUTUAL SECURITY, where round and round like a slow radar scanner went the news in lights that the temperature was 72° and the time was 4:59. And when the lighted time flicked to 5:00, there in the silence with only the mutter of traffic far below and the click-clack-clank of the tall narrow elevator mechanism jutting from the roof, another noise came suddenly from somewhere across the street: a jangling tuneless cracked-bell sound that became recognizable, in a little while, as soupy hymns played from some kind of electric campanile. I looked out at the orange sun, dropping lower now; and beside it, on a roof over the source of the tinny hymns, between the two great winged red horses of a Mobil Oil sign, two giant words sprang suddenly into brilliant neon life. They seemed to summarize something, in that warm smoggy evening—because I could read them, but only from behind. They said:

ᒐႮᒐᒣ ᒐᘓᐴᒐ

It is not uncommon, especially in condemnations of "athe-istic Communism," for Americans to speak of God as if he were the country's own property. The expression ubiquitous on public platforms, "this republic under God" (with almost as long an ancestry as "one nation under God") tends to give the same im-pression. And indeed organized religion does make up a far greater part of life in the United States today than in many countries with an established state church. The land in which school prayers were declared non-compulsory by the Supreme Court, in 1962, is also the one which probably goes in more for communal prayer than any other Christian nation. St. Patrick's Cathedral in New York, tucked down between the commercial cliffs of Fifth Avenue, is a symbol of the way in which spiritual values, in the United States, have been kept on terms with the other side of life. No godless materialism for the Americans. It is on Sunday that they can feel themselves a staunch God-fearing bastion against the over-sophisticated world-weariness of Europe. (Normally, I do realize, this is a comparison no American would think to make, but one heard it quite often during the trial of Dr. Stephen Ward—a gentleman who, with Mr. Profumo and Miss Keeler, gave Britain a prominence in the American press that she had not achieved since the headlines that read MEG WEDS PHOTOGRAPHER.)

On Sundays, the American churches are filled, everywhere from the sleepy white spires of small New England towns to the brand-new cathedral that dominates San Francisco from the top of Nob Hill. Of a population well on its way now to 190 millions, some 65 per cent goes to church; within the last twenty years there has been a stupendous rise in church-going in America, reaching a peak in 1959 and afterwards slackening; only the Episcopalian and Eastern Orthodox churches now are still growing faster than the population. One of the country's most lively minded churchmen, Dr. James Pike, the former Episcopalian Bishop of California, says that the peak was largely an after-effect of war: "There was a considerable increase in awareness of personal anxiety, so that people felt the need for religion. And it was a period in which the churches themselves were finding better ways of being articulate—better public relations, if you like. Then there was the self-saving element, the fear of Communism. A very irreligious reason for going to church, when you come to think about it. Some people disparaged the boom all along. They said it was no more than a phase. 'You've tried tranquilizers, why not try God?' That sort of thing. All the same, the more people a church has around, the more chance it has to consolidate, and that's our job now. With"—he grins an amiable unclerical grin— "a lot of nice new buildings as a result of the last few years."

The churches in America, and those who run them, give an impression of being much more open-minded than many in other countries (despite the well justified gibe, current in Negro and liberal white circles, that eleven o'clock on Sunday morning is the most segregated hour in the nation). The most obvious difference is in manner; the clergy, from Roman Catholic cardinal to Baptist minister, seem to the foreigner a jolly and unpretentious lot, notwithstanding the frequent and paradoxical efforts of many of their flocks to treat them as apostles reincarnate. It is not uncommon for clergy in the Episcopalian Church—the American cousin of the Church of England—to come into the church relatively late in life, from another career: Dr. Pike, for instance, was formerly a lawyer and Naval Intelligence officer, with a doctorate in law from Yale. And there is not only increasing interrelation between the country's proliferating Protestant churches, but between Jews, Protestants and Catholics. In America today you can find Christians taking doctor's degrees in Hebrew seminaries, rabbis reading lessons in Episcopalian cathedrals, Protestants and Catholics working together in civil rights crusades, or preaching in one another's churches.

Beside this open-mindedness—perhaps because of it—there is a tangible feeling of self-sufficiency about religion in America. Although almost every denomination in the world is represented there, they have been isolated by distance long enough to develop a distinct character of their own. The aura is perhaps most noticeable around Roman Catholicism, which is the biggest single faith in the country, embracing about 30 per cent of the population, and which naturally has the highest weekly church-going figure—about 72 per cent—of any major denomination. It is also by far the wealthiest church, and in many ways the most self-confident. The impulse towards liberalization sparked originally by Pope John XXIII seems to have led in the United States to a more vigorous conflict within the church than in some other, stuffier countries. The most striking example is probably the controversy over birth control, with discussion and rebellion against the continuing official view of Rome reaching such a pitch within America that *Time* magazine was able to publish in August 1964 the bold, if unattributed, statement: "It is estimated that about half of married Catholics use some form of contraceptive sometime during their lives." This same magazine, the Lucepapers being always religion-conscious, provided a side-illustration of the American qualities of American Catholicism in a typical anecdote about Richard Cardinal Cushing of Boston, head of the third largest Catholic archdiocese in the country. In Rome in 1963, they said, "when President Kennedy visited the North American College, Cushing was on hand to greet him, with a group of sobersided clerics looking on. Instead of offering the episcopal ring to be kissed, Cushing squared off, aimed a mock right hook at the President's solar plexus, and bellowed: 'Hi, Jack!' "

But perhaps *Time* came nearest to the point in observing that "inevitably, millions of U.S. Catholics are . . . the born-and-bred bead-sayers for whom faith is simply a comfortably furnished apartment of the mind." This is no doubt true all over the world, yet at the same time it is probably the main reason why, in the U.S.A., the most supranational of all the Christian denominations can seem to be so essentially American, as firmly rooted behind the Golden Curtain as the economic system. Distance and lack of casual interplay have their effect again, and the American Catholic is not a being who strikes one as having much in common temperamentally, beyond the basic tenets of faith, with his Irish or Italian counterpart—unless, that is, they too have emigrated and become part of the golden fold.

This same elusive individuality exists in the American branch of the Anglican Church (that is, the Church of England), which is a relatively tiny denomination in America; 45 per cent of the population is Protestant, but less than 3 per cent Episcopalian. The historical background gives more apparent importance to the church than it really possesses, since three-quarters of those who signed the Declaration of Independence were Anglicans, and the resulting residual social and traditional appeal meant still that about half the children at the best-known preparatory schools (America's nearest equivalent not of English prep schools, but of English public schools), and at many non-denominational colleges, will be Anglican as well. "It means," says one bishop, "that in a funny way we're still regarded as the established church. As an Episcopalian bishop you're still treated as Mr. Religion—partly also, I suppose, because you're both Catholic and Protestant at once."

The Episcopalian Church in America tends in many ways to be more closely identified with the way of life around it even than the Anglican Church in England—which, being the established state church, is as undeniable a national symbol as the English monarchy or the American flag. The church's fastest rate of growth in America is found not in the cities, but in the suburbs, where for the swift-shifting families of the United States the church is often the only element in life—except the family itself—which provides emotional continuity. So it must work to embrace all those who move, within it, from one unit to the next; satisfying, as one clergyman puts it, "both the high church guy from Milwaukee and the low from Virginia." Perhaps it is for this reason that the Episcopal Church, like the Catholic, seems to have a peculiarly American face. "One of the dangers of the American church," says James Pike, "is that through this period of trying to keep up with success, and to provide people with roots, we've become overly busy. Often an ordained man trained in theology finds himself involved in a sense of haste and rush, in being a businessman. Partly it's a matter of catching up in staffing, getting the laity into roles of delegation—we've not quite caught up with ourselves. But as things are, we still rely very heavily on the Church of England for thinking and theology. In America, we're occupied with putting those things into effect."

The most obviously American characteristic of religion in the United States is its astounding variety. There are more than 250 known religious denominations in the country, and at least 100 others which are not registered anywhere. In order of magnitude, after the 45,500,000 members of the Roman Catholic Church, the list runs thus: 23,500,000 Baptists, 13,000,000 Methodists, 8,500,000 Lutherans, 5,500,000 Jews, 4,400,000 Presbyterians. After these six there is then a gap of more than a million before the next denomination on the list, and many of those which follow can be classified as Protestant: varieties of nonconformism which are divided often only by very narrow doctrinal differences, based generally on their country or district of origin. It is not easy, for instance, to tell the difference between the Calvary Pentecostal Church, with 20,000 members, and the Pentecostal Holiness Church, with 47,000; or between the 204,000 members of the Christian Reformed Church and the 205,000 members of the Reformed Church in America. There are not many successors to the really determined Protestant rebels; the puritanical extremists who not only came from Europe seeking religious freedom, but proceeded at once to isolate themselves from their fellow Americans to be sure of keeping it. The Shakers are almost entirely extinct, and though the Amish still flourish in Pennsylvania and Ohio they could not, with their total of 50,000, be called a large proportion of the Christian population.

The sects which grow fattest and strongest in the great fish-tank of American religions are not like this. They are instead the products of two hundred and fifty years of Protestantism in the American milieu; they are what America has done with nonconformity. They appear to resemble the more orthodox Protestant denominations, yet have fundamental differences; they are curiously old-fashioned, yet are all, in competitive America, very rich. They are also influential, and have found a way out through the Golden Curtain. We talk a lot in Britain about the insidious spread of Masscult out of the United States: the rock'n'roll beat, the Hollywood treacle, the alleged vulgarizing of practically everything. But we seldom think to attach any significance to the fact that this same country has also produced the world's only major *new* religious denominations of the last hundred years. Once upon a time the freedom of the U.S.A. attracted minority sects from other countries; now its own minorities send missionaries back out again. And these new sects, born and bred in America, have enough in common to make them a kind of living commentary on their homeland.

The Big Three of the self-exporting minorities are the Mormons, the Christian Scientists and the Jehovah's Witnesses, all fairly familiar by now in Britain—though not perhaps in quite their home form. The best-established in the United States are the Mormons: the Church of Jesus Christ of Latter-Day Saints. There are 1,800,000 of them in America, and three-quarters of a million in the rest of the world. Salt Lake City, in Utah, has been their headquarters (and the home of the current head of the church, known as the Prophet of God) ever since Brigham Young made its site the end of their first famous and polygamous trek over plains and Rockies in 1847—though their overall distribution has followed the pattern of the population explosion, and today there are more Mormons in California than in Utah, Idaho and Arizona put together. The Mormons' history was somewhat bumpy from the beginning, possibly because they regard themselves as a chosen people who have established the new Jerusalem. The Book of Mormon, which they use alongside the Bible, and which you are likely to find at your bedside in many western hotels, charts the history of an alleged ancient American race in a parody of the style of the Old Testament; the sect's founder and first Prophet, Joseph Smith, claimed to have found it inscribed on golden tablets (thus going one better than Moses) on a hilltop in New York State. All their way west the Mormons were persecuted, and Smith was killed by a mob in Illinois. When his fol-

lowers finally settled Utah, as determined and industrious farm-
ers (they still constitute 72 per cent of its population today), so
many more unnerving incidents followed that federal troops
were sent into the state, which was not admitted to the Union
until 1896. By that time the Mormons had abolished their practice of polygamy; not, they now claim, because of civil pressures,
but because "it had accomplished its purpose, which was the
same as that in ancient Israel—to raise a righteous posterity."
Many of the early Mormon elders—though only 3 per cent of the
whole church, they say—had several wives, and Brigham Young
had seventeen. Today's Latter Day Saints limit themselves to one
each, and make their background sound like a series of highly
moral and rather dismal stud farms. "Plural families have made
relationships kinda complicated now," said one youthful Mormon elder to me cheerfully. "My great-grandfather has five thousand living descendants—if we want to have a family reunion, we
have to rent a park."

Certainly there is nothing wild about modern Mormons;
they don't smoke or drink alcohol, tea or coffee; they are polite,
restrained and anxious to please—about a thousand earnest
young American Mormons are scattered across Britain at this
moment working as missionaries. The church is highly prosperous, receiving a loyal 10 per cent tithe from all its members; not
only does it own most of Salt Lake City, but it has recently begun
building a fifty-storey skyscraper in Manhattan, whose lower
floors will become the headquarters for the 300,000 Mormons in
the eastern U.S.A. It appears to be on good terms with all other
denominations; it has no particularly peculiar religious practices;
it is in all apparent respects an image of what might be called
religious regularity. "He's a Mormon," said an American lady to
me once in casual conversation, speaking of some local lad. "He's
a *good* boy." She, so far as I remember, was a Baptist.

Not every American speaks with such warmth of the second
of the Big Three minorities, the Christian Scientists, whose hopeful little reading rooms and Churches of Christ, Scientist, are dis-

tributed halfway across the world. America has more than two-thirds of the 3,300 branch churches (they keep no membership figures), and though the sect began in New England its largest concentration, predictably, is along the Westcoast.

Christian Science was founded—or as they say, "discovered" —ninety-eight years ago by Mary Baker Eddy, a remarkable lady of forty-five who cured herself of a serious illness, spent years digging into the Bible to find out how she thought she had done it, wrote a book called *Science and Health,* and proceeded to teach others how to heal. "She was convinced that this was no such thing as a miracle in the ordinary sense," says Robert Peel, one of the church's administrators, "but that healing happens according to law and principle. Hence Christian *Science.*" Peel, who works with about a thousand other fulltime Scientists at the large and splendid headquarters of the sect in Boston, was formerly an English lecturer at Harvard and a leader-writer on the *Christian Science Monitor.* He says that the church doesn't proselytize, but grows mainly through the healing work of its "practitioners," which appears to draw unbelievers into the fold through gratitude and wonder. "My own father was healed of acute appendicitis. And my grandmother was healed of an inoperable cancer after the doctors had given her only a few days to live. She survived for twenty years. . . ."

Christian Science practitioners are, in effect, faith healers, with no medical training; anyone who goes to them for a cure need not himself be a Christian Scientist, but is expected to give up all medical treatment. "We find that medicine and Christian Science treatment simply lessen one another's efficacy. So we rely on spiritual healing—except for childbirth, because we aren't trained obstetricians. And Christian Scientists with broken bones may sometimes prefer to have them set by a doctor, though a great many bones are healed by practitioners. We aren't *against* doctors, we very much appreciate what they do—for those who want them."

American doctors, however, do not often appreciate Christian Scientists, especially when called in to a case at the last moment by a desperate family. They have been known to refuse death certificates when they feel a Christian Science patient has died for lack of medical attention—the disease most commonly involved is pneumonia. But the church is undisturbed. "We don't claim to be 100 per cent effective," says Mr. Peel. "And after all, for every case that fails we have a great many that succeed."

The Christian Scientists meet, at their 3,300 churches, on Wednesdays and Sundays. There are no ministers, only readers; there are prayers and hymns, and on Sundays a set "lesson sermon"—Mary Baker Eddy wrote twenty-six of these, to be used twice a year. Members have to study the sermon during the preceding week: "You really have to work at it. The drifters tend to fall off." On Wednesdays they give testimonies.

"One morning our little daughter woke up in pain and holding both ears. I recognized the trouble as abscessed ears. She had had two ear operations before I had found Christian Science, but still she often complained of earaches. Now I had the truth to rely upon. . . . This time I called for the help of a practitioner. Within half an hour the child was at peace. That took place about nineteen years ago and she has had no further trouble with her ears. . . ."

And so on. By establishing man's right relationship with God, says Christian Science, "healing just flows in"—to bodies, relationships or nations. The members do not smoke or drink, these being regarded as enslaving habits; they do have a kind of service for those who die: "though people tend to say 'pass on' rather more." They too are a prosperous church: "Most Christian Scientists are awfully grateful for some case of healing and just want to pay." During the desperate Thirties they raised several million dollars to build their headquarters simply by asking once for it. "If people are poor when they become Christian Scientists," says Mr. Peel somewhat enigmatically, "they tend not to remain poor. Poverty is a sickness, a denial of the goodness of God."

The third of the Big Three, the Jehovah's Witnesses, clash
more often and more openly with authority than either of the
other two. In the ninety years since they were founded by a
group of Bible students near Pittsburgh, they have grown to a
strength of about 315,000 in the United States and more than a
million throughout the world, with some 50,000 of these in
Britain. This gives them an American clergy equivalent to the
population of Omaha, since every Witness—after being publicly
baptized by total immersion, usually in a convenient swimming-
pool—is regarded as a minister and missionary. All over America
they tramp the streets devotedly knocking on people's doors, and
write "messages of comfort" to anyone who puts a death notice in
the local paper. They telephone strangers, they chat hopefully
with their neighbors in aeroplanes, and once a New York cab-
driver offered me a sheaf of Witness literature with my change.
They do not believe in the Trinity or the immortality of the soul
(adding, rather confusingly: "Man doesn't *have* a soul, he *is*
one.") but think that the purpose of their lives is to spread God's
Word to the rest of us by preaching a literal interpretation of the
Bible. They say that we are approaching Armageddon, but add
comfortingly: "This sphere isn't actually going to be destroyed,
only the Devil's rule."

The Witnesses have an imposing headquarters in Brooklyn,
with a magnificent view of the Manhattan skyline; a training
school for the "overseers" who supervise the Witnesses at each
local Kingdom Hall; and eighteen rotary presses turning out
some twenty-five million books and pamphlets a year. They are
strongest in California, the Midwest, and the Northeast, and
weakest in the Deep South, possibly because of the rival pull of
the Baptist churches. "People down there just say they have their
Bible already and don't want to talk about it." And they claim
that they are persecuted, almost everywhere:

> In the last twenty-five years we've met violence in at least
> forty-four states of the Union. Mob violence stirred up by belli-
> gerent opposers, mostly members of the American Legion. Mili-
> tarists. You see, we don't take part in the things of the world,

and so we claim exemption from military service. All persons in the ministry are exempt by law, and every Witness is a minister, so . . . . Several thousand Witnesses have been imprisoned on that question. We meet hostility from the clergy of other churches everywhere too, especially the Catholics because we draw so many people from them. Up in Quebec we've had twelve hundred arrests just for preaching.

Jehovah's Witnesses also appear in the headlines at regular intervals when one of them dies because he or his parents declined a blood transfusion. They are not, in principle, against other fleshly doings—"The Bible condemns drunkenness, not drinking"—but they say flatly that "the Bible prohibits Christians from taking blood—and the United States guarantees freedom of worship. Taking blood, either in some kind of food or as a blood transfusion, is the same as committing murder or breaking any other kind of rule. We just can't do it. And anyway transfusions have their own dangers. You can get infected with hepatitis."

Many of the minority sects of the United States thrive on insecurity, anxiety, prejudice or fear. The Witnesses unhesitatingly claim the first two:

As Revelations Twelve says, the Devil knows he has a short time to go. So there's a tremendous amount of comforting that can be done, to all these people afraid of the future. Jesus pointed out that the sign of his second presence would be a world war followed by pestilence—we mark 1914 as the beginning of that period. Then he said that this generation would not pass away until all these things are fulfilled, which means that some people alive in 1914 will still be here to see the destruction of the Devil's rule. So we know that the world now is near the time of God's kingdom, when men will live for ever. It makes us kind of a happy people . . . .

The range of minority religion in America spreads, of course, far wider than this: from Black Muslims to Holy Rollers, from Yoga to Zen. But the Big Three hold a particular interest because they are home-grown, not merely variants on imported ideas and practices. If they have anything significant in common, it is a close involvement of religious belief and way of life. Their ideas tend not only to be brought out and polished on Sunday, but to affect the whole week—something which is true of some of the orthodox denominations more in theory than in practice. Most of them are exceedingly eager and unself-conscious about discussing what they believe. In each of the three main groups religious belief is a central support for everyday life; two of them believe themselves to be chosen peoples, and the third denies the strength of most of the ills under whose pressure the rest of mankind totters along. When I met members of all three in America, I realized why their respective subsidiaries had always seemed slightly incongruous to me in Britain; it is because they are all primarily an answer to American needs, expressed in American terms. It is more than a matter of the geography of administration which makes foreign members of all three regard the United States as a kind of Mecca. It is that there, and only there, they find themselves surrounded by the raw material of their faiths: something which a Christian Scientist described to me as "a kind of natural expectation of good in the American character—which can seem a naïve optimism that grates terribly on the European." He added that he noticed this especially when invited to speak to youth groups: "I'm always very impressed by the way they're willing to consider *anything*. They don't automatically rule out any form of religion. . . ."

Here is the sense of freedom again. And for the same reason religion, like most other things in the U.S.A., is a fertile field not only for new ideas but for the entrepreneur. It is a fair bet that anyone of suitable loquacity, whackiness or even sincerity can go to America today, particularly to California, set himself up as a religious leader, and soon acquire an appreciable number of followers—most of them, to begin with, female, elderly and prosperous. In fact almost every one of the American-founded minority groups did begin with a single prophet or teacher; they are all, as it were, examples of private enterprise, and many of them are incorporated in exactly the same way as business organizations. At intervals, one of these newer groups will reach the headlines when some enterprising reporter discovers that it practises voodoo or "glossolalia" (speaking with tongues). But always the less colorful examples are there, quietly flourishing in the background.

One catches brief glimpses of them by accident. Enclosed in a hotel room in the Midwest one Sunday morning, I turned on the television set—an instrument as well geared to the pattern of Sundays as its audience. On every channel some kind of religious service was in progress. Most were recognizably denominational: a mass, or a nonconformist-type oration. But one was different.

It seemed to be taking place in a kind of concert-hall, with a stage; three young men sat up there with electric guitars, playing a folksy, neo-religious song. Soon a man of about forty replaced them, and turned to the leading guitarist: "Victor," he said earnestly, "I want you to know we *enjoyed* that . . . he could be playing for other places, friends, but I'm glad he's playing for the Lord."

He read through a list of events for the coming week. He said: "We've got something for every member of the family." He used exactly the same tone of voice as if he were in a supermarket or a variety show. He had an air of the wholesomeness which is praised by many Americans, but it was not altogether convincing. Shortly he introduced three more singers, a trio of teenage girls looking like less attractive versions of Doris Day; they were called the Golden Triplets, and they sang in ambiguous close harmony:

> Since he put his arms around me
> And he took me in his care;
> Set me free from condemnation,
> Gave me joy beyond compare . . . .

The man in the dark suit rose again, and began talking about money. "Our budget calls for seventeen thousand five hundred dollars," he said. The cameras switched briefly to his audience; they looked middle-aged and respectable. Five thousand dollars were for payments on the building, he said; the rest for missions and other expenses. "Well, the first week's up to date. But last week we fell short by twenty-two hundred and thirty-eight dollars. Now that's *terrible*. . . ."

He went on in this vein. It was as if he had finally reached the point of the whole proceedings. He said: "I have a text for you: The Lord loveth a cheerful giver. . . . If you want a record for tax purposes, you'll find an envelope on your chair."

You could see the middle-aged ladies reaching into their handbags as the picture faded, and a voice announced that the service had come from a certain local "religious non-profit-making organization." This was religion behind the Golden Curtain, with a vengeance: all denominations must depend on the charitable impulse, but not all try so openly to prod it. Inevitably, in a competitive, consumer-conscious society, the churches are led not only to compete with rival calls on their congregations' pockets, but to compete, often, in their rivals' terms. And just as inevitably, other institutions which are kept alive only by the religious impulse, the Christian humanitarian instinct, are found traveling even further along the same road. Thus the pleas of charities arrive daily in every American home with the morning post, couched in very much the same language as advertisements, and with the same plethora of "soft sell" literature.

Some charities include up to six pieces of persuasive literature in each appeal, all loaded with exclamation marks; and may send an appeal to anyone on one of their lists three or four times a year, irrespective of whether the recipient has contributed to their funds or not. Also, anyone who has once given money to a cause linked with his own religion—particularly if it happens to be Roman Catholic or Jewish—will receive thereafter, as well as the general appeals, numerous letters from other organizations connected, or claiming to be connected, with that religion.

At Christmas and Easter the volume swells, and begins to include books, ties, boxes of Christmas cards painted by somebody's toes. "Here," said my husband to me one day as I sat writing letters, "use these," and he tossed across a package of about fifty bundles of those little gummed labels printed with one's name and address, to be stuck as "return address" on the outside of envelopes. I had never seen them before. There were among them at least twenty different kinds of typeface and design, which seemed puzzling: surely he would not have bothered to have such remarkably unnecessary objects printed in twenty different ways? I then discovered, of course, that he had not bothered to have any of them printed at all; the little bundles had been sent to him in twos and threes, at various times, unwanted and unsolicited, by charities. "We hope you will wish to send us a donation in return for these," said the accompanying message each time, in effect, "but if you don't, please keep and use them anyway." Inevitably, when this happens, most people send their donation. There seems, of course, no point in sending the labels back; they would be no use to anyone else, being so obviously "personalized"—that process by which the American consumer is endlessly wooed, by salesmen eagerly offering to stamp his name or his initials on his doormat, his matches, his shirts, even his wallpaper. The charities, by adopting yet another of the processes of commerce, have found an improved way of making the American householder either pay up, or feel like Scrooge. It is a more up-to-date (and therefore far more wasteful) version of that classic piece of Christmas blackmail, the sheet of Christmas seals.

Many Americans have come to lean on this system for stimulating their annual output of charity; they take the promotional literature for granted, as they do the ordinary advertising, and send a couple of dollars to anyone who solicits help. This, naturally, is why the system survives. Others will choose a few charities which seem to them particularly worthy, divide among these all the money they feel disposed to give away each year, and ignore the pleas of the rest. But many are so baffled by the plethora of good causes, and often so disturbed by the proportion of charitable funds that appear to go not to the good cause itself, but to promoting it, that they give up the problem of trying to distinguish between any of the competing charities at all. The only rational way out is to send one composite check to the United Fund, and transfer to them the job of discovering which charity is worthier than the next. But still the varied literature continues to arrive. There is no help for it.

Charities and churches, the two visible expressions of the religious impulse, have to be geared to their surroundings in the land of free enterprise. I remember in England once, years ago, discussing politics with a charming woman who happened to be a life-long supporter of the Labour Party, and hearing her remark disconcertingly: "The first Socialist, of course, was Our Lord." It is difficult, sometimes, looking at the United States, to decide whether its system is devoted to proving her right, or to proving her wrong.

Certainly religion is one of the cornerstones of the American Way; the stern, self-confident Christian faith of the founders of the republic breathes from every clause of the Constitution, and one can still believe in its survival however much corruption and violence one may now see flourishing at its side. Thus the young American is reared in constant contact with a religion that teaches unlimited brotherly love, universal understanding, general benevolence—but that does so in the language and terms, often, of unmitigated materialism. It cannot help but do so. As a result, religion in America acquires a curiously individual holy bounce which you will find nowhere else in the world.

At one extreme, it can produce a phenomenon like the American Christmas, which is an eye-opening experience for anyone who complains that the occasion has been adulterated by commercial values in Britain. There they all are; the glaring displays in early November shop-windows, plastic poinsettias in pots, recorded carols played on electric organs, hugely increased amounts of advertising, and strange eruptions at all the large shopping centers: "Boys! Girls! Santa arrives Saturday November 21 with Mrs. Santa Claus at North Shore Shopping Center! Come and greet them as they fly in from their North Pole headquarters!" So Santa duly descends by helicopter, accompanied by a pneumatic Mrs. Claus and assorted gnomes, and throughout the ensuing store-crowded weeks small shrewd children will climb recurrently on his lap to be given "a candy treat and a free ticket for a kiddy ride." Outside, the Huge Forty-Five Foot Christmas Tree dominates the rows of stores with its Dramatic Fourteen-Foot Toy Soldier Honor Guards, and the whole commercial campus is lit by "70,000 miniature Italian lights twinkling merrily," and scattered with "Lilliputian telephone booths for youngsters to phone and talk to a pre-recorded Santa." And as the harassed mothers drag little Johnnie away from the Toy Fair, they may cast a cursory glance at a Magnificent Life-Size Crèche, "including the Wise Men, the Shepherds, the Mother and Infant as well as the camel, cow, donkey and sheep. All dramatically lighted."

In no town center can one escape the streamers and bells and tinsel, swaying over the streets from November onwards. In the city shopping districts, a Santa Claus stands on every street corner, endlessly clanging a handbell, collecting for charity as much of the Christmas spirit as may spill out. It is not until night, generally, that the American Christmas takes on a real enchantment—especially in New England, which is like as not deep with crisp white snow. Wreaths of holly, evergreens and red ribbon hang from front doors, and in many houses a single golden light glows like a candle in each window. And here and there in a front garden, trees are starred with sudden bright flowers where the family has hung their branches with white, blue or rainbow lights. The sight is more peaceful than that of the giant papier-mâché crèches set up outside most of the gas-stations, with tinny recorded carols blaring out over the pumps; or than that of one house which I noticed last Christmas. It was a large house, in a prosperous neighborhood. For twenty yards or so on either side of it, trees and hedges were as thickly studded with colored lights as Times Square. The house itself was floodlit, and in the middle of the front lawn—which lay open to a main street—two spotlights were trained on a gigantic crèche. The strongest spotlight of all was directed up at the roof, where there hung from the chimney a large metal star.

The overall effect of this, as of all displays like it, could not have been described as religious. Yet its owners no doubt set it all up with the best of intentions. They may even have been deeply devout. For who can say that the religious impulse is made less valid by gaudiness, or more valid by dignity? The Americans may have given it some strange forms of expression, but at least they have not caused it to disappear. There are some remarkable anomalies involved in finding Michelangelo's "Pietà" on show at the New York World's Fair, or a whole issue of *Life* magazine devoted to the Bible, but these do not essentially differ from the anomaly that is Esso World Theater, or the sign announcing in neon that Jesus will save Los Angeles. Religion, in America, must naturally wear American clothes. The only sad thought is that there are so many million Americans who will never understand why these clothes should not seem natural to all the rest of the world.

7 ∗ School

*"The public school is an educational agency
of the community established to maintain,
strengthen and improve our American
Democratic way of life."*
**High school handbook
Virginia**

When I was about twelve, in my third year at an English grammar school, one of our history teachers disappeared to the United
States for a year and was replaced by an American "exchange"
teacher of equivalent ability. The American was a dynamic lady
with a bun; very fluent and bubbly, and generally liked. But
there was one disconcerting thing about her; at the end of each
term we were left vaguely aware that although we had heard a
great many chatty stories about the period of history we happened to be studying, and had produced two or three "projects"
involving much cutting out of magazine pictures and discussing
of corporate ideas, we had learned hardly anything at all. It had
been a period of marking time, much unlike the year before or
the year afterwards; without realizing it, we were baffled, and
spoke of the American after her departure as "that funny Miss
Thing." Five or six years later I happened to mention her in
passing to one of the other members of the staff. The teacher
chuckled. "Poor Miss Thing," she said. "You all scared her stiff.

She seemed to think the school was full of young geniuses. I don't think the teaching here was at all what she'd been used to. . . ."

This is the kind of incident which goes to make up part of the paradoxical image of American education which exists on the British side of the Atlantic. It is a false image, but very firm. (So is the false image the Americans have of British education.) It is based on two beliefs, each of which tends to contradict the other. The first, current among the champions of grammar schools, states unequivocally that the overall standard of American education is much lower than our own. The second, loudly trumpeted by whichever political party happens to be in opposition, states that because 40 per cent of all American children go on from school to college, as against only 7 per cent in Britain, America's educational situation must be much better than our own. Each statement is partly true, but so horribly over-simplified that on its own it makes nonsense.

The same can be said of the American image of British education. Most Americans know very little about the system of education in Britain, beyond a rather vague picture of regimented children in unbecoming uniforms; but those who have ever given the subject any thought tend to consider the system snobbish, unfair and old-fashioned. They assume that all children of rich or aristocratic families go to expensive private schools like Eton; that the rest are all brutally divided at the age of eleven and sent into either superior or inferior schools; and that since the vast majority of children leave school at fifteen, the average exposure to education must be very low. Over-simplification, again, has run wild. And for the sake of a proper comparison, I think it is worth describing the British system here at some length—just as, in the British edition of this book, I described the American system instead.

Ninety per cent of all the children in Britain receive a free state education, in schools financed out of tax money by the Ministry of Education, and administered by the local County Education Authority. (Britain is divided into thirty-two counties, each possessing far more power than an American county, and rather less than an American state.) This education starts at the age of about five, in a coeducational "infants' school." (Many children start at four, three or even two, generally in a "nursery school," but this is not always available.) At seven or eight, the child progresses to a primary school, where he will stay for three or four years, still among both boys and girls. Already, here, his education begins to differ from that he would receive in the U.S.A.

Take an example; call him Bill Smith. He is eight years old, and sits in a classroom with a group of about forty other boys and girls, which he describes as "Miss Robinson's form." (About 80 per cent of all primary school teachers in Britain are women.) Miss Robinson is wholly responsible for this group; she teaches them everything except gymnastics, games, and one or two specialized subjects like—for the boys—woodwork. They will go on up through the school together, these forty children, and each year only their teacher will change; for already they are a product of the system basic to most British education, known as "streaming." That is to say, they have on entering the school been roughly sorted out according to their ability, so that each is likely to be working at more or less the same speed as his fellows. The bright child will not be chafing in a group of children slower than themselves, and the slow child will not be unhappily struggling to keep up with a brighter form. Bill Smith's group is known as Form 1R, from Miss Robinson's initial; it does not wear a label that shows it as obviously better or worse than any of the other two (or three, or one, according to the school's size) Form Ones. But in more realistic and less merciful days the "R" would have been "A" or "alpha"; for this is in fact the top group of the year, and nearly all its children will prove bright enough to go on to a grammar school when they reach the sifting process which waits at the end of their three primary school years.

This sifting, at the age of eleven or twelve, has been a point of huge controversy in British education for twenty years or more; but for all that it is still the key point of the system—which is based, roughly speaking, on the maxim that although all men may be born equal, not all are born with equal kinds of brains, and that different brains require different kinds of education. The traditional method of sifting is a composite examination known as the "eleven-plus," which is a series of short English, arithmetic and intelligence tests complemented by a confidential report supplied by each child's teacher—but which is being widely replaced now by a series of tests or reports on the child's work throughout the previous year. Suppose that there are three forms taking the eleven-plus in Bill Smith's school: probably twenty-five or so children from the top group will "pass"; about ten from the second, and perhaps two or three from the third. Even in those areas of Britain where the eleven-plus has been replaced by another means of selection, the end result—classification—is the same. Then, secondary education begins.

Bill Smith may go to any one of four different kinds of secondary school. If he passes the eleven-plus or its equivalent, he will be offered a place at the nearest grammar school for boys. Grammar schools, which are the most academically-oriented in the system, are not often coeducational, though the boys' and girls' schools in the same town almost always join forces for after-school debates, dances and so on. He will stay there until he is sixteen, and longer if he decides to apply for a university place. His parents will pay for nothing except his school uniform (cap, blazer and tie)—all books, paper, pens and such implements are provided free.

If Bill Smith fails the eleven-plus he will probably go—as do about half of all British children—to a secondary modern school. His education here, again free, will be more vocational and less academic than at a grammar school; secondary modern teachers work with the knowledge that most of their charges are determined to leave school at fifteen and go straight into a job. Those who were misdirected by the eleven-plus, and who turn out to have been academically minded after all, can take a "late-developers" examination at thirteen and be transferred to the grammar school; those who are not suitable for this, but who want to do something more in life than working at a stenographer's desk, or a factory lathe, can work towards qualifying for some kind of vocational higher education. (In American terms, that is, they can go on to college; for Britain, unlike America, tends to restrict its university teaching to academic subjects, and to teach the rest in specialized colleges.)

A third kind of school is available to Bill Smith if he appears, at any point after the age of eleven, to be deeply attached to technological subjects; he can go, like 5 per cent of the children in the country, to a technical school. The subjects taught there will vary widely, but will be concentrated after the first two years on the vocational; the technical school produces, or sends on to higher education, anything from plumbers and electricians to textile designers and civil engineers. It also attracts back to evening classes a number of children who have left grammar or secondary modern schools at fifteen.

These are the three main categories of secondary education. But there is one other kind of school in Britain which has been spreading since the war, and to which 10 per cent of our children now go: the comprehensive secondary school, which combines grammar, secondary modern, and technical brands of education under the same roof in separate streams, and which is popular among educators for its obviation of parental snobbery. ("Our Johnnie goes to the grammar school, her Mary's only at the secondary modern.") It is also praised for the greater ease with which, within it, a child can transfer from one "stream" to another. Some education authorities in Britain, particularly those which are Socialist-controlled, have decided that eventually all the schools in their area shall be comprehensive; London, for instance, has been building nothing else for years. In size and variety, the comprehensive school is closest of all British brands to the American high school, though the manner of its teaching is not at all the same.

These then are the proportions of British secondary education: 17 per cent of all children aged eleven and beyond go to grammar schools; 58 per cent to secondary modern schools; 10 per cent to comprehensive schools, and 5 per cent to technical schools. The remaining 10 per cent are the "privileged few" who attend private schools—which we, in our perverse British way, call public schools. (They are in fact independent fee-paying schools, known in the beginning as "public" because none of them is run for private profit.) Though some of these schools offer a few free places to children from grammar or even secondary modern schools, most are limited to those whose parents can afford the fees—and who can pass the school's entrance examination. They are nearly all single-sex boarding schools, and there are far more for boys than for girls. All of them teach both academic and vocational subjects. The best offer the equivalent of an excellent grammar school education, and are highly selective; Winchester, for instance, has very high academic standards and is said to take only the top 1 per cent of all public school applicants. At the other end of the scale there are public schools containing boys who would probably not have passed their eleven-plus, and who have been sent there less for the sake of an academic education than to acquire the socially-useful accent and undeniable self-confidence which all public schools manage to supply. Their age range is that not of the British grammar school but of the American four-year senior high school; they take children between fourteen and eighteen or nineteen, and are generally fed not by state schools but by other fee-paying independent boarding schools, called preparatory schools, which take children from eight to fourteen—and which work towards the public school "Common Entrance" exam just as the state primary schools work, with younger children, towards the eleven-plus. The British public schools are of course undemocratic institutions, like your own private schools, and the Labour Party would like to abolish them (though it shows no sign of doing so, and indeed some of its more affluent members send their children to be educated at one.) However, there they are.

This is the external framework of British education. It is, as you will have observed, more convoluted than the framework of education in the U.S.A. The kind of teaching and learning which goes on within the framework differs more widely still— and perhaps its differences have more significance.

When Bill Smith reaches his British grammar school to begin his secondary education, he will be "streamed" just as he was at his primary school; the children in his year, that is, will be divided into three or four groups—forms—of thirty or more, so that they will be working with others of roughly the same ability. Bill Smith's form no longer has a Miss Robinson teaching it all day and everyday; instead different specialist masters take this complete group for every different subject. And the pattern of the curriculum presented to these eleven and twelve year old boys of Form One will not have changed very much by the time they reach Form Five; they learn English, history, geography, French, arithmetic, algebra, geometry, general science, music, art, R.I. (religious instruction—compulsory, if perfunctory, at all state schools) and athletics including cricket and football. The teaching of all these subjects will follow a continuous sequence throughout the next five years. In the second year trigonometry and a second foreign language (usually Latin or German) will be added, and general science will be split into its component parts, so that the child of thirteen will find himself studying chemistry, physics and biology under different teachers; but still all the different subjects continue simultaneously. And just as primary school education reached its climax with the eleven-plus, so when Bill Smith is sixteen his secondary education will reach a climax in the Ordinary Level examination of the General Certificate of Education, known throughout Britain as the G.C.E.

The G.C.E. has no equivalent in the United States; it is a national examination, with papers set by five regional boards whose standards are all more or less the same. They are high standards, on an international scale: "O" Level, the sixteen-year-old's first rung of G.C.E., is roughly on the level of the German *Real-examen,* the first part of the French *baccalaureat,* and the entrance requirements of all but the most demanding American universities. It is the nearest thing we have to a school-leaving exam, and a useful guide for future employers, though no child is compelled to take it; we do not graduate from our secondary schools in Britain, we merely leave, with no diploma to show that we have been there. "O" Level G.C.E. might, however, be called a kind of diploma-substitute; it can be taken in any number or combination of subjects (seldom more than nine at a time) on any number of occasions, and it is taken in every kind of British secondary school. Although nearly every child at a grammar school takes at least some "O" Level subjects, far fewer choose to take any at secondary modern or technical schools—in educators' language, many of them lack the motivation. Also, the latter schools tend to concentrate more—naturally—on vocational examination subjects like Homecraft or Mechanical Drawing than on academic ones, and to offer fewer at a time.

But for children reaching the school-leaving age of fifteen, G.C.E. "O" Level is a hurdle available to anyone who cares to try to leap it, with secondary education a complex unbroken slope leading up to that point. Examination preparation is not the raison d'être of the slope; the child who never contemplates sitting for any exam will be taught in the same pattern as those who do, with each subject developing continuously through the years. British education has always taken that pattern, long before the General Certificate of Education or its predecessor, the School Certificate, were ever born.

Bill Smith, let us suppose, is now sixteen. He has taken and passed his "O" Level G.C.E. in perhaps eight subjects; he could now, if he liked, leave school and take a job. But Bill Smith is a bright grammar school boy and wants to go to a university; so he must stay at school for another two years to take the next rung of the G.C.E. examination, Advanced Level, on which all British universities base their judgment of candidates. He remains at school, therefore, and passes into that peculiarly British institution, the grammar school (or public school) Sixth Form.

To go into the Sixth Form is a rather more momentous-feeling step than to become a senior at an American high school. The Sixth is an entity; there is no remnant of "streaming" inside it, the only division being between first, second or third-year Sixth-formers; and each of its members has his own individually-designed curriculum. Unless both school and Sixth are very large, teaching is done in small groups more nearly resembling tutorials than classes; the Sixth-former learns to study hard alone, as he will have to do later as an undergraduate, and his relationship with his teachers becomes more like a friendship between equals. He learns, in fact, many of the things which an American child cannot learn until its first two years in college, for he is now being educated in something which is nominally only another class in a secondary school, but is in fact a unique institution halfway to a university. This is just as well, since the Advanced Level G.C.E. examinations which he will take when he is eighteen or so are of the standard reached by an American college sophomore.

Not all grammar school Sixth-formers are destined for the second part of G.C.E.; most schools have a "General Sixth" for boys or girls who want an extra year or two of advanced education in a fairly wide range of subjects, without working towards an examination. But for most, the range of study narrows suddenly, giving ground for the accusation of over-specialization which is leveled at grammar school education by critics within Britain. The standard of the "A" Level exam is so high that few children can manage to take it in more than three subjects at a time, and those three are studied in such depth that they will take up the greater part of the working week.

So Bill Smith, bearing in mind his own preferences and the combination of subjects he is likely to need for university entrance, will probably find himself squarely on either the arts or the science side of the Sixth Form. On the science side he might combine physics, maths and chemistry; on the arts side, perhaps English, history and French. The choice is his own, but the school will make sure that he also fits several classes in general, non-examination subjects into his specialized weekly syllabus, their number varying with the time available and the school's concern over the need to prevent the great Two-Culture divide —to prevent, that is, the emergence of illiterate scientists or of scientifically ignorant artists.

At eighteen, Bill Smith duly takes his examination papers. (At neither level of the G.C.E., by the way, is there ever an exam of the kind that can be marked by machine. All subjects except mathematics and certain sections of the sciences demand nearly all their answers written in well ordered essay form—which is one reason why English is so carefully taught in English schools.) Unless he chooses to stay for a third year in the Sixth Form, to add to his total of "A" Levels, to take them again, or to work for an open scholarship to a particularly demanding university like Oxford or Cambridge, he will then leave for university, training college or job. There is, again, no ceremony attached to this departure; his last day at school does not differ from that of his fellows—except for his own awareness, gleeful or nostalgic, that he will not be coming back. (The whole procedure is very casual and British, with the exception of one after-effect: the hymn "Lord, dismiss us with thy blessing" is sung on the last day of term at so many British schools that it can, if heard unexpectedly, evoke a remarkable emotional response in half the adult population of the British Isles.)

Bill Smith is informed of his "A" Level G.C.E. results by postcard some weeks after leaving school, and if they are good enough his chosen university will offer him a place. (If he cannot manage to find one on his own, he may also be found a university or college place by a central clearing-house financed by the Ministry of Education, to which students can send one composite application instead of applying to several universities themselves.) He is unlikely to be kept out of a university by poverty; both state and county authorities in Britain offer scholarships on the results of the G.C.E., and even if he does not merit one of these any boy (or girl) who has been accepted by a university will be given a "county grant" of public money to pay his tuition and residence fees—the amount of the grant being worked out on a sliding scale according to his parents' income. When he does reach university, he will usually take a three or four year honors degree course, and specialize still further in his chosen field: entering the world of scholarship or research of which he has already had a taste in the Sixth Form.

It is of course even more difficult to generalize about universities in Britain than about schools. Some offer a general degree incorporating a fairly wide range of subjects; some require one or two subsidiaries to be studied continuously alongside the main subject; some, particularly the newest universities, allow a cross-disciplinary degree which might combine, say, history, biology and German. But many, especially in the arts and pure sciences, probe fairly strictly into the restricted area of the chosen specialist degree. For the degree in English Language and Literature which I acquired at Oxford, for instance, one took examination papers at the end of the first year in English, Latin or Greek, French and Anglo-Saxon, and then concentrated further. The nine three-hour papers of the final degree examination, supplemented by a viva voce exam, were entitled Anglo-Saxon Literature, Anglo-Saxon Language, Middle English, Chaucer and contemporaries, Spenser and Milton, Shakespeare, English Literature 1600–1700, English Literature 1700–1870, and Literary Criticism. This does not, I suppose, sound to American ears much like a liberal education; but under the British system it is not the universities which are designed to provide that, but the secondary schools.

And in essence if not in content, British further education, be it academic, technological or vocational, is the same as that given in the schools; it is not cellular but successive, working towards one or two climactic points at which everything must be combined into an integral expression of knowledge and understanding. All along the way, the structure by which this is supported is that of hurdles required to be jumped: the eleven-plus, the G.C.E. "O" Level at sixteen, the G.C.E. "A" Level at eighteen; the university first or second year examination, and at twenty-one or twenty-two, the first degree. The idea behind this structure is that of exercising the muscles of the mind; of giving it incentives to stretch to its full capacity; and no amount of democratic reform within the system has ever really changed that basic idea. The process of growth in British education has been one of abolishing forms of irrelevant privilege in order to extend—not to alter—the species of education available. It has become a matter of treating every child as if it were a plant: of making sure that it is given the right environment, and of then proceeding to feed it so that it will grow as fully and as fast as it possibly can. Those unfriendly to this system call it forcing, and claim that far too many potentially useful plants droop down into oblivion under its pressure. Others, who approve, claim that it is simply a matter of giving education to each according to his capacity, and that it is foolish to pretend that the capacity of every child is equal to the next. But either way, it provides a useful comparison with the American system.

For in the United States, the process has been different from the start. The sense of privilege, and exclusion, is not there. Admittedly American private schools are much like English public schools, and the Ivy League universities like Oxford and Cambridge, in being both older and more academically geared than the rest, with an aura of social and economic privilege which is diminishing but still survives. But these make up a very small minority. In America, the healthily democratic determination of the first settlers was soon applied to education. Education meant Opportunity; and each new generation of immigrants has been determined to make sure that its children should have easier access to this particular kind of opportunity than their parents had in the land from which they came. So it is, I assume, that 95 per cent of all American children attend more or less the same kind of school: the public high school (or the parochial school, where the control may differ but not the education). And so it is that the control of these schools is, by European standards, so remarkably localized, even taking into account the standards imposed by federal government or state. The Englishman visiting the U.S.A. is astonished at the varieties of power exercised by a school board or school committee, by their superintendent of schools, and by the local P.T.A. At home, his own closest contact with his child's education comes in meeting teachers, headmaster or headmistress; he is very remote from the administrative processes of the Ministry of Education, or the county education committee, who control the school's resources, and he can exert no influence over general educational policy except by his choice of party at the General Election. The American, knowing that he pays a direct tax for schools, and that perhaps a member of the school board lives next door, can feel far more inclined to make his own demands on the system. The phrase "our schools" bears more weight in an American community. They *are* your schools: a local facility, like the public library or the roads. And like these last two, they are open to everyone and must cater for everyone's needs.

Now a system which must begin with this premise—and very many American schools systems have of course had to begin comparatively recently and very rapidly, especially in the western states—cannot possibly operate on the "stretch" principle. It cannot afford the time or money needed to develop different kinds of education and schools for children with different kinds of ability; and even if it could, it wouldn't want to, for its first concern, in a self-consciously democratic atmosphere, must be with the good not of a number of minorities, but with the overall majority. So in almost every way, American education must be designed for the vast majority. There are no built-in labels which mark the schoolchild as anything different from the average. It is symbolic that while the American child is in high school, he does not live and work with a class of other children of similar ability. If you ask him, as you might an English child, "Is George Brown in your form?" the answer cannot be yes or no, but is likely to be "He's in my biology group" or "I see him in French Two." The most significant of all the characteristics of the American educational system, to my foreign eye, is the pattern of its teaching. The basic unit of the British secondary school is that of the miniature community of children working together at a continuous curriculum, and the pattern in general is like that of a woven fabric, with the threads of all the major subjects running unbroken from beginning to end. In America, on the other hand, the pattern is more like that of the kind of open-work wall one can build in one's garden with bricks; and the individual brick, the unit of education, is the "credit" or "course." These two words, which dominate American education as the expression "eleven-plus" dominates our own, are not interchangeable. A course is a quantitative unit: one subject taken for one year, generally about four or five lessons a week. The credit is the unit of value then set on the course: as a year's biology, for instance, might be worth five credits, or a year's woodwork be worth two. And the pattern of school education is made by setting one course on another and adding up the total of credits at the end.

Thus the bright college-aiming American boy of fifteen is not in Form IVA, or whatever it might be in a British grammar school, studying along with the rest of the form the nine or ten subjects he has been studying throughout his five-year journey towards G.C.E. "O" Level. Instead he is a sophomore in senior high school, studying three, four or five major subjects which will not necessarily (apart from English and a foreign language) be the same as those he took the year before, or will take in the year to come. The years do not interweave in the same way for every child, as they do in British schools. No strong regulation governs the order in which the American child puts the bricks into his educational wall, so long as he accumulates in the end the number of credits officially required for him to graduate, and to receive his high school diploma. Although he will have to work to a comparatively rigorous timetable if he hopes to meet the entrance requirements of one of the better universities, the demands he must satisfy in order to graduate from high school are not great.

James Bryant Conant proposed, after making his famous 1957 survey of American high schools, that the minimum graduation requirements of every high school should consist of "four years of English, three or four years of social studies—including two years of history (one of which should be American history) and a senior course in American problems or American government—one year of mathematics in the ninth grade (algebra or general mathematics) and at least one year of science in the ninth or tenth grade, which might well be biology or general physical science. By a year, I mean that a course is given five periods a week throughout the academic year or an equivalent amount of time." This, he suggested, should account for more than half the student's time. The rest should be taken up with at least seven elective courses, not including physical education. *"All students,"* he added in hopeful italics, *"should be urged to include art and music in their elective programs."* It is of course in the range of subjects available as "electives" that the American schools show most clearly their comprehensive character; the range available is huge. The aim of catering for every kind of child within the one school is thus met, though there is no standard means of measuring the amount of each subject which the child is actually taught.

Some of the recommendations in the Conant Report criticized particular aspects of U.S. education; Conant commented sorrowfully, for instance, on the "widespread feeling in the United States that there is considerable merit in a student's studying a language for two years—and only two years—in a high school." It would be far better, he pointed out, either to give a child three or four years of a foreign language, or to give him none at all. But in general, the Report was throughout a mirror for the pattern of American school education, with its stress on the course as unit and—even more significant—its strong plea for "an individualized program" for each student, rather than any setting of obvious divisions (like the "streaming" of British schools) which could be labeled as "college preparatory," "vocational," or "commercial." And although Conant's list of graduation requirements was put forward not as an average sample, but as a desirable norm, again it showed the pattern. Some high schools demand more of their pupils, some less; but always a set number of units is required. One fairly typical high school in Massachusetts, for instance, requires for "regular standing" at the beginning of each year 17 credits for sophomores, 38 credits for juniors, 63 credits for seniors; and the high school diploma, mark of graduation, goes only to seniors who have completed 90 credits, "of which 55 must be in major academic courses." But the total of courses and credits which adds up to a high school diploma will not necessarily add up to college entrance. This particular high school warns its pupils at fourteen that four-year colleges, though varying widely all over America, have certain basic demands in common: they require "sixteen college units for admission, consisting of four years of college preparatory English; three years of one foreign language, preferably four; two laboratory sciences, biology, chemistry or physics; three years of social studies; three years of mathematics. Students preparing for engineering and science must complete four years of college preparatory mathematics, one year of chemistry, and one year of physics. . . ." And though each of these subjects is not judged through a separate externally set examination, as is the case with the British G.C.E., most schools do offer—and most colleges demand—the Scholastic Aptitude Tests and the College Board Achievement Tests. Neither of these, again, bears much resemblance to the G.C.E.; they consist—for those of you who have forgotten—mainly of long strings of brief questions, and demand quickness of wits rather than any ability to express oneself coherently; breadth of knowledge rather then depth. For a great part of its length, American education is essentially generalized.

As a result, the standard reached in each subject by most children who go through this high school unit-collecting process is not high. No one has been pushed; many of the brighter students have not even been stretched to the possible edges of their abilities. Only an exceedingly unusual American high school graduate would have the smallest chance of entering any British university, since in all academic respects the college entrant in America is at least two years behind his counterpart in Britain. This is not a smug private assumption on my part, but a generally accepted fact; you can find it stated over and over again in American works on education. Also it is standard practice in most American colleges to give credit for two years of college work to any student who enters a first degree course straight from a European secondary school. This time-lag of two years is the one basic difference between the educational system in the United States and those on the other side of the Atlantic, especially since it does not change very much during the four years of the first degree course—American college education being far less fiercely specialized than the work leading to a British degree. Except at a few of the best universities and liberal arts or technological colleges, the American with a bachelor's degree is still, in his major field, two years behind the British B.A. or B.Sc. This is the principal reason why one finds, at any given professional level, so many more Ph.D.s in America than in Britain; it is only by doing graduate work that the American makes up the specialist gap. In the arts subjects especially, a graduate in Britain will very seldom go on to work for a doctorate unless he proposes to teach at a university; his bachelor's degree serves as sufficient guarantee of competence in most other professional fields. But in America, as proof of the same degree of competence, these same professional fields often demand that an American graduate shall have taken his doctor's degree.

From all this comes the first of the false images on the British side of the Curtain: the flat assumption that American education is poorer than our own. The image is false because it is incomplete; and it is incomplete, probably, because the reality is so horribly complicated. But there is no need to brush aside all the complications with the decision that the Americans' two-year lag must be a result of inferior teaching, or of a defective sense of overall educational values. A foreigner can accuse the American system of wasting time, as I think it does, but he can't accuse it of being worse than any other—because, quite simply, there is no point at which direct comparison is possible. The patterns of education are too different. In Europe, especially in Britain, we give children an intensive early general education and allow them to specialize as soon as they seem capable of close, mature involvement with a subject; in general, standards are geared to the quickest brains and trimmed downwards for the slower. But the self-consciously democratic system here in America is pretty well the reverse of this, since it begins by offering the same kind of education to everybody, as a constitutional right, and then lets the best brains float gradually to the top, like cream. The floating, not unnaturally, takes time (and there is a danger that sometimes it may never happen at all, and the best brains be left to drown in mediocrity.)

For one thing, education in the United States begins, by international standards, comparatively late. The first grade, the first year of primary education, is not usually open to children of less than six years old. American children do not generally learn to read and write until they are six, or even seven, whereas most British children begin at five, or even four. In the middle 1950s American parents rushed—and are still rushing—to buy a book called "Why Johnnie Can't Read", by one Rudolf Flesch, which suggested that this difference was part of the reason why many American children seemed to be handicapped by an inability to read fluently even in their teens. "You say your child isn't ready at the age of five?" cried Mr. Flesch wrathfully to the parents.

"Don't be ridiculous. Are you trying to tell me that your child is inferior to every single child born and brought up in Great Britain?" He then proceeded to attack not only this initial one-year difference, but also the actual American method of teaching children to read, which he claimed was so faulty that it added a second year's delay to most children's mastery of the language. Poor reading is still a matter of concern in American schools, though much work has been done in the last ten years; teaching methods have been improved, and although only two-thirds of the country's public school systems have pre-school kindergartens for five-year-olds, these are now trying much harder to give their children some ability to read and write before they go on to primary school.

Whether or not this matter of reading is a basic cause of the overall two-year lag, it certainly adds to the impression abroad that the educational process in America is, through its efforts to cater for all children in roughly the same way, inevitably slower and less demanding than that elsewhere. Even the school day is shorter. The average American high-school child goes to school from 8:00 A.M. to 2:30 P.M., compared to the average hours of 8:30 A.M. to 4:00 P.M. in the British secondary school; and the distribution of his holidays is such that he has a far longer break in the summer. The American public school year ends in the middle of June and begins again in the second week of September, giving a total of about three months—compared to an average six-week summer holiday in Britain. No doubt this long non-academic American summer was connected, in the beginning, with the need for releasing children to help harvest crops and so on—as they still do in some agricultural states. In most areas now, however, the necessity is gone, and the long holiday is simply part of the traditional pattern; with the result that there is not only a very thorough mental break in the child's educational year, but also a good chance that he will be found—with the approval of his parents and teachers—earning pocket-money in some kind of summer job. This is, after all, the land of opportunity and enterprise, and any evidence of either is naturally considered a good thing. In Britain, on the other hand, school-children in nonagricultural areas are rarely to be found working except for a few days at the local post office during the Christmas holiday; only university students work in the summer, and that with only the grudging approval of their teachers, who usually set long vacation reading lists and sometimes essays as a deterrent. But in America, the paid holiday job seems to be the norm. Perhaps I have the wrong kind of friends, but the only American students of my acquaintance who appear to do more than a token amount of university or school work during their summer are those high-school or college unfortunates whose marks have been so low in some particular subject that to gain their required total of credits they must attend that sad revision-cramming session known as summer school.

There is much to be said in favor of this system; at any rate, much *is* said in favor of it, generally mixed with references to the unhindered development of personality, and the virtues of a broad, humane, liberal education. The most relevant point about it in this context, however, is the fact that these differences in speed and intensity of education make it impossible to draw any direct comparison between the standards of schools on either side of the Atlantic. In the United States, education is necessarily spread more thinly on the bread. Even though he may have taken special advanced courses designed for what Dr. Conant calls "the academically talented," and even though he may have sailed easily through his ninety credits, the American high-school child leaves for college—or his job—without having experienced education as a *continuous* broad spectrum of many subjects, and without having had any taste of the close involvement with a few subjects which is offered to British Sixth-formers. In America, the college has to serve as an extension of the high school in the way that the British Sixth Form is an extension of the grammar school; and even so it must go more slowly than the Sixth Form, since the credit-and-course system continues at college level, with each student taking a varied range of subjects which sometimes bear no relation to one another at all. At many American colleges, the student is not involved in the study of a particular subject in any real depth until he reaches the graduate school. Thus it comes about that the second popular image of American education which has crept out through the Golden Curtain—and which also prevails inside it—is as false as the first. The United States has an admirably large total of universities and colleges; at the beginning of the 1963 to 1964 academic year, 4,528,516 students were enrolled at a total of 2,080 institutions of higher education. But the total is large not only because of the democratic concept of opportunity for all, but because the whole system depends on higher education and its products. If all the universities and colleges in Britain were to disappear tomorrow, we should still be turning out each year, from the secondary schools, a generation capable of meeting the challenge of tough educational standards; but if all America's colleges disappeared, you would be left only with a great cheerful mass of children who had never yet been faced with any great challenge at all. Their first real intellectual involvement with study comes only after they leave school, as many college freshmen are alarmed to discover in that first traumatic year. This is, moreover, often an involvement which in many other countries would take place in some institution other than a university—so that it is wise, before sitting comfortably back when educators praise the fact that the United States has proportionately more universities than any nation in the world, to examine precisely what they mean. What is a university: what is a degree?

During the academic year 1963–64, some 502,104 first degrees were awarded in the United States. It is an imposing total; far more imposing than that in Britain, which with a population one quarter the size of that of the U.S.A. should, to be able to boast a similar total have had 125,000 degrees in that year, but instead had only 22,000. Consider, however, the nature of the American degrees. By far the highest number, 112,993, were awarded in education. But in Britain, education is not a degree subject; secondary school teachers tend to take a degree in their own specialist subject and follow it with an education diploma course, and the great bulk of teachers are trained in specialist three-year training colleges, and qualify without the label "A.B." (In Britain, as a matter of fact, we say "B.A." for Bachelor of Arts; A.B. stands for Able-Bodied Seaman, which must cause some confusion to American academics traveling on British ships.)

Then, on the American list, there is "business and commerce," in which 58,964 degrees were given. In Britain, no university yet offers a first degree in business management, though one or two post-graduate institutions have recently been set up. Business training there is acquired through various training schemes within industry or commerce, or by accident (which is no doubt one contribution to Britain's sad slither down the business efficiency path).

Then again, 35,226 degrees in engineering were awarded in the U.S.A. In Britain, only about a third of our degree-level qualifications in engineering are acquired in universities; one of the recommendations of the Robbins Report on higher education in 1963 was that the Colleges of Advanced Technology, which supply the other two-thirds, should be granted degree-giving status. Making allowance for this last complication, one can estimate that these three fields alone amount to about 177,000 peculiarly American degrees; and in fact when you add up all the rest of a similar nature, it turns out that about half the first degrees in the United States are awarded in vocational and commercial fields which in most European countries are not treated as degree subjects at all. Britain and the rest give the same training in these fields, but consider them not academic enough to wear the label of a degree; it seems an excessively purist attitude, but there it is. It is probably one reason for the scepticism the foreign academic tends to feel towards scholarship in America—or at least scholarship outside the more renowned institutions like Harvard and M.I.T. "In the States," he says loftily, not without some accuracy, "you can get a degree *anywhere* for *anything*—even basket-weaving."

But the main point is that at the level of the first degree, higher education in the United States differs very widely from that in Britain and other Transatlantic countries, in kind as much as in quantity. It is not useful, and certainly not fair, to expect the same things of each. I recall an American contemporary of mine at Oxford who was reading an arts subject; since he already had his first degree from Princeton, he was expected to acquire his Oxford first degree within two years instead of the usual three. But by the time he was halfway through his first year he had been thrown into deep gloom by the kind of work required of him, and before long he had switched to the normal three-year course. Only at post-graduate level can the average American student cross without difficulty to the British system, for only then do the kinds of education in the two countries coincide.

It is as though the two systems were two travelers bound for the same point: the one walking steadily all the way, the other making short swift hops in an automobile in order to be able to stop at intervals en route for other activities. They both reach the same destination in the end, and the only difference then is the possibility that the walker may have done more for his muscles and general well-being than the man who hopped in and out of the car. Thus, in the end, the British and American systems both reach the same point. Each method has its drawbacks: Britain's proud walkers may never have the (mental) muscle-power to start the journey, or may tumble at any one of the examination hurdles along the way. But nor is it as simple as it might seem for the American education-travelers to clamber back, after each interval, into their car.

Since there are no forcing or sifting processes built into the long American system of education, those who are to benefit fully from it must be educated for a long time. But a great many are not. They fall, as it were, out of the automobile. Only half the children of the United States graduate from high school. Of these, only 40 per cent then go on to at least one year of higher education; and a quarter of this 40 per cent goes only to a two-year college. Of those who go to a four-year college, one in three will have dropped out by the end of the first two years, and only half will graduate. By the basic democratic standard, of course, none of this matters very much. Each child is capable of absorbing only a certain amount of education—well, he is given the chance, and even if he doesn't stay in a particular course, that certain amount of education will probably have rubbed off the system, and on to him, while he was there. Unfortunately, however, this matter of "drop-outs" is not quite so simple as it appears either. It is not merely a question of different amounts of talent. Nine out of ten of the brightest schoolchildren in America (of, that is, the top academic 30 per cent in the schools) graduate successfully from high school; but within this group only two-thirds of the boys and one-half of the girls then go on to college. Of these, only half the boys and one-third of the girls then proceed to graduate. As a result, more than 400,000 of the cleverest children in the country not only fail to reach the graduate training which crowns the American pattern—but do not even finish their college education. Why?

According to one substantial American reference book, the *Modern Family Guide to Education,* by Benjamin Fine, part of the reason is financial. "Huge numbers of talented youngsters from low or average income homes will never get to college," says Mr. Fine flatly. "The deciding factor, unfortunately, is money, not brains." Eighty per cent of all families in the five thousand to ten thousand dollar a year income bracket, he claims, say that they plan to send their children to college; but only 40 per cent manage to do so. In the income brackets over ten thousand dollars a year, 70 per cent of the families send their children to college; but in the bracket of three thousand dollars and below, only 20 per cent. It is possible, though arduous, for a student to work his way through college, and more than 50 per cent of all of them do earn at least part of their expenses, though only 30 per cent manage to earn more than five hundred dollars a year. But Mr. Fine is despondent over the general picture. "To a distressing degree," he says, "the economic status of the parents determines whether a boy or girl actually does go to college. And this situation is likely to worsen in the years ahead, with the middle classes hardest hit."

The Conant Report, however, contains one observation which—although it has nothing whatsoever to do with finances—probably comes nearer than anything to the central drawback of the American educational system. "In all but a few of the schools I have visited," wrote James Conant, "the majority of bright boys and girls were not working hard enough." He took care to qualify this statement by pointing out how easily, with shifts of emphasis, the situation could be remedied; and in many parts of the United States it is in fact continually being remedied, not only by the introduction of more and more accelerated courses for bright children but by the development of entirely new methods of teaching them. There are also those schools, nearly all on the Eastcoast, which use selective entrance requirements deliberately to limit themselves to academically talented children, and which in this sense differ very little from British grammar schools. But all the same there is no denying that the overall American pattern handicaps the proper development of many children who could have gone much further, much faster, if they had not been held back by teaching standards designed for the average student. It is not a worse failing than others abroad; Americans can just as easily accuse the British system of denying, through "exclusive" practices, the chance of higher education to many who would have had the talent to benefit by it. I am not trying to throw bricks; the most interesting point seems to me to be the *kind* of failing that exists in the United States' system, since it has much in common with those aspects of the general American Way which have woven, and help to preserve, the complex barrier I am calling the Golden Curtain.

The American is accustomed to his kind of education. "I minored in psychology in college," he says proudly, and is genuinely disconcerted when the visiting English doctor is, equally genuinely, not impressed. "Come visit at our P.T.A. meeting," he says, and is baffled when the visitor expresses horror afterwards at the influence parents appear able to exert over the running of the school. Not unnaturally, he finds it difficult to look at his own familiar system through a foreigner's innocent eyes. And as a result, he often does not notice that system's close and curious relationship with the image of his own way of life. American education is a very American institution indeed. The box-of-bricks educational concept of courses and credits may not offer any obvious challenges to its students, but it is one which makes it very easy to set up an educational system where there has been none before—as each state of the U.S.A. has had to do during the last century or so. It is far better adapted to a new and growing society than the British concept, which for those purposes depends far too much on the individual excellence of teachers. It can be easily prefabricated: set up without any slow-filled foundation. But unavoidable dangers go with these same qualities. When the "stretch" concept is absent, and no obvious prestige is attached to superior talent, it is perilously possible to assume as a result that education is not an exercise, but a commodity, to be acquired in packages. The store is set up; one buys the goods; *et voilà*, an educated public. I have heard American high-school teachers describe a tendency among their charges' parents to complain, if the child does poorly at school, in the same terms as if they had been given short measure at the supermarket; since they have paid their taxes, the half-conscious reasoning runs, since education is there to be acquired, their child is entitled to a high-school diploma. What does it matter if one or two of his grades aren't good enough? They should still let him graduate, like the other kids. . . .

It might be argued that dim-witted parents of any nation might pursue this kind of argument, but I think there would be a difference. The Englishman, and more particularly the Welshman or the Scot, instinctively accepts the implications of a pattern of effort and reward—perhaps through a new equivalent of the old sense of degree. However loudly he may complain that little Johnnie at the secondary modern should instead have gone to the grammar, or that little Mary at the grammar should stop messing about with chemistry, and leave school at sixteen to get a good solid job—however he may carp, he tends to understand that education is a demanding occupation, a respectable exercise, rather than a thing. He may misunderstand the procedures of education, but he accepts its purpose. The American tends instead to understand the procedures very well, but to forget what the purpose of education ought to be.

For in the United States this purpose is sometimes curiously blurred. In general, American schools and colleges appear to give as much emphasis to training the personality as to training the mind; to producing good American citizens as to producing good engineers or doctors or priests. To doing all these things, that is, not by mere implication, as a valuable side-effect—but by design, as a necessary aim. It is not just a matter of the deliberate teaching of Americanism fostered by Freedoms Foundation and others of a similar turn of mind. There is instead, among many people involved in American education, a sincere belief that perhaps the most valuable function of the system is the preparation of young men and women to play a useful part in the life of the United States—founded on an appreciation of, and respect for, the ideals upon which that life is based. This kind of thinking, admirable enough *in vacuo,* can quell the distracting suspicions that a great many students may never have the best brought out of them. If a boy is happy, and a good all-rounder, and completing all his courses satisfactorily, need any more be expected of him? He may never set the Hudson River on fire, but he will be a pleasant, well integrated American, a regular fellow; he will get on well with his boss and his neighbors, never shake the economy, never rock the boat. . . . He will privately understand the aims of his government, as he has understood those of his teachers; he will not suffer from neuroses over not having accomplished all that was expected of him. He will be likeable, as are most Americans, and he will probably spend much of his most enjoyable leisure time in the only occupation which is preserved, in American schools, as a matter of challenging individual achievement, rather than something served out in easily digestible dollops— sport. For the American schoolchild, the only model which the system seems to offer is that of the Great Average. When each generation graduates from high school, leaving behind its Year- book, "presented by the Class of 1966," or whatever, there in the year's descriptive roster of departing seniors appear over and over again the key words: "Goodnatured . . . sincere . . . popular . . . easy-going . . . well-liked . . . friendly . . . witty . . . cute. . . ." It's no more than a lighthearted tradition, but it has its significance. Undoubtedly the epithets are all accurate; un- doubtedly these qualities are all valuable in the production of attractive, harmless citizens. *But is this what education is for?*

The boy who emerges bearing the accolade of the system and the school, who is on all counts an admirable product, can also be a boy who seems a little disturbing to those who are not them- selves products of the system's standards. Just as most Englishmen cease in early childhood to see anything ridiculous about the rules of cricket, so the average American is unlikely to think that there could be anything worrying in the boy who is in every way a normal, average product of the high school—least of all the boy who "does well." He will worry enough about the delinquent boy, especialy the one who comes from a prosperous home and appears to have no reason for delinquency; but he would not worry at all about, for instance, a perfectly normal boy I once met called Tom Wilberforce.

Tom Wilberforce was seventeen years old, student president of a high school of about 1,500 boys and girls on the Eastcoast of the United States: a thin, earnest, self-possessed boy with a long neck and cropped hair. Set in a wide grassy campus among fall- scarlet trees and timber houses, the school was long and low and brick-built, full of burly youths without ties and pretty girls in long white socks. "We are," said Tom Wilberforce sincerely, "very proud of our school." And certainly he meant it; and certainly there was nothing wrong with that.

He led the way through gleaming woodwork and metalwork rooms; past a clock with "Coca Cola" written across its face; past a language laboratory, full of long desks partitioned by glass into individual places fitted with earphones and a microphone; through the rehearsal studio of an orchestra ninety-two strong. (Very impressed, I asked the music master how many visiting teachers he needed to cover such an enormous range of instruments. "Oh," he said proudly, "I teach them all.") The students' Code of Honor was inscribed, very large, along one wall of the main corridor; it began: "To be honest in thought and deed. . . . To promote clean wholesome thought and speech. . . ."

We passed a part-time class for children who had already left school to take jobs, but who had been persuaded to come back several hours a week to study certain courses. We passed a suite of rooms for "guidance counselors," six members of the staff who were employed not to teach, but to spend all their time giving advice on careers and curricula, and to form a halfway house between teachers and parents. ("We also," said one of them in a startling casual phrase, "work in close touch with the courts.") We passed the gymnasium, with three bouncing physical-education teachers wearing sweatshirts that showed the names of their own former universities inscribed across their chests. As we went, Tom Wilberforce explained it all; and gradually, as he talked more and more of the way he and his fellows were "exposed" to influences, education, traditions, he began to seem strangely unreal: adult and childlike at the same time. Above his head in the corridor a notice read in foot-high letters: THE ONLY WAY TO HAVE A FRIEND IS TO BE ONE. In the room where his student government met, a list of imponderables pinned to a board was headed: "What We Can Do To Strengthen America."

The visitors were a motley group from several nations, for

this school was used by officialdom to demonstrate what they had decided was American education in typical action. In the school canteen, Tom Wilberforce shepherded us expertly to collect our set lunches on trays: huge tuna-fish sandwich, French-fried potatoes, apple sauce, hunk of pie, milk, coffee. He greeted the scattered members of staff and exploding groups of children as if they were all the same age, and then sat talking over lunch. He explained solemnly, looking round the room for a particular teacher, that he had had to cut some classes that day in order to act as guide. "It's a pity, this being a Friday, because we're given weekend tasks."

He was a very ancient and disturbing young man. When we reached the subject of segregation in the Mississippi schools, then in its first welter of publicity, he said: "We all think it's *dreadful.*" He spoke with such heat that one felt compelled to ask why, all day, no Negro boy or girl had been visible in his own school.

"Oh, there's no segregation here at all. There's nothing to stop them coming. We do have one girl. Haven't you seen her?"

Only one? Out of 1,500?

"They don't come," he said obliquely. "They live other places. It's a great pity. But Mississippi, now. . . ."

Tom Wilberforce was a pleasant lad, really. He said that he wanted to be a teacher when he was through college, or perhaps a guidance counselor. He was the perfect embodiment of all those notices on the school walls. He was a conscientious school president, elected by his fellows; he went to church each Sunday, he enjoyed football, he loved his family, he was visibly pleased with the idea of being a young American showing his school to a group of foreigners. And there was not an ounce of curiosity in him. One might have been talking to him through a thick blanket. He never discussed his facts, his ideas, or his judgments; he merely uttered them; pleasantly enough, but without interest in what one might make of them. He had never been outside America, but it did not occur to him to extract any useful information from the Turkish, Iranian, Filipino and English strangers around him. Occasionally one of us would offer a tentative comparison between something in the school and something abroad; but Tom Wilberforce would never return more than a polite: "Oh yes." And one saw that the observation did not register in his head; it bounced off, like a tennis ball. He was simply not interested in anything beyond his own immediate horizons. There was nothing in him to which anyone could take angry exception: no boorishness, no malice, no overt prejudice; he was a good product of the educational system and Transatlantic Christianity, and he was already a hopelessly insulated American. I shall never forget him; I think he frightened me more than the whole Cuban episode did.

But when I mentioned this to an American who had accompanied the group of visitors to the school, he stared at me in astonishment. "What's the matter with you?" he said. "That was just a regular kid."

8 ∴ Sport and the Regular Guy

> *"Are you bothered by feelings of insecurity
> or inferiority? Do you make friends easily?
> Do you enjoy recreation in groups?"*
> —Questions on a college registration
> form for freshman students

> *"Sport in America has the vices of a
> religion . . . it is not in the least sportive."*
> —G. K. CHESTERTON

Earnestness is probably the great American sin. It isn't a bad
one; there are many far more irritating, including, no doubt, the
reticence of the Englishman. But it is this earnestness, not necessarily humorless, often endearing, which gives a strange inflexi-
bility to the American ideal of personality and behavior. Kooks
and screwballs and wild youngsters certainly exist in large quan-
tities in the United States, and appear in the headlines (especially other nations' headlines) with monotonous frequency; but
when the foreigner goes there he finds that Americans in general
seem not to harbor the sneaking admiration for the eccentric that
one finds in many parts of Europe. Sometimes, indeed, they will
not even tolerate the oddball. Admiration is reserved for the man
who in all respects approximates pretty well to a wholesome
norm; who has nothing strange about him. And inevitably this
same ideal is instilled by a kind of educational osmosis into the

young. The girl collecting her college credits in psychology and anthropology and ancient history knows at heart that she is really only preparing to be a Good Wife And Mother, with the side ability one day—when the kids have all been sent off to college—to provoke admiration from the local women's club study group with interesting little papers on psychology and anthropology and ancient history. And the activities which most closely involve her male counterpart are those of the regular guy: the All-American boy, whose image comes perilously close sometimes to that of the All-American football player.

The nearest English equivalent of this somewhat sinister word "regular" is "ordinary"; but the American term, unlike the English, has no pejorative overtones of the dull, the uninteresting, the commonplace. On the contrary, it is generally used as a compliment; William H. Whyte's *The Organization Man* is a horrific testament to the extent to which business, public administration and even university administration in the United States have come to value the quality of being personally unremarkable.

The regular guy is the one who can be relied upon never to throw any kind of spanner into the works. He is predictable; he is a credit to the norm; he is the salt of the Transatlantic earth. "My proudest boast," said a high school principal to me once, "is that we turn out a batch of fine regular kids each year, ready to make a great contribution first to their college and then to society." Depressingly, one knew that he and his pride were typical of the personal values widespread among American educators; such people do not want to turn out Freedom Riders, or poets, or any kind of disturbing individualist. They want to produce sturdy but comfortable persons who are not so spineless that they could be labeled immediately as conformists (a term bandied so often now by distressed sociologists that to use it is to conform) but who can be relied upon never to rebel.

The male members of this species are more unnerving than the female—it being fairly natural, after all, for most girls to ex-

pect a single set pattern from life—and you can recognize them
in every high school and university in the land. The regular boy
is tolerably good at his work, but seldom brilliant in any subject;
his grades will be a predictable permutation of As, Bs, and Cs,
and he will graduate from high school without difficulty or great
distinction. He is a largish boy, sometimes slightly overweight; he
drinks a great deal of milk, and likes to eat fried chicken, steak,
hamburgers, peanut butter and jelly sandwiches, and apple pie
à la mode. He wears his hair very short, his denim trousers (or
dungarees, or "chinos") very tight, and no tie except on Sundays.
He goes to church once a week with his family, but spends all his
free time with a small group of "buddies" of his own age and sex.
He is never a solitary; to prefer to be much alone is not to be
regular. At the age of sixteen, in most states of the Union, he acquires a driving license, and henceforth drives the family's car, or
second car, at every possible opportunity. He will probably have
several small accidents in the next two or three years; he may get
a speeding ticket, and may even lose his license temporarily, but
this will do him no real damage in the eyes of friends, school or
family. It is too close to the norm; the regular boy is expected to
have spirit, of the Tom Sawyer variety, and this is an accepted
modern outlet. It is also generally accepted that he will begin to
have dates now and then at about fifteen or sixteen. He is expected to have several girl-friends; to date only one is to "go
steady" too early, and to cause general alarm. He will take his
girl, generally, to treats such as dances or movies; he is not accustomed to theaters or concerts, and if he began listening to classical music his friends might think him odd. He cares deeply for
the good opinion of these friends, and discusses the engine capacity of motor-cars with them incessantly, often on the telephone.
With them, in due course, he learns dutifully to smoke cigarettes
and to drink beer; now and again in sufficiently prosperous areas
half-a-dozen regular guys will acquire a case of canned beer,
drive to some secluded spot, and proceed to get mildly and self-
consciously drunk, tossing out their flip-top cans to decorate the

side of the road. Generally the boy who is driving will have the sense to remain sober. Parents seldom hear about this custom unless a policeman happens to come upon the boys and their beer, or to stop the car; but except in those cases where one of the boys inadvertently kills a pedestrian or another driver, nobody takes the crime too seriously. The assumption is, often accurately, that this will turn out to be the regular boy's one wild oat.

The regular boy's home life is depicted, in essence, in the kind of pictures the American artist Norman Rockwell used to draw for the covers of the *Saturday Evening Post*. (To borrow a quotation from Dwight Macdonald: "There's this magazine cover," says the comedian Mort Sahl, "and it shows this kid getting his first haircut you know and a dog is licking his hand and his mother is crying and it's Saturday night in the old home town and people are dancing outside in the streets and the Liberty Bell is ringing and, uh, did I miss anything?") It is the kind of home in which one is more likely in fact to find the *Post* than a copy of a recent novel, though it is by no means always the home of insulated parents. It has never bred in the regular boy any great intellectual curiosity, and he is never likely to feel any particular interest in any of the fine arts; his passionate devotion to pop music belongs in quite another category. He may experience some pangs of an emerging social conscience in his late teens, but this infant will die soon after birth, unless its owner is inspired to join that excellent opener of young American minds—though still a regular organization—the Peace Corps. Probably, however, he does not feel inclined to join either the Corps or any organization of a slightly more offbeat nature; his ambitions are more likely to be limited to going to college, joining a fraternity, buying a car, getting a good job, marrying a regular American girl, raising some regular kids in a good home, becoming as prosperous as possible, and so dissolving invisibly into the American way of life.

There is one other ambition; he will, nine times out of ten, assiduously involve himself in some kind of sport, first as participant and then, when business conferences or martinis take their toll, as spectator and knowledgeable critic. For the particular aspect of the American way which is most ardently proselytized in the educational system, as a form of character-training attracting adulation of a kind granted, in England, only to the Oxford Greats course, is sport.

Most countries have a national game, which reflects to a fairly significant extent the temperament and inclinations of the nation concerned. Cricket is still the most peculiarly English of English games, though the whole athletic spectrum has been used to indicate the Anglo-Saxon's scale of values: the concept of fair play; the virtue of concealing huge effort beneath desperate nonchalance; the images of the modest winner, the stoical loser, and the crowd that cheers the plucky underdog. The vocabulary of sport, when applied to life in general, covers a great deal of the traditional equipment of Englishness. But still more revealing, in the matter of illuminating a nation's standards, is the way in which Americans tend unconsciously to treat sport not as a mirror for manners, but as an actual container for all the emotion, romance and solemnity they feel life has to offer.

> Above the south-western rim of Green Bay's City Stadium a halfmoon looks as though it is pasted against the blue-black sky. Under the lights the grass is greener than grass-green, and Zeke Bratkowski, who is a quarterback for the Green Bay Packers, is kneeling and the Packers are huddled in front of him, their pad-broadened, green-jerseyed shoulders touching, their yellow-helmeted heads lowered to hear him.

> "All right," he says. "Red Right. The 49 Option, on two! Let's go!" It is the play that Vince Lombardi, who coaches the Packers, brought with him to Green Bay five years ago and put in just for Paul Hornung . . . . More than 42,000 people fill the stands and they are waiting to see the Paul Hornung they remember . . . .

> "Golden Boy is Back,"
> *Life Magazine,* August, 1964

A football game in the United States is almost as difficult to believe in, the first time you see it, as a political convention. It is not the professional game that shakes you, but the college and high school variety: the kind which—that strain again—the American takes most for granted. Every Saturday, from mid-September to the end of November, in every town and campus of the United States, football stands of varying size and splendor fill with children, teenagers, men and women—far more women than you would ever find at a European football match; far more parents, and far, far more personally disinterested townspeople. And although you can hardly fail to know what a high school football game is like, I propose to include my own description of one here to demonstrate what the sport would look like to a new arrival from the moon—which, in this context, a visitor from Europe might just as well be. There seem to be six teams on the field rather than two, to a foreign eye; American football allows so much switching of players during a game that there may be more than a hundred players out, all with space-helmets, wire-masked faces, vastly padded shoulders, and so many other pads and guards scattered about their anatomy that their tight shirts and shin-length trousers seem ready to burst. Eleven of each are on the field at a time; the rest sit hunched under long splendid cloaks in a line at either side, with their high school coach bounding up and down exhorting the playing spacemen, muttering to non-players, summoning two or three of the giant boys off the field and sending others hurtling out to take their place. It is a rare player who spends the whole forty-eight minutes (sixty minutes for college and professional games) in play; it is a rare stranger who can extricate the significance of the game, which began as a semblance of rugby football but has been so rationalized since with rules and ramifications that it seems, in comparison with modern soccer or rugby, curiously slow. The two lines of spacemen crouch, facing, like wrestlers; a center flicks the ball; the whole game erupts as players all over the field fling one another to the ground; the crowd howls; and within seconds the whistle shrills and the ball, which had at once vanished, is revealed beneath a heap of padded bodies. It seems, by some weird magic, considerably nearer the opposing goal than when the center passed. Two brisk be-jerseyed men rush on to the field with a tape measure, and with the referee, umpire, timekeeper and linesman bobbing round them like wasps they measure the distance the ball has traveled. "Second down, one yard to go," booms a great voice inscrutably over the field from the loudspeaker system. The crowd wildly cheers or nervously groans; the brass section of the school band, visible as a large colored patch of uniform among the crowd, blows huge discords on its tubas and trombones; and the cheerleaders bound out in front of the stands while the players are forming their lines again.

They are the most disconcerting phenomena of all, these cheerleaders: half-a-dozen boys in white jackets and trousers, perhaps, at a college game; or at a high school game, girls in bright abbreviated skirts and shirts that would have them shivering in the autumn wind if ever they stood still. But they are seldom still; they leap and dance and turn cartwheels before the crowd, exhorting support for their team with strange shouted runes that bring a trained chorus of response not only from the schoolchildren but from large enthusiastic men who have not stopped shouting them, at such games, since they left school themselves. Perhaps they have never left school themselves.

> Ipso razzo
> Teddy boom bazzo
> I skiddy I sky
> Teddy boom bah
> Teddy roo
> Teddy rah
> Teddy rub-a-dub fub-a-dub
> Chicka boom bah
> Midville High School
> RAH RAH RAH . . . .

Or as the sweating giants work their spasmodic way up the field, with referee and umpire and timekeeper and linesman darting round them now like snapping terriers, the crowd breaks into a long growing chant: "We wanna touchdown . . . we wanna touchdown . . . we wanna touchdown . . ." And the cheerleaders prance and wave their arms and lead the incantation through their megaphones, until either some desperate ball-carrier manages to make a touchdown, or the maddened defense drives the line back. But the relentless girls and the exuberant crowd are still chanting away:

> You add a little pep
> You add a little might
> You put it all together
> And you FIGHT FIGHT FIGHT . . . .

At half-time, between the second and third quarters, when the acres of players stream off the field (half of them not yet having played at all) gigantic school bands march raucously on to give successive displays: each vying with the other in magnificence of uniforms, complexity of marching and counter-marching, volume of sound, variety of instruments—saxophones, clarinets and gigantic euphoniums are much in evidence among the more usual brass-band range—and in the agility of the group of acrobats or plume-decked baton-twirlers who march at their head. At the same time each school's corps of cheerleaders crosses to the side of the field where the opposing team's supporters are thickest, and gives them a complimentary, meekly received display.

All this malarkey, all this expense, training, effort and talent is subsidiary to one thing: the football. Far more people than the players take an active part in the game. Some of them, like the band, might exist anyway without it; but as things are, most of their time is taken up with practicing for the entertainment that forms the icing on the cake of sport. "Ah," say the game's organizers warmly, "the good thing is, it gives so many kids a chance to participate." And so it does; but again, the thing in which they are participating, whether or not they would prefer something else, is sport.

This scale of values is necessarily assumed, by the American

schoolchild, to be part of the natural way of things. If he is one
of the several hundred involved in playing football (for there are
teams of like size for each year, though only the major team,
mainly of seniors, represents the school with such ceremony), his
life is geared to the game and ordered by the school's football
coach. He must stay at school for football practice every day from
two-thirty until five; he must be in bed by ten-thirty; and he
must not smoke or drink beer. He is, as if he were professional,
strictly in training. For football, in the United States, can pay off
in ways unfamiliar to an Englishman:

> They call Paul Hornung the "Golden Boy." He is one of those
> people born to be winners and for most of his 28 years he has
> been just that. He is good-looking, intelligent and highly person-
> able and he has that great gift for the game of football. He played
> it first as a sixth-grader at St. Patrick's School in Louisville,
> Kentucky, and two years later his coach let him make up his team's
> plays. When he was the star of the Flaget High School team,
> colleges from coast to coast were running at him with scholar-
> ships and the governor of Kentucky visited him twice to try to
> get him to go to the University of Kentucky. At Notre Dame he
> was twice All-America, and at the end of his last season—1956—
> he was voted the Heisman Trophy, awarded annually to the
> outstanding college football player in the country . . .
>
> *Life Magazine, loc. cit.*

So it goes. Scholarships for football and other kinds of sport
are no longer the simple handouts they once were in many American universities and colleges; no completely witless numbskull
can today find himself studying physical education or wood-
carving at some reasonably distinguished institution simply because he happens to be a brilliant quarterback. But the scholarships are still there, albeit with rather higher academic requirements attached; and many colleges will still send sweetly persuasive letters, generally signed by the football coach, asking juvenile football stars on the verge of graduating from high school
whether they wouldn't like to try for a place. College football is

no longer a simple sport; there is too much money involved. At even the wealthiest of British universities the football pitch is generally a bleak muddy field somewhere, its only difference from any other field being two or three sacrosanct patches of grass marked off for use as the wickets in summer cricket games. But the great football stadium at the University of Michigan seats one hundred thousand people, is never used except in the autumn, and then only for the major Saturday college games; and the price of its seats is never less than five dollars each. . . .

With the seasons, the focus of sporting attention changes in America. Basketball and hockey take over, then baseball and track. The girls of course have their own sports: softball or tennis, field hockey or lacrosse, but I suspect there is more prestige attached to being appointed cheerleader or drum-majorette than to reaching the girls' hockey team. The American schoolgirl can still be deemed regular without taking part in any organized school sport.

But here more than in any other country, girls and boys alike have very often indeed a genuine interest in at least one sport, either as participant or spectator, outside school hours. Beyond the organized activities of schools and colleges, the mystique has two great spheres of influence in the United States. The first is that of spectator sports. In Britain, these days, only first division soccer, major rugby matches and Test cricket draw really large crowds; there are always spaces in the stands at minor soccer and rugby games, and the county cricket grounds suffer from a chronic and depressing disease known as Low Gate. But in America, large fervent crowds travel miles to see professional football, baseball, basketball, ice hockey: television not withstanding, the crowd at the Rose Bowl football game in California in January each year contains many among its hundred thousand who have come two or three thousand miles to watch the game. The great god Sport is a relative of the great god Entertainment, and similarly lucrative; so that when C.B.S. in 1964 bought the Yankees baseball team lock, stock and barrel for $11,200,000, they were not only acquiring what is commonly known as a hot property, but were perhaps putting it in the right category at last.

But the second sphere of sporting influence is more lucrative still, in the long run. Since the Second World War there has been much talk in the United States of education for leisure; of preparing people to make good use of the increasing amounts of spare time they will have as automation spreads and the human working week dwindles down. But before working weeks dwindle, pay packets usually increase, so that greater prosperity has begun to have its effect before greater leisure can spread. And in a country where physical activity, *doing* things, is already respected as a laudable and worthwhile way of spending one's time, the result as far as leisure occupation is concerned has been, in the last twenty years, a growth not so much in peaceful intellectual activity as in the more expensive kinds of sport. It is encouraged, of course, by the vast range of climate and topography in a country so large, which offers a wide choice of activity from the outset; when the mountains of New England have more than six feet of good snow every winter, for example, it is hardly surprising that people living within reach should flock to ski down them. Everywhere in the mountainous United States, in fact, skiing has become a good example of the new preoccupation, particularly among the young. In Britain, it is only just ceasing to be a "snob" sport; our climate does not provide enough snow for skiing, except in very remote areas, and the average man has rarely been able to afford the fare, hotel bill, clothes and other appurtenances of a trip over to Davos, or St. Moritz, or Zermatt. Even the multiplying thousands who now can afford to head for the Alps must generally spend most of their year's allowance of holiday time and money in order to ski. And British roads being what they are, one does not often pop up from London for a weekend's skiing in the north of Scotland, even when there is enough snow.

But in America, at least 30 per cent of the population has skiing within fairly easy reach. All the New Englanders, all the Bostonians, all the New Yorkers can drive in three or four hours, or less, to the ski slopes of Vermont, New Hampshire, Maine, Massachusetts or New York State; the western and central states have ski areas multiplying each year in the Sierras and the Olympic Mountains and every attainable part of the Rockies; in Michigan and Colorado and Idaho. So it is that when November comes, and the lists of snow depths begin to appear in the major newspapers, in half the states of the Union the mass weekend trek begins on the expressways that lead to the mountains, and every third car has skis strapped to its roof.

The ski-resorts to which these cars joyously slither and climb would not look familiar to the European accustomed to the Alps. Many are large and well appointed enough, to be sure, with large hotels, crowded bars and prosperous, suntanned faces; some, like Aspen in Colorado and Mount Snow in Vermont, lie beside flourishing year-round towns. But most of the American ski centers are small and comparatively new, the fruits of the new affluence, like automobiles and washing machines. And they are all deliberately made resorts. "In the Alps," says a German-American friend of mine nostalgically, "you go up on the lift once or perhaps twice a day, and you know you can ski off somewhere over the mountain and find a little village and a glass of wine, because people have been living in those mountains for two thousand years. But here it is up-down, up-down, like a yo-yo. Perhaps fifteen times a day on the lift, or more."

For in the United States most skiing is done in country which has only begun to be settled, and that sparsely, in the last two hundred years; and in country which is for the most part below the timberline. The Americans ski not over open slopes but down trails and runs carved out of thick forests of pine and maple and birch. It does not take them long to come down from the point at which the ski lift sheds them; they have a limited choice of directions in which to go. So the word that goes round at the beginning of a winter tends to be: "There's a new T-bar at Pleasant Mountain . . . they've cleared a new trail at Wildcat . . . ." and the pleasure is all, to this extent, man-made.

It is also a pleasure for the ordinary man in a way that it cannot be in Britain. The small ski resort in, say, Maine is a startling sight at first; the first overwhelming impression that of a kind of brilliant scruffiness. The long wooden building at the foot of the slopes, holding restaurant, snack-bar and ski shop, booms and clatters with the sound of snow-dripping ski boots as panting crowds push and queue towards the counters for their hamburgers and hot dogs, clam chowder and French fries, tuna-fish sandwiches and bowls of chili. There are tubby fathers in ancient parkas and baggy ski pants; pink-nosed mothers in Norwegian sweaters shepherding small determined children whose ski boots seem twice as big as their heads; loud grubby-jerseyed eight-year-olds from the rabbit slopes. And there are endless groups of teenagers, the girls with bright flowered and striped parkas and sweaters, immaculate bouffant hairstyles built carefully round their earmuffs, and the boys in the tightest of ski pants or carefully casual denim trousers, vast yellow goggles dangling round their necks, and an assortment of jerseys and jackets ranging—according to personality—from curious three-quarter-length garments of battered corduroy to baby-blue anoraks that blend oddly with near-bald crewcut heads. Outside the hut, a forest of skis and ski poles bristles out of brown trampled snow, left stuck on end by their eating owners; there is seldom a theft, due partly to skiing camaraderie and partly to the fact that anyone arriving without skis would be conspicuous from the start.

Twenty yards up the slope, long shuffling queues wait for the T-bars and the chair-lifts; the clanking groans of the machinery make a continual background that is noticeable only when it stops; and in hardly broken sequence the ski-dangling couples are hoisted up the hill. It is when they come down again that the broad democratic spread of American skiing makes itself most obvious of all. These people are not elegant experts, well taught by expensive instructors; they are there because they can afford the equipment and the cost of reaching the area, spending a night or two, eating, using the lifts. But that is all. They are affluent, but ordinary. So, in general, is their skiing. Ostentatious teenage boys with more nerve than skill shoot vertically down the slopes like unguided missiles; happy novices bounce up and down like ungainly snowballs, or stand paralyzed in the middle of a slope; truly accomplished skiers are not common, and the majority are content if they are able to stay on their feet. It is rather like the overall standard of drivers on American roads: there are far more bad ones than you hope or expect to find. For although these skiers are the sport-hungry Americans who can afford now to spend their winter leisure as their parents could not, their occupation is not cheap. The scruffiest of the skiers must spend not only several hundred dollars to equip perhaps a family of four for skiing (skis, ski poles, bindings, ski boots, parkas, pants, mittens, goggles, and so on and so on . . .) but must then pay some twenty dollars a night for two motel rooms excluding all meals, and five dollars a day for each skier's use of the lifts. Not many are then prepared to fork out an extra eight dollars an hour for individual skiing lessons. But some do, of course; and rather more than this take cheaper lessons in classes. At one northern resort a young Swiss, Hans Jenni, married to an American girl, runs a ski school: teaching groups of middle-class Americans to ski during the winter, and reverting to his homeland trade of cabinet-making in summer. The pattern is much the same as it could have been for him in the Swiss Alps, but there is a difference which Jenni puts succinctly. "Here more people spend more money," he says.

The other most notable combination of prosperity and sport-worship occurs on the coasts and inland lakes of the United States. Every weekend between about March and November, and all the year round in Florida and California, the great streams of cars turn towards water like a dowser's divining-rod. Fishermen head for lakes, with a canoe strapped to the roof of their car; children flit through the waves on Sailfish or Sunfish. And everywhere sail-boats have multiplied as astonishingly as they have in

Britain since the last war. The boom in boats in Britain, however, is concentrated on the smaller dinghies; in America, the
range is wider, and the year-round boat-advertising columns of
the *New York Times* are full of offers from owners of boats of
seventeen feet and up . . . and up. . . .

> Rhodes 44-ft Masthead Yawl. An excellent opportunity to get a
> first quality cruising racing auxiliary at a steal. Price has been
> dropped by $15,000 to only $20,000 for action. Layout is stand-
> ard 5-berth, very spacious due to broad beam. Much bonus gear,
> such as: 15 bags of sails, mostly new dacron, phone, depth finder,
> Kenyon, gust wind indicator, RDF, dodger, awning, bow and
> stern pulpits, lifelines, roller reefing, geared winches, gimballed
> oven and stove, etc. Survey invited . . . .

Boat Shows are held every year all over the place, even in
cities which may be miles from good sailing water; and for those
who prefer to indulge their sporting instincts at one remove, professional sailors offer berths on windjammers, "U.S. Coastguard
approved vessels," cruising the remoter parts of the coasts. "Sail,"
lure the advertisements: "Explore. Relax to guitar music under
the stars. $125 weekly, includes hearty meals. . . ." Altogether
there are 7,678,000 recreational boats in use in the United States,
and about two and a half billion dollars a year are spent on
boating.

But there is one aspect of this water-borne craze which seems
to have intriguing undertones, and to be significant of more than
the traditional American reverence for physical exertion and the
outdoors. I have been noticing it in different ways ever since I
arrived: when, one early day, I was sitting in a bus traveling
alongside the Potomac river in Washington, D.C., and my guide
said: "That's our boat club over there." I peered over the bank,
with my British assumptions, and said: "Where? Can't see a
single mast." The guide looked at me with a mixture of wonder
and scorn. "O, not *sailboats*," he said. "*Power*boats."

The powerboat in America is at all levels more widespread
than the sailing boat. In Britain, perhaps significantly, there is

no real generic term for the species; motorboats and speedboats, those effervescent inescapable wasps, are not recognized as being related to the chubby cruisers which wash away the banks of the upper Thames; and the most complicated outboard motor is allowed no description in common with a launch. These do not make up a distinct race of boats as they do in the U.S.A. with all the tough implications of the mighty word "power." Nor do they contribute to a new and fascinating version of nautical leisure which money, or the mentality bred by the automobile, or simply the attractions of the American household way, have carved out of the American pastime and sport of powerboating. One American writer and sailor, Morton M. Hunt, discovered this in full flower when he set out to cruise all the way round the coasts of Long Island Sound, which is probably the most thickly populated maritime playground in the whole of the U.S.A. Everywhere, especially at weekends, he found the water cut choppy by hundreds of powerboats, rocking the similar hordes of boats under sail; but also, in the harbors, he found something else. The most splendid example of this new phenomenon was in Manhasset Bay, at a marina called Club Capri (the marina, which is spreading now to Britain from America, being a kind of watery parking-lot for boats, with enough quays and small cross-quays to provide moorings for an astonishing number of vessels in a smallish space. There are about four thousand of them in the U.S.A.).

A small barge with a store on it—it looked like a houseboat—was moored in the middle of the harbor; colored pennants flapped from halyards running to the top of a short mast, the doors were beach-house jalousies, and signs above the cabin proclaimed the vessel to be Cap'n's Galley. Two power-boats were tied up alongside and their occupants were ordering snacks or lunch. We dropped sail, motored up, and hove a line to an attendant, who, in return, handed us a menu offering soft drinks, sandwiches, French fries, shrimp, a "He-Man's Fried Seafood Plate," and ice cream. We bought some ice cream and shoved off. A short distance further on was a second and somewhat larger float, whose sign read "Gulf Marine Service Station." It had gasoline and diesel-oil pumps on deck . . . .

The Inland Sea

Around this unseaman-like centerpiece, the marina was almost entirely filled with powerboats, tied up at cross-quays which were all labeled with street signs bearing names like Bahama East and Tahiti West. Mr. Hunt observed a hydrofoil passenger boat which carried commuters from the marina to Wall Steet every weekday morning. And among the high-heeled women and flowery-shirted men, the swimming-pool, the dance floor and the store selling red carpets lettered "Welcome Aboard," he found one of the boat-owners: a husky, T-shirted man on a glistening white-and-chromium sixty-six-foot cruiser:

The boat, he told me, had everything that he and his wife— who was sunning herself on the foredeck—could want; it was a real floating home. The saloon, which he showed me first, was carpeted in gold from wall to wall and had gold-and-beige-upholstered furniture; there was also a television set, a cocktail table, a liquor cabinet, and a gateleg dining table. The master stateroom, forward, was also carpeted in gold; it had twin beds (not bunks), a vanity, a chest of drawers, two large closets, two electric heaters, and a bathroom with a stall shower, and, in fact, was indistinguishable from a room in one of the better motels. The wheelhouse, aft of and above the saloon, was a marvel of chrome handles, buttons and dials; from this vantage point the skipper could operate twin engines totaling five hundred and fifty horse-power, with which he could cruise comfortably at twenty knots or achieve a top speed of about twenty-five. Cruising in such a boat burns up about twenty-five gallons of gasoline an hour.

Ibid.

But this owner did not use much gasoline. "All summer long," he told Mr. Hunt, "we like to run down here in the evenings and sit on deck and smoke and talk to our neighbors, or watch television. . . . We use the boat primarily as a means of transportation to different eating places, though sometimes on a weekend we'll go a few hours away and stay overnight in another marina. . . ."

To the multiplying American powerboaters of this kind, a boat is not an object of glory, or something to mess happily about in: it is much more like a car. They can take it out to make a noise in it—which will prompt their sons to murmur admiringly: "Gee Dad, that's cool." They can zoom up and down feeling powerful in it—and indeed the better designed big boats do give one a few glorious moments of feeling like the skipper of a PT boat. Or they can catch a few large impressive fish from it—fish much too large to eat, so that later they will be thrown away. But otherwise it can be nothing but a means of transport; or a houseboat. Before leaving the remarkable Club Capri, Morton Hunt found a sailing acquaintance who had known the place for some time.

> "It's full of kids, dogs, organized play groups, dances and barbecues," he said . . . . "These people think of their boats as summer homes. Hell, I know one fellow—an engineer—who had a thirty-five-foot power cruiser here two years ago and kept her tied down all summer. He'd run up the engines once in a while, and he even went out in the bay a couple of times, but he didn't try to go out on the Sound until the end of the summer, and then, when he got to the mouth of the bay, he saw a few whitecaps outside, so he came right back. As for the women sitting around here, most of them love sitting on deck in nice clothes and looking chic, but they hate to go out, especially if there's any kind of a little chop . . . ."
>
> *Ibid.*

All this is the inevitable extension of the mystique of sport. The regular American has a healthy interest in playing games, in keeping fit, in doing things; he knows he has, he has been brought up to know it. But his prosperity can get the better of

him. He is still paying lip-service to the ideal; he has bought a
boat, he is out in the open air, more or less; he is a sportsman.
And he is able to gloss over in his mind the fact that this boat
involves him in no exertion or display of skill; that it is, in fact,
no more than an enjoyable and faintly glamorous way of doing
nothing. His boat-owning ranks with the neat little electric bug-
gies to be seen on American golf courses, which have turned up
in increasing numbers ever since former President Eisenhower,
that image of regularity, took to one after a heart attack. "Played
two rounds of golf this weekend," says the sportsman, beaming
with healthy pride; and neglects to mention that after every
stroke he hopped back into the electric cart driven by his caddy,
and buzzed away in idle comfort down the fairway to catch up
with the ball. It ranks with the "camping trips" taken in sup-
posedly remote areas of the American national parks; during
which a family drives with its loaded car to a special camping site
supplied with running water, lavatories, and sometimes a small
general store; sets up its tent in a space so crowded that the guy-
ropes will sometimes overlap those of the tent next-door; sleeps to
the strains of somebody else's transistor radio; and clambers the
next morning back into the car to drive on. "Spent this summer
camping in Yellowstone," says the proud paterfamilias, back at
his office. "Great to get away from civilization. Helps toughen up
the kids, y'know."

In such ways as this, certain varieties of sport in the United
States have become fakes: cushioned, smoothed-down versions of
the less comfortable real thing. And this was the reason for the
paradoxical situation in 1963, where, in a country more overtly
infatuated with sport than ever before, President Kennedy grew
sufficiently alarmed at the state of the nation's health to issue his
famous recommendation of twenty-mile hikes. The regular guy
was quite satisfactorily involved in the world of sport; in golfing
or boating or cheering a football team; but this didn't seem to be
keeping down the incidence of coronary thrombosis. The values
of speed and comfort had begun to infiltrate the older and basi-

cally more American values of the mystique of sport; and whether or not this was bad for the health of the nation, it was certainly bad for the health of sport itself, the only native cultural development of the U.S.A. It was perhaps a little too much like the way the canned arts, films and television, had by their premature dominance stifled the fine arts from growing to a proper height at a proper speed.

But however the corners of its structure may be smoothed away, the American sporting mystique itself grows sturdier every day. It is a live and flourishing part of the American culture, as the theater is a live and flourishing part of the British. Of course sport has always made up a formidable part of the life of modern Britain too, at either end of the social scale; the Cup Final, Royal Ascot, the dog-tracks, the Varsity Match are all focuses and symbols—but mainly social symbols, gathering-places for cognoscenti of many different kinds but of a remarkably single intention. The cloth-capped crowds on the terraces at a British Saturday afternoon soccer game are taking part in exactly the same sort of spectator ritual as the somnolent old gentlemen in the Members' Enclosure at Lord's Cricket Ground. And indeed cricket, I sometimes think, is hardly considered as a sport at all, but as an art. Strength, there, is a far lesser criterion than skill, and Denis Compton's execution of a leg-sweep can produce much the same reaction as John Gielgud's reading of one of the Sonnets.

The British have a curious attitude towards sport. They take it seriously, but seem to offer it love rather than respect; which is perhaps why Britain is one of the last strongholds of the amateur. Even though cricket is so much a part of the schools, state and public alike, it leaves most adult males not with a love of hearty outdoor exercise but with a romantic image of sunlit summer days, the smell of grass, and the click of bat and ball. The idea of stretching the abilities to the limit, the Teutonic idea of tough training, is confined in Britain to education of the mind; the Gordonstoun-Outward-Bound syndrome of character-building

through body-stretching is not related, there, to the overall concept of the purpose of sport.

But within the American mystique, physical exercise,
whether observed or performed, seems to be given an intrinsic
value which is more than therapeutic. Sport is all kinds of things
in the U.S.A., but seldom merely a frivolous business of playing
games. For many it is a proper emotional object for hammed-up
myth-making like that of the *Life* magazine article quoted earlier
in this chapter; a properly wound-up sports commentator of this
kind, operating at full blast during a football or baseball game,
can seem exquisitely embarrassing, uproariously funny, or rather
disturbing, according to the mood one happens to be in while listening. Then too there are all the people for whom sport is big
business: the managers, the promoters, the resort operators and
sports-goods salesmen, the bookmakers and sports-magazine pub-
lishers—all of them devoted to making sport appear not as a
lighthearted extra, but as something on which time and money
can be spent with true advantage. And perhaps the most astonishing thing to the stranger is the extent to which many Americans still half-consciously identify the conventional image of the
sportsman with the conventional image of virility. This takes us
straight back again to the "regular" norm, of course, since its
male version must necessarily appear to be not only resolutely
heterosexual, but manly—one of the many echoes of Victorian
England that one finds constantly in the modern U.S.A. Robert
Anderson's 1953 play *Tea and Sympathy* is by no means as outdated as in my innocence I thought it was until I came to America; there is still immense probability in its portrait of the manly,
wholesome American males who believe a boy capable of homo-
sexual practices not because they have any incontrovertible evidence, but because he prefers guitar music to football and
"doesn't even play tennis like a regular fellow, no hard drives
and cannon-ball serves. . . . He can put more damn twists on
that ball. . . ." Through the close marriage of the images of
sport and regularity, the regular guy must not only take part in

sport, but must do so in a regular way. At what point, I wonder, did the ideal of straightforward male virtue become so curiously fossilized, like petrified wood?

Whenever and whyever this did develop, and with it all the other perilous edges of sport-worship, it certainly plays a healthy role today in perpetuating the insidious anti-intellectualism that is nibbling at America's attempts to develop a live culture. While flourishing as a genuine and lively part of the culture itself, it keeps the whole unbalanced, unintegrated. And what is sport likely to do for America in the future, besides multiplying her crop of Olympic gold medals? A few years ago a sociologist at Johns Hopkins University, Dr. James S. Coleman, published under the auspices of the United States Office of Education a survey called *Social Climates in High Schools*. It was based on studies of ten thousand high-school students, up to eighteen and nineteen years old, and its findings showed very clearly one effect of the high status of sport. All the boys involved were asked what, given the chance, they would most like to become when they left school or college. Thirty-seven per cent of them chose to become a nationally famous athlete—the most popular category at every school questioned. Thirty-one per cent opted for "jet pilot," and 25 per cent for "atomic scientist." (When the girls were asked the same question, 33 per cent chose modeling as the ideal career, 26 per cent nursing, 10 per cent acting and 10 per cent teaching.) All the ten thousand students were then asked which of two alternatives would make their parents most proud of them: if they were to do particularly well in any one subject at school, or if they were to be chosen as a member of the school basketball team or a cheerleader. Without hesitation, the boys said that their parents would be prouder if they made the basketball team, and the girls said the same of being chosen a cheerleader. "The importance of athletics in these cultures is striking," observed Dr. Coleman mournfully, "particularly when we realize that the school as an institution is designed to focus attention on studies, and presumably upon the brilliant student."

A society shall be known by the things it values. But I doubt whether many Europeans realize, until they go to the United States, that the voice which speaks out most accurately for American values is that not of Abraham Lincoln, or Thomas Jefferson, or John Fitzgerald Kennedy, but Ernest Hemingway.

9 ✢ Freedom for Violence

> *"In memory of Mr. Nath. Parks, aet. 19,*
> *who on 21st March 1794, Being out a*
> *hunting and conceal'd in a Ditch was*
> *casually shot by Mr. Luther Frink."*
> *Epitaph,*
> *Holyoke, Mass.*

In April 1964, a curious kind of extended credo appeared in the American sportsmen's magazine, *Field and Stream*. It was spread over two pages, with fierce orange stripes at top and bottom, and decorated with an inset portrait of a modern huntsman, carrying a gun, and his huntsman forefather. (You could tell the two apart by their hats.) The credo was headed "FOR A STRONG AMERICA," with a subheading taken from Article Two of the Bill of Rights: ". . . the right of the people to keep and bear Arms shall not be infringed. . . ." The text which then followed began thus:

> WE BELIEVE that the future safety of the United States depends on a responsible citizenry skilled in the sane and effective use of personal firearms and alert to the threat of extremist groups that would change our form of government, and that this responsibility should cut through all strata of our society and transcend any personal prejudice for or against firearms . . . .

196

It went on to summarize a great many arguments in support of free public ownership of firearms. "The right of each citizen to own guns," it said, "is still the strongest deterrent to criminal entry of our homes or to the subversive overthrow of our Government." The licensing of personal firearms, it claimed, was unfair to responsible citizens and did nothing to handicap criminals; indeed, this held the seeds of "police-state government and the eventual corruption of both police and judiciary." Of course, it said, young people shouldn't be allowed to buy guns without their parents' consent, but there should be nationwide facilities for teaching them to shoot. There should be strict laws against the criminal misuse or theft of firearms, and people such as "fugitives from justice" and drug addicts should not have access to them; this should not be done, however, by passing any law that would "turn law-abiding citizens into either deliberate or unknowing violators." And the credo ended:

> WE BELIEVE that the views expressed here are substantially those of all the readers of *Field and Stream,* and of the great mass of some 50 million hunters, shooters and sportsmen of these United States, and we call upon them to impress their views on lawmakers who would mistakenly abridge their right to bear arms.

This remarkable document was followed in the magazine by an article headed "The Anti-Gun Extremists Are At It Again," written by one Richard Starnes. Mr. Starnes was incensed at "the senseless and shameful torrent of anti-gun hysteria that swept the country in the wake of the assassination of President Kennedy," and most of his space was taken with attacking both the idea and the letter of firearms legislation. On the question of crime, he stood firmly on the familiar ground of don't-blame-the-gun-blame-the-gunman, and though his first concern was for the preservation of unfettered gun-buying by sportsmen, he didn't hesitate to jump into the deep waters of justification.

> I believe a man's right to the means of defending his family and property goes back a good deal further than any written instru-

ment of government . . . . The unfortunate reality is that we
live in a predatory world, and one not likely to change within
any near centuries. I would count myself an unfit father indeed
if I did not instruct my children in some of the rudiments of
survival in a hostile environment . . . . Let me hasten to aver
that I also try to arm my kids with faith, hope and charity, plus
an abiding passion to meet others more than halfway in trying
to create a better world. Until that happens, however, they must
be granted the ancient right to have the means of defending
themselves and their homes in a world that still falls far short of
being ideal.

It would be charming if it weren't horrific: the picture—
straight out of *Hudibras*—of Mr. Starnes' kids going out more
than halfway to meet the other guy, demonstrating how well
equipped they are with faith, hope and charity by carrying guns.
His assumptions, and those of the main *Field and Stream* article,
are typical of the things that seem most shattering when one
comes as a stranger to the United States. The only argument used
which employs anything like familiar terms is that concerning
the freedom of the individual, which runs, in effect: "If a man
wants to buy a weapon for lawful use, why should the law com-
pel him first to apply for a license?" Whether or not you agree
with this, it is at least a point that can be argued along rational
lines. But the other points offered are not at all like that. Starkly
they imply the existence of a society so fragmented and perilous
that all its citizens must be armed, both against invaders of
homes and against fanatics likely at any moment to threaten
armed revolution; in which education must include the teaching
of lethal self-defense; and in which it is safer to promote the widespread distribution of weapons than to put faith in those appointed and paid to administer law and order. Each man for
himself: trust no one, even your protectors. The whole thing has
a flavor more of ninth-century England, disorganized and beset
by marauding Danish pirates, than of ordered, powerful twentieth-century America. It also brings a distinct echo of the mores

of the Wild West era, the period when the law was perforce homemade and a rifle was as necessary a piece of domestic equipment as a cooking pot. But the Wild West breathed its last, in theory, fifty years ago. How can anyone utter such views in the modern United States, let alone claim that they represent the beliefs of more than a quarter of the population? If Americans themselves think in these terms, says the outsider to himself, can it be that America is, behind its Golden Curtain, a wild and vicious place, terrorized by subterranean violence?

It isn't, of course. That is to say, one does not go about in the United States with the everyday uncertainty of survival that has beset many in the Congo, or in a newly revolutionized South American state, or for that matter in wartime Europe. But nor does one feel altogether safe there, from the very first moment of seeing a revolver on every policeman's hip. The assumption that policemen must be armed is one of the basic symbols of the disquiet that tweaks at the mind of nearly all the British who visit America; I couldn't begin to count the number of times I have argued the benefits of a revolver-less police force with American friends, smugly pointing out how unthinkable it is for a Londoner to picture holsters suddenly sprouting at the sturdy waists of the members of the Metropolitan Police. It is easy to classify the kind of arguments I hear in return. One or two bold idealistic spirits (not policemen) enthuse over Britain as a model: "We should be like you—issue cops with guns only when they're out after a dangerous armed man." But most either go off into detailed praise of the noble restraint of American police forces, which is not only irrelevant but largely inaccurate (considering the frequency with which some American policemen shoot at escaping traffic offenders or shoplifters, quite often hitting passersby instead) or to offer gloomy excuses: "It would be great if we could do without guns, but you can't expect the police not to go armed when they know most criminals will be. Police recruitment would drop right away, and it's bad enough now. And the crime figures would go up. . . ." The users of this last group of arguments do include policemen; though they, rather than stress-ing the deterrent theme, tend frankly to observe that as things are at present, they just wouldn't like to be without their guns. They know, unlike the average member of the public, that whether or not the ubiquity of guns has anything to do with it, the crime rate in the United States is in fact rising steadily. In the last five years alone it has risen four times as rapidly as the population.

In 1964, the latest of those years for which the F.B.I. has released fully detailed criminal statistics, crime in the United States increased by 13 per cent over the 1963 total; and in the first half of 1965, by a further 5 per cent over that. There were 9,250 murders during 1964: 25 every day: one every hour. The cities with the highest murder rates were, in descending order: New York, with 636; Chicago, 398; Philadelphia, 188; Los Angeles, 177; Dallas, 149; Baltimore, 144; Houston, 137; Wash-ington, D.C., 132; and Detroit, 125. (In the whole of Great Britain, with rather more than a quarter of the population of the U.S.A., there was a total of 148 murders in the year 1963.) St. Louis had 120; Cleveland, 116; New Orleans, 82; and Fort Worth, 68. All these cities except the last have populations of more than half a million, and their murder rates correspond roughly to their relative sizes—except in Dallas and Fort Worth, which stand respectively fourteenth and thirty-fourth in the list of largest cities, but are fifth and thirteenth among those with the highest murder rate. Chicago, whose gangland image still persists in countries outside America (and for that matter in a great many parts of America as well) is second in both size and murder rate, but has an annual robbery total which is by far the highest in the country. During 1964 there were 16,832 rob-beries in Chicago, compared to 7,988 in New York, the next city in the list. And among totals of car thefts, only New York's 32,856 exceeded Chicago's 31,878; Los Angeles had 19,532, Boston, 10,202, and Detroit, 9,610. This last category of crime is a fair index of juvenile delinquency, since almost 90 per cent of all arrests for "auto theft" in America are of people under twenty-five, and 63 per cent involve boys or girls under eighteen. Arrests of American juveniles have been rising steadily for fifteen years, twice as fast as the population growth in that group, and rose by 12 per cent in 1964.

Of the total of murders, more than half involved firearms, and about a quarter some kind of cutting instrument.

About one in ten of all police officers in the country was attacked in the course of duty, most frequently in the southern Atlantic states. And 88 police officers were killed. (Of the unarmed policemen of Great Britain, three were killed in the same year.) In addition to all this there were 184,900 cases of aggravated assault in the U.S.A. during 1964, and 20,550 cases of "forcible rape."

This undertow of criminal violence has to be taken for granted by anyone living in the United States. Only in specific cases of multiple murder does it seem to arouse universal fear: as in Boston in 1963, when the list of murders attributed to the unknown and uncaught Boston Strangler had risen to eleven, and any woman left alone at night in a house or apartment kept her doors and windows carefully locked and jumped at any unaccountable noise. Generally, the awareness of possible violence is limited to a phlegmatic indifference; it is a commonplace in New York City that one does not walk in Central Park alone at night, and preferably not in daylight either. And in few American cities does anyone look up with more than a flicker of interest or alarm at the sound of a police siren wailing from a rushing car; this too is a commonplace of life. You get used to it. The city nights of my first week or two in America were a sequence of sudden nervous awakenings out of sleep; the undulating howls of police cars or ambulances seemed to come so often that it was like being back among the air-raid warnings of wartime childhood nights. But when I had lived in America for some time, I too was hearing them without much more than a twitch. They mean nothing; they are merely a noise; if they imply a crime, it is somewhere else, someone else's concern. This kind of indifference is so common now in the great cities of America that only a really horrific jolt can make people realize what is happening to them, and how perilous a callousness their bored assumptions can breed. New York City had its jolt halfway through 1964, when a girl named Catherine Genovese was attacked and stabbed one night in the thickly populated street where she lived, and where no less than thirty-four people heard her screams for help. They heard—and ignored her, or glanced to make sure that their doors were shut. One brave spirit did throw up a window and yell; and the attacker backed away. But even then no one came to the girl's aid, so he came back with his knife and finished her off.

For days and weeks after that, outraged sermons on the inhumanity of man to man rumbled from pulpits and radios and newspapers; but it was not very long before similar incidents, less spectacular but equally appalling, began to be reported again. The only difference now was that the newspaper writers were able to point out similarities to "the Kitty Genovese case." The background to this kind of event was summarized very neatly by Nora Sayre in the *New Statesman:*

> Considering the English a violent race (historically, ethically, emotionally) I'm impressed by their disregard for the simple danger of Manhattan's streets. There have been several cases concerning newly arrived Englishmen who were hit on the head while admiring Central Park at sunset. But trained New Yorkers choose their itineraries with care. At my good East Side girls' school, we were advised at twelve to carry a rolled copy of *Vogue, Harper's Bazaar* or *Fortune* dangling casually at our sides; if assaulted, we were to heave it up beneath the villain's chin, coincident with swift action of the knee. (Some parents thought this excessive; mine asked me to be certain that the menace was not a family friend.) Recently, I've had two robberies within six months (and now keep my amethysts in the oven, on police advice), have been attacked at a Garbo film (*Mata Hari*), and have twice been most unpleasantly trapped in vestibules—in one case, escaping only by pretending to have cancer, which

caused a wonderfully quick recoil. All my assailants were white, clothed in decent sportswear, seemed educated; they were perhaps a trifle drunk but clearly crazed. The point is that my neighbourhood (East 75th Street) is supposed to be safe—so safe that the police are rarely around when we want them . . . .

New York City, Chicago, and all the other big cities of the United States are not places of unmitigated terror and things that go bump in the night. It is as possible for a lone female to travel all round the country without getting raped, robbed or murdered as it is in Britain. All the same, with the sense of freedom and speed there is also an undeniable sense of suppressed violence; compounded partly of the sight of those police holsters, and partly of a patchwork of smaller details. In most American cities, for instance, it is not uncommon to find a drunk or two rambling along a main street at any time of the day from breakfast on. There are obvious reasons why this should occur more frequently in America than in Britain; for one thing, the licensing laws in some places make it possible for bars to open at nine in the morning, and for another, alcohol is relatively much cheaper in the United States. But whatever the reasons, the result is one of many small additions to the feeling of the new arrival that the ground of America is undulating slightly, as if something were about to burst explosively out from underneath.

And although it may seem strange to say so, considering America's persisting external image of gangsterism and wild exuberance and civil affrays, I do not think many Americans have been aware of this sensation. You lose it, when you live behind the Golden Curtain for long; and if you are born and brought up there, in small-town or suburban security, you may never feel it at all. If the dwellers in big cities have a protective shell of indifference, the population of the rest of the country—dwellers in what the politicians would call grass-roots territory—have a great sense of safety, a trust in the general benevolence and protectiveness of their system. Perhaps it is because they know they have things so much better than their parents had them; perhaps it is a relieved reaction to memories of the Thirties, when this sense of safety had not yet arrived. At all events the American dream presents a peaceful image to these people, and they believe that this already exists. They would probably never have thought of stating the *Field and Stream* credo quoted earlier, but if they read it they would see its belligerence mainly as a means of preserving the dream of peace, without examining its implications.

But others, I think, are troubled, and cannot think of these placid assumptions of safety now as they could before the bitterly relevant events of November 1963. They do not cherish a fierce independent pride in pioneer methods of preserving individual rights; they are left only with uneasiness. In however small a degree, many of them have the disturbing suspicion that within the nature of their system there is perhaps something destructive and perilous at work, which they can neither see nor understand. It is probably another version of what the incoming stranger feels. And by "something at work" I do not mean the familiar and ridiculous whisper of a dark conspiracy in high places; I mean the spirit of violence. Through the shock that rocked the country to a standstill when John F. Kennedy was assassinated, you could from the very beginning see this deep uneasiness beginning to spread, and making, ironically, one of the vital but uncommon chinks in the Golden Curtain that are broken through when Americans are suddenly faced with themselves.

On the afternoon of November 22, 1963, I was in Washington D.C., crossing the lobby of a downtown hotel with that idle attention that one pays, in American hotel lobbies, to the glossy miniature shops, the motor-car on display in the middle of the carpet, the restless dark-suited men who wait, mysteriously and interminably fidgeting, beside pillars and huge potted palms. At the hotel news-stand my eye caught a glaring black headline filling half the front page of an evening paper. "JFK IS SHOT IN DALLAS," it said. In that first irrational moment which tries to deny disaster, I thought it must be a practical joke: really, said a small stupid voice in my head, they shouldn't go that far, it's not funny. Then one of the girls at the newsstand said quietly to another, with the flat emptiness of shock: "It's so terrible." I picked up the paper; it had a picture of a windswept Kennedy taken on arrival in Texas, and then, headed BULLETIN, the first hasty agency report hurled over the wires and into print:

DALLAS, Nov. 22 (UPI)—President Kennedy and Gov. John B. Connally of Texas were cut down by an assassin's bullets as they toured downtown Dallas in an open auto today.

The President, his limp body cradled in the arms of his wife, was rushed to Parkland Hospital. The Governor also was taken to Parkland. Clint Hill, a Secret Service agent assigned to Mrs. Kennedy, said "he's dead," as the President was lifted from the rear of a White House touring car, the famous "bubble-top" from Washington. He was rushed to an emergency room in the hospital. Other White House officials were in doubt as the corridors of the hospital erupted in pandemonium.

It was impossible to tell at once where Mr. Kennedy was hit, but bullet wounds in Gov. Connally's chest were plainly visible, indicating the gunfire might possibly have come from an automatic weapon.

There were three loud bursts.

Dallas motorcycle officers escorting the President quickly leaped from their bikes and raced up a grassy hill.

At the top of the hill, a man and a woman appeared huddled on the ground. In the turmoil, it was impossible to determine at once whether the Secret Service and Dallas police returned the gunfire that struck down Mr. Kennedy and Mr. Connally. It was difficult to determine immediately whether the First Lady and Mrs. Connally were injured.

Both women were crouched down over the inert forms of their husbands as the big car raced towards the hospital. Mrs. Kennedy was on her knees on the floor of the rear seat with her head towards the President.

Reporters about five car-lengths behind the Chief Executive heard what sounded like three bursts of gunfire. Secret Service agents in a follow-up car quickly unlimbered their automatic rifles. The bubble top of the President's car was down. They drew their pistols, but the damage was done. The President was slumped over the back seat of the car, face down. Gov. Connally lay on the floor of the rear seat.

Vice President Lyndon B. Johnson was in a car behind the President.

There was no immediate sign whether he was hurt. In fact, there was no evidence at all of what might have happened to Mr. Johnson since only the President's car and its Secret Service follow-up car went to the hospital.

A screaming motor-cycle escort led the cars there.

The President had landed only a short time before at Dallas Love Field and was driving to the Trade Mart to deliver a luncheon speech sponsored by three Dallas organizations.

The largest turn-out of the current Texas tour was on the streets to greet Mr. Kennedy.

An estimated 250,000 people lined the streets. At 12:50 P.M. Central Standard Time, acting White House Secretary Malcom Kilduff was asked whether the President was dead.

"I have no word now," Mr. Kilduff replied.

A Secret Service man said "He's dead" as the President was lifted from his car. A few minutes later, Rear Admiral George Burkley, USN, the White House physician, rushed into the hospital. He headed for the emergency room where the President and Gov. Connally were taken.

I suppose no reporter's story anywhere can ever have been thrown so rapidly into print; and the bleak, anxious bewilderment given the words by their speed was an exact prefiguring of the expression on the faces of Americans all around. Across the hotel lobby, there was already a crowd round the Telex machine.

"How bad is he? How bad is he hurt?"

"They don't know."

Question and answer twitched to and fro; nobody felt able to mention the word death. At a flowerstand in a far corner of the lobby, someone had a radio running, and another crowd gathered quickly there too, craning in silence to listen. The descriptions that are now so familiar flowed incoherent and strained over the chrysanthemums and the roses; distant crackling voices from Dallas, taut with anxiety and disbelief. And then an announcer broke in grimly: "We have just heard that the flag on the White House roof has been lowered to half-mast. It is being lowered now. The news is official. The President of the United States is dead."

Outside, in Washington, there was a clear blue sky and the bright sunshine of the East Coast fall; the traffic was flowing normally in Pennsylvania Avenue, and the people who did not yet know were passing in the streets, chatting amiably to one another. But outside the White House, police had already roped off the sidewalks, and a crowd was beginning to collect, a straggling line of figures under the trees. It was not a crowd like any I had ever seen before. It wanted nothing, looked for nothing, did nothing; it simply stood there. There were businessmen, housewives, soldiers, sailors, tourists; white and Negro, young and old; and, inevitably, reporters and television cameramen multiplying by the minute, with little to provide them with copy. At intervals, swift black limousines swung in through the White House gates; sometimes a small group of people drifted together round someone with a portable radio. But nobody said a word. These people were not the usual crowd familiar to all journalists: the ghoulish and the curious, feeding on trouble, attracted by disaster. They knew that they would see no one and nothing; they were certainly not waiting for the President to be brought all the way back from Dallas; they looked at nothing except, sometimes, the flag. You could see the heads tilting towards it almost furtively for a quick glance, over and over again, as if trying to convince themselves that the next time they looked, it would be flying normally. They wanted nothing else, and they knew they wouldn't get even that. They simply seemed to feel that they ought to be there. So they stood together in silence, more and more gathering each moment, as the last late leaves fell round them from the trees.

All over Washington other flags on government buildings and stores were coming down to half-mast, and the streets were beginning to fill with grim, disbelieving faces. The stillness did not last long. Within an hour, the whole city was a chaotic mass of milling bodies and hooting metal; for the government offices, which employ a huge percentage of Washington's population, had instantly stopped work at the announcement of the assassination; and homegoing workers, who usually are sent out in carefully staggered waves, all poured out at once. Fifty-yard queues stood at bus-stops, filling the sidewalks, waiting for buses that would be for a long time stuck several streets away, immobile in the hordes of cabs and cars. It was as if the surface of the day and of the country had cracked, shaking all standards of reality; the bemused people swarmed through their suddenly meaningless city, and over it all the shouts of the newsboys rang out in a bleak rhythmic dirge: "Dea—eath of the President . . . Dea—eath of the President . . ."

Naturally, that first surge of disbelief was primarily personal and emotional; the aura of the Presidency in the United States is as strong and symbolic as that of a monarchy, and most people (with only some chilly exceptions who could not even then forget their disapproval of Kennedy's path to power) were stunned as any nation would be at the loss of a vital young leader. Although there was immediately dark wild talk everywhere of politically motivated conspiracy, the full enormity of it as a manifestation of the spirit of violence did not perhaps finally overwhelm people until the next day, with Jack Ruby's murder of Lee Harvey Oswald. In a way, that second shock was the moment of awakening from shock. In many households in America the circumstances were the same, that day: the television set running continuously, with subdued members of the family drifting in and out irregularly at intervals to see what was happening; and then perhaps an eruption from a child watching alone: "Look, *look,* someone's shot the man who killed the President—"

"Ah come on now," from a weary parent.

"He has, he has, they were in the police station, and he shot him, come and see—"

"*What?*" The first reaction, punchdrunk disbelief. The second, more horror even than at the death of the President: the horror greater because the presence of a live television camera involved the affair so completely with the everyday pattern of life. How could things like this be? What was happening to the country? And at once, for many Americans, the first immediate defensive reaction was to turn this to "What's happening to Texas?" —since the East of the United States has always a tendency to raise its eyebrows at the West, and the North at the South; and people had already remembered that Adlai Stevenson, ambassador to the United Nations, had been spat on in Dallas four weeks before. They had already begun to make Dallas their scapegoat. But there was not really any way of forgetting that Dallas was part of America, Texas was part of America, that there was a chance all these terrible things were happening because of something in the nature of America. . . . Do you remember them, the complex emotions of that day?

In his book *Dallas Public and Private,* Warren Leslie tells of hearing the news of President Kennedy's assassination in the Club Imperial at the Baker Hotel in Dallas, a principal meeting-place for members of the city's Establishment. The Presidential motorcade had passed down Main Street; all was cheerful and serene; and then a man burst into the club yelling that the President had been shot. They turned on the television set, and found that it was true. "In back of me, a man threw his head down on his arms against the table. 'This God-damned town,' he said quietly. . . ."

But Leslie's remarkable book, despite the appalling nature of many of its revelations about the background of Dallas, is at heart more nearly a vindication than an accusation. Although he points out that a group of leading citizens of Dallas very nearly warned the President not to visit their city, he also gives an American perspective to the whole picture:

It is an extraordinary thing when an American city does not trust itself to receive the President of the United States in dignity. Dallas did not so trust itself—and with reason. This book is an attempt to show why. If it is a Texas story, it is also an American story. To place a local guilt and exonerate the rest of our country is as naïve as some of the people of Dallas have themselves been during the years when the storm clouds were banking. The forces of violence exist everywhere. Unchallanged, unrepudiated, they grow and fester, gaining in confidence, attracting new strength . . . .

And when I went to Dallas some three months after the President's assassination, one of the huge crowd of journalists dispatched from all over the world to cover the trial of Jack Ruby, there was indeed the sense of finding oneself at the center of a sore: an eruption which happened to have broken out at this particular spot because, as it were, the skin was not clean, but which was fed by a deeper, more general infection. I had never properly been to Dallas before; I had only whiled away an hour between planes there once, sitting in the great shining airport under its statue of the Texas cowboy with his six-shooters at the ready, and discouraging the hopeful advances of another cowboy whose clothes and accent were probably his only professional qualifications. It had been just another airport then, just another city. And so it seemed at first the next time: a bristling of big buildings in the middle of nowhere, after the usual long dull ride in the airport limousine. Most of the major skyscrapers, ironically—but then, Dallas at that time was brimming with ironies—belonged to insurance companies. There were streets called Commerce and Prosperity; there were the usual broad windy main streets, and if some of them were battered and sleazy, they were no sleazier than others in Chicago or Boston, London or Liverpool, or a thousand other towns. There even seemed fewer potential trouble-spots than elsewhere, when one found that racial integration appeared to have been peacefully and fairly fully accomplished in Dallas—albeit for commercial reasons, rather than any sense of idealism—and that nothing stronger than beer or wine was allowed to be sold in any bar, saloon or hotel. But hand-in-hand with this last discovery came the inevitable information that it was very easy indeed to dodge the liquor-serving law, since there were more than two hundred "private clubs" in town—some on the level of Jack Ruby's own establishment, some more restrained. It was as easy to become a member of most of these, said one's Dallas informants wrily, as to board a bus. And so it was: in the hotel where I stayed, one such club led off the lobby as if it were an ordinary bar, and between deadlines and dinner, journalists found it equally natural to meet there—either as instant members or as one another's guests. This accepted law-evasion was a small thing, easily forgotten after the first mildly ridiculing comment; and yet somehow, for the incoming stranger, it began after a few days to seem typical of other more perilous things in Dallas—and as in Dallas, so in many parts of America—which appeared perfectly ordinary but were not quite so ordinary when taken apart.

We learned, for instance, how easy it was to acquire a gun; you could walk into any of a hundred gunsmith's shops and buy a neat little pistol for twenty-five dollars cash down, with no more asked than that you should leave your name and address —which could, without too much difficulty, be a false name and a false address. And there was a distinct element of frontier morality in what you could then do with that gun. You could legally keep it, loaded, in your home or in your office desk; you could even carry it with you if you were, in a loosely interpreted phrase reminiscent of the old West, a "traveler." And under certain circumstances, you could kill someone with it and never even stand trial. Of the 104 murders committed in Dallas during 1963 (which included not only a President, a policeman and an assassin, but four burglars or hijackers killed by the police in the course of duty) some 30 per cent led to no convictions for murder. More than a third of those who committed the murders, that is, went free, as having committed "justifiable homicide." This proportion is partly a substitution for a manslaughter verdict, which does not exist in Texas law; but it is also a legacy from the rougher justice of other days. In Dallas, you can kill a man and get away with it if he was committing adultery with your wife. You can kill him not only in actual but in apparent self-defense: that is if you can prove that you *believed* him to be threatening your life, the lives of your family, or your property—whether he really was doing so or not. And even if the killing is not "no-billed" as justifiable homicide, but goes to trial, the killer is not necessarily liable to a grave penalty even if found guilty. For one thing, the law in Texas has a flexible element: its juries pronounce not only judgment, but sentence. For another, as the Dallas district attorney Henry Wade pointed out in court: "The law has provided a wide range of punishment in murder cases." Thus after a verdict of "guilty of murder with malice"—which was eventually brought in against Ruby—a prisoner can be sent to the electric chair, or be given a term in the penitentiary ranging from life down to two years. "Murder without malice," on the other hand, carries a sentence only of two to five years imprisonment. And in either case a sentence can be suspended; a two years' suspended sentence, the minimum penalty for someone found guilty of murder, becomes no more than a token obeisance to the cold immoveable core of the Law. Also, murder is not the only capital offense in Texas. During the short time I was in Dallas, two cases of rape were given small spaces in the morning paper: a twenty-three-year-old Negro boy was electrocuted for raping a white woman, and a nineteen-year-old white boy, also convicted of rape, was given a ninety-nine year jail sentence. ("Prosecutors did not seek the death penalty in this case," added the paper, "because of the youth of the defendant.")

Considering all this, it was perhaps understandable that one should have developed, in Dallas in 1964, a feeling that nothing was likely to be as one expected it to be. During the first hearing in the Dallas courts, held to consider a change of venue for the actual trial, Ruby's attorney Melvin Belli called as one of his mixture of witnesses a young law student, a thoughtful-seeming lad who in the course of testifying said hesitantly from the witness stand: "I think anyone who commits a murder must be temporarily insane." It was not an uncommon or revolutionary statement; I had heard it often enough before and so probably have you—and not only from the young. But as this boy said it in Dallas, the district attorney and his assistants raised their heads suddenly and stared at him in a mixture of disbelief and pitying wonder; and I don't think they were doing it for the benefit of the court. It was an instinctive reaction to what seemed a ridiculous statement. They knew their Texas legal code, and they shared its laconic Western assumption that the sound of shots is from time to frequent time an ordinary—sane—part of life. It was not perhaps so very different from the New Yorkers and their assumptions concerning Central Park.

I have never felt the ubiquity of violence more strongly than during those days in Dallas, and I heard other far more seasoned reporters say the same, including Americans and foreign correspondents, and including those who had covered riots, revolutions and wars. In a time of overt violence you expect horror, indignity and a loss of all normal standards of behavior; in time of peace you expect something better. But although the physical horror was over, in Dallas then, with the three killings three months past, the air was not clear. There was something disturbing about even the smallest things. From the beginning it had seemed ominous that we should have had to apply to an advertising agency for our passes to the courtroom: the two giant badges that we had to wear on our lapels all day, four-by-three-inch cards enclosed in plastic, one bright green, stamped COURT-ROOM, and the other bright orange, stamped—beside a photograph of the owner—PRESS. But this could be argued down into normality; the officers of a Texan court are not, after all, geared to organizing journalists from almost every major newspaper in the world—what harm in their accepting professional help? The things that were more difficult to rationalize were those connected with the trial itself. Badges notwithstanding, we waited in line morning, afternoon and evening at the door of the court, while the sheriff's deputies searched everyone who entered the room to make sure none was carrying a gun. They found an unloaded pistol in the handbag of one of Ruby's strippers ("It'd been there so long," explained a detective, deadpan, "that she'd forgotten all about it") and a water-pistol, also unloaded, in the handbag of one spectator—a divinity student's wife, who had impounded it in church from her small son the previous Sunday. They did not, so far as I know, find any offensive weapon on a journalist, though they seemed to expect dark things; one woman deputy displayed deep suspicion over a pocket torch from my handbag, until I took it to pieces to prove that it was neither a camera nor a gun; and another relieved me accusingly of a three-inch nailfile. Then they frisked every part of one's anatomy that might possibly have hidden other weapons. Judge Joe Brown was standing a few feet away watching the details of the search with interest, that morning, which didn't make the process more agreeable. He was chewing a plug of tobacco, as he did much of the time in court, and he wore heavy make-up, which pleased those television teams planning to interview him after the day's work. He looked rather like a creamed and powered bloodhound, and very little like an image of Justice. And as the defense counsel Melvin Belli approached, wearing fur-collared overcoat, black shirt and a Stetson, the judge's face lit up and he cried: "Hi, cowboy!"

Apart from the daily searches, they were thoughtful of the press in the Dallas courts—as thoughtful as they had been in bringing Lee Oswald up from the cells in public on the day when Jack Ruby happened to be among the reporters and cameramen with his gun. In the courthouse corridors, crowded with reporters and television and radio equipment, hot and brilliant with arc lamps, chaos was allowed to break loose before and after each day's session. Often, before a session began, Ruby would for five minutes or so be the center of a pushing, shouting group of re-

porters and photographers; of men trying to scribble in note-
books with their arms pinned to their sides, and of others thrust-
ing out microphones in an attempt to catch Ruby's almost inaudible answers to questions. (One morning, during the change-
of-venue hearing, a microphone thwacked one of the attorneys
hard across the ear.) Then the cameramen would be thrust un-
ceremoniously out of court, the reporters would scramble for
places, and the day's incredible proceedings would begin. And
when there was not the violence of counsel shouting at one another, there was always the immanence of suspicion; for you
could seldom look up from a notebook without encountering the
eye of one of the stony-faced detectives who sat facing inwards all
round the room, paying no apparent attention to the circus
going on in front under Judge Brown's laconic eye, but staring
continually at reporters and public to catch any movement that
might herald the production of a gun.

There was no sense ever of that counter-balance of violence,
the remote awfulness of the Law. How could there be? At the
end of each day, the moment Ruby was hustled off after adjourn-
ment, the doors of the courtroom burst open, and in flooded the
press of cameramen and photographers who had been milling
outside all day. Within seconds the courtroom was draped with
wires and blazing with light, and there were great shoving eddies
of bodies and microphones and cameras round Belli, round the
district attorney, even round the judge—who would come wandering casually back from his chambers, or pop cozily sometimes
into the press room, "to see how you fellows are getting on."

As for the proceedings themselves, whose story everyone
knows: they had, hidden behind that familiar narrative, a chill
of their own, not least in the assumptions of those conducting
them. It was not only Melvin Belli's deep velvet voice, handsome
gray head and remarkable courtroom presence which made him
seem notably often an island of civilization in a kind of ghost-
ridden tundra; it was the occasional incident in which his op-
ponents suddenly seemed—though probably not to themselves—

to have dropped their guard. One such moment came to the district attorney's lean, dark assistant Bill Alexander, an unsmiling, tight-faced man looking as though he were being played by Jack Palance. During the first hearing he was questioning Mrs. Doris Warner, the nineteen-year-old who managed the apartment house in which Ruby had been living, on whether she thought Ruby could be given a fair trial in Dallas. Had she heard anyone say that Ruby should not be punished for shooting Oswald? Yes, she had.

"There are some, then," said Alexander, coldly but utterly naturally, "who don't want to burn him?"

Almost as soon as the shiver started down one's spine, Belli was up on his feet, shouting: "What? *What?* Burn him?"

Alexander looked at him. "That's a shorthand rendition," he said, unmoved.

The day before this, his superior, Henry Wade, had also used the term "shorthand rendition" in describing the statement that "a man is innocent until proven guilty." This did not, somehow, seem quite the same.

From where the press sat, there was no telling what effect this exchange had on Ruby. Nor, for that matter, could one tell how he reacted later, when the time came at the beginning of the trial proper to pick a jury, and Belli was on his feet again, shouting at a prospective juror: "You want to get on this jury to put this man in the electric chair. . . ." Ruby was only a small still figure, the back of a bald head plastered over with a few lank strips of dark hair. The dim little man who had sought the limelight now had more of it than he could cope with; he might seem ebullient enough at some moments, coming into court with a smile and a wink for the journalists and the public, but always sooner or later he appeared as meaningless an object as the rubber ball bounced about by a troupe of performing seals. His part in the play of violence was over; he was no more now than the object of possible retribution. And the cameramen instinctively treated him not even as a character in black comedy, but as a suitable recipient of the familiarity they are all accustomed to use towards inmates of showbiz. "Over here, Peter," they call to the film stars they have never met. "Pull your skirt up a bit, Shirley!" They can be confident that these, being slaves of publicity, will often enough do as they are told; and they made the same assumptions in Dallas about Jack Ruby, though whether because he was trapped in publicity or because he was merely trapped I do not know. Only once did Ruby turn on them, his eyes bright with resentment or self-pity: "Instead of yelling Jack, Jack, say 'Mr. Ruby, turn this way,' and I'll be glad to." But the circus was too far on its way for him to slow it down then. At some point in the proceedings he had ceased to appear as a full-grown human being; now, to photographers who would think twice about calling to Mr. Belli, "Hey, Mel!" Mr. Ruby would always be "Hey, Jack!" Of all the remarks I heard made by or quoted from Jack Ruby in the course of the trial, the one that sticks most persistently in my head was recorded by Murray Kempton in the *New Republic*. It came from a Dallas artist who had been sketching Ruby's portrait for a magazine. "At first," said the artist of his sitter, "he mumbled away about what a fearless fellow he was, and then he began talking the way most subjects do, asking if the double-chin would show too much and wondering if I could draw him a little less bald. And then, as I was leaving, he said: 'Don't make it too rough. Leave me a little dignity.'"

But Jack Ruby had hardly a tatter of human dignity left to him by the end of that trial. Somewhere, somehow, the process of the entertainment that was called Law had wrenched it away from him. He was not properly cast in the role of President's Avenger; he was a very small actor in a very large part. So he became almost irrelevant to everything that was going on, and one felt he would have had more dignity if he had been a corpse. But outside the courtroom, the world of violence seethed on. During the trial, in Dallas, four men and a woman were arrested for holding up a bank with sawn-off shotguns. A café-owner was accused of murder and arson after four Dallas firemen died in a fire that burned his café down. An unsuccessful jail-break kept the courthouse atmosphere taut, and gave some unexpected pictures to cameramen waiting in patient boredom for the day's hearing to end. A woman was arrested at Dallas Love Field, the airport, for shooting at a passenger; she missed him, and in any case was firing at the wrong man, for the senatorial candidate she was hoping to shoot ("because he's in charge of a gang which is trying to prove me mentally ill") was not even at the airport at all.

Shortly afterwards a store was robbed by two armed men, and the manager's wife beaten up; and a hospital porter named Grant was sentenced to ten years in prison for killing his wife as she lay in bed. The couple's children, said the *Dallas Morning News,* "testified they heard their parents quarreling in another room of the house over a pistol which had been taken from Grant's tool box, before the fatal shot was fired. Grant . . . told the court he shot his wife in the head with a .22 caliber rifle because he thought she had the pistol and was going to shoot him."

We are back again, you will observe, at the guns. If I seem to be making a great fuss about firearms, it is not because of any particular personal phobia (there is a target rifle in our own house, for potting at marauding squirrels) but because they form one obvious bridge between the worlds of deliberate and accidental violence: the world of crime and the world of the common man. And the fact that these two worlds are not separate and distinct, but are very much interrelated, is something which Americans, wrapped up in their own insulated country, have until now tended to forget. It will be a better monument to President Kennedy than any number of street-names and airports if the circumstances of his death have caused them to think again. For those Americans who do still feel a sense of disquiet about the assassination and its subsequent events do not, I think, find that this is the same emotion that they felt about Chicago in the Twenties, or about the surviving remnants of gang warfare today. This time, they are not merely clicking their tongues over one regrettable but distinct part of their world. The disquiet goes deeper, and is related to the uneasiness which is expressed from time to time on the European side of the Golden Curtain—the feeling that beneath the exuberance and sense of personal freedom that shouts cheerfully out of the United States, there is a violence of emotion, a potentially destructive force, which has its roots in almost every corner of life. Above all, this is the kind of violence which is still thriving and bubbling towards new outbreaks in places like Mississippi; for it feeds greedily on any sense of difference between one man and the next man—and such differences, in polyglot America, can be found vulnerably obvious in every town and street.

The food of violence, the prelude to violence, is nearly always prejudice in some form. And prejudice, in democatic America, is common in many more forms than the stranger expects. It exists, for instance, as anti-Semitism, which lingers in golf clubs and country clubs which "happen" to have no Jewish members, or in towns where a Jewish Businessmen's Club exists alongside the other businessmen's organizations which were formed, once, to keep them out; and which occurs in the conversation of otherwise rational people (in remarks of the "O-well-he's-a-Jew-what-can-you-expect" variety) with a frequency which still startles me. And in everyday life, inevitably, it takes some crude forms. A Jewish friend of mine whom we will call Joe was once sailing off the coast of Florida with two or three others in a sloop belonging to a man we will call Smith. They put in at a smart yacht club one night, and were greeted through a megaphone by the harbor-master, who recognized the boat. "Ahoy, captain, we have a berth for you," boomed the voice over the water. "Have you all Gentiles aboard?"

Smith yelled back: "Yes, all Gentiles," and turned to the others to make what Joe expected to be a caustic apology for the club's bone-headedness. But instead Smith gave them all a big cozy grin. "No goddam Yids on *my* boat," he said proudly.

"I hadn't realised he didn't know I was a Jew," Joe said afterwards. "I was so angry that I nearly did let him know properly, but it would only have ruined the trip for the others. You can't do anything with characters like that anyway. Maybe he wondered why I never went sailing with him again."

But this irrational, vicious resentment, or hatred, or whatever it is, does not limit itself to the ancient nastiness of anti-Semitism. You can find a related variety of anti-Catholicism; I once spent a distressing half-hour in which the director of a large American city library explained to me nonstop how the Catholics held 30 per cent of all administrative posts in the United States (not so remarkable, since they make up 25 per cent of the country's population), how They were planning to take over the whole country, and how They would eventually force everyone else out of any sort of office. I have sometimes wondered how this man reacted to the assassination of President Kennedy, whom he seemed to regard as the spearhead of this sinister Catholic invasion.

Alongside this kind of thing goes the matter of nationality. It is an extraordinary thing in, say, Boston, to hear second-generation and even third-generation Americans decrying one another as Italians—more often, "guineas"—and Irishmen. The present nationality is fully accepted, yet the old nationality is not dropped, but used as a weapon not only for goodnatured jokes but for antipathy, particularly by roving groups of belligerent teenagers, or, naturally, by drunks. Always, in America, there seems to be some kind of racial, nationalist or religious bellicosity ready to bubble up to the surface; curiously ready, readier than one would expect. Only in the remotest areas, untouched by most facets of the usual pattern of American life, do the animosities lie quiet. Another American friend of mine was born and raised in a small isolated town in the French-speaking part of Maine, near the Canadian border. "Perhaps we were backward or something," she said once, "but there never seemed to be any kind of name-calling there. The best doctor in the place was a Negro, but we never thought anything of it. I only once heard

the word 'guinea,' and it was years before I knew what it meant."
Then she added thoughtfully: "There was one thing, of course.
In that town you were either Catholic or Protestant, and a Cath-
olic girl had to marry a Catholic boy or else. . . ."

Color prejudice of course enormously overshadows all of
these. We have our own variety in Britain, as every West Indian
knows, and to encounter it is as appalling an experience as it
would be anywhere else. But it does not tell you what to expect
in the U.S.A. The Negro who has lived in the worst slum in Not-
ting Hill, or in Birmingham, England, will still not be prepared
for the way of life offered him in Birmingham, Alabama; the liberal white who has fulminated against the stupid cruelty of land-
ladies, employers, trades unions or men-in-the-street in Britain
will still be utterly disconcerted when he meets, in the North of
the United States, the calmly reasoned arguments which otherwise gentle and sane people use to explain why they don't want a
Negro family to move into their street; or, in the South, the overwhelming conviction with which otherwise intelligent and civilized whites explain—just as firmly as stupid and crude whites—
the utter impossibility of black and white races ever co-existing
on equal terms. Once in Atlanta, Georgia, on my first visit to the
South, I spent a long weekend with an attractive young couple of
about thirty, whom I had never met before. Grateful for their
hospitable friendliness, and for the way in which we seemed to
think alike on topics ranging from opera to international politics, I had trodden delicately around the one subject with which,
someone in the State Department had taken care to warn me,
foreigners always manage clumsily to offend the people of the
South. But at dinner on the last evening, someone did begin
talking about Negro-white relationships for the first time; I think
the young wife had complained wrily that her Negro "daily" was
unable to understand the simplest instructions without hearing
them repeated five times. And before I had quite grasped what I
was hearing, the husband had begun explaining to me earnestly
and with complete certainty how Negroes were irrevocably an in-

ferior race. "It's been medically proved—there was a very sound report published by a group of doctors. Nigras skulls are thicker than ours, and their brain capacity is less. They're biologically inferior—so they can't ever catch up with us." And so on and so on, with a plethora of improbable pseudo-medical details, so that one could only listen in silence; and then, correctly interpreting the silence, they began inevitably explaining to me how "the problem" is something that no foreigner or Northerner can ever understand. Which is, in all parts of the South, the great false, hollow, callous piece of self-trickery that forms the worst of all the results of American insulation.

Like any other traveler I have encountered enough examples of the "color problem" since then, in both North and South, to become utterly convinced that the complex thickness of the Golden Curtain, which has for so long kept America enclosed in thoughts only of her own mores, her own assumptions, is principally responsible for the centuries during which Negroes have been refused their due of human dignity. It is the inbreeding of ideas and prejudices, the introverted refusal to be influenced by the standards of the rest of the world, which have made it impossible for white Americans to realize not only their own hypocrisy in the treatment of black Americans, but the way in which this makes a far greater impact in Europe and Africa—especially Africa—than the fine words of the Declaration of Independence. There are several reasons why I may seem to have left a gap in this book by not including an entire chapter on the life of the American Negro, and the largest is the fact that no one can show it properly without writing a whole book on the subject. But there are three other points. First: the rest of the world knows much about America's treatment of those Americans who happen to be black; perhaps too much, for it inclines us to throw up our hands in horror without investigating the nature of the atmosphere which allows such prejudice to thrive. Second, something has already happened to those Americans who happen to be white; through the demands of the Negroes themselves and of the

Kennedy and Johnson administrations, and through the unselfish idealism of some of their own number (like the young civil rights workers murdered in 1964 in Mississippi) they have at last grown aware of what they should be doing, and have begun—still too slowly—to do it. And third, this book is about all Americans, not merely The Man, and except in dealing with their treatment by white bigots there is no earthly reason for splitting off the Negroes as if they were a separate nation—they are as much a part of the American Way, and as much involved in its values, as anyone else.

But it looks like being a long time before this last point is recognized by the entire population of the United States; or even before the violence bred of prejudice will end. I once asked a Negro doctor in California how long, in the normal course of evolution, he thought it would take for racial antipathies in America to die. He was much involved in the civil rights movement, and a great optimist; I expected him to be either condemnatory or crusader-hopeful. But instead he shook his head quietly. "I think," he said, "that while our skins are different colors, such an obvious symbol of difference, you will find that nothing can ever be done in this country to touch people's minds. Long after we have attained complete equality, life will still, for both races, be a matter of We and They."

The Episcopal Bishop of California put it a little differently. "When we can all tell one another Negro and Jewish jokes without self-consciousness," he said, "then I'll think the Kingdom's come."

Coming to the U.S.A., you expect in this independent, enclosed land to find everyone speaking of We. Instead, everyone seems to have his own They. No doubt the same may be true in different degrees in every other country—but in no other country is it so important that it should *not* be so. The grouping that is everywhere in the United States, this melting-pot full of recalcitrant unmelted lumps, produces rivalries and resentments and hatreds to an extent that a great nation cannot afford. I can see where it came from easily enough, but I cannot understand why it perpetuates itself; unless the American dream has ceased to be anything but a dream, and touches no one's heart any more. And in the reality that one sees instead of the dream, it is the multiplication of prejudices and animosities, between one American race and another, and one American group and another, which seems to produce that strange sensation of immanent smouldering violence. Intermixed like hardwoods and softwoods in a forest, there are among all the examples of warmth and openheartedness an astonishing number of half-hidden dislikes: of Left for Right, Right for Left, white for black, black for white, Gentile for Jew, Protestant for Catholic, Northern-European-American for Southern-European-American. They are all far older than America, but why do they thrive so well in this new land which should have no place for them? Such dislikes are all said to spring from subconscious fear; but an awareness of difference has to come before the fear, and why should Americans be so conscious of fundamentally irrelevant differences among themselves? Is the sense of We-They built into your system, by the stress laid in the beginning on states' rights? Is your revolution too recent, leaving you still sensitive to the idea that you must guard at all costs against the chance of ever again being controlled by unsympathetic minds? Or is it that you are simply so remote from the rest of the world, through an accident of geography, that you lack the healthy easy rivalries of contact with foreign neighbors, and seek substitutes among yourselves?

Perhaps time will provide the solution—though time is busier these days than in the long leisurely centuries which smoothed the edges of older nations. In the meantime there remains the undercurrent, and the warnings that jut out of it like wrecks: the crime rate, the juvenile delinquency rate, the perilous nights of cities, the hate organizations, the assassination of a President, the racial battles, the impossibility of having a police force which is not armed. And for some people, there is the uneasiness that grows from awareness of the warnings, and the fear of whatever such warning will come next. For most, there is instead the illusion of safety and tranquillity, the stability of the family or the group; the world of Tom Sawyer rather than of Huckleberry Finn. The majority can disregard the matter of diagnosing sources of violence. They have enshrined President Kennedy as a martyr with President Lincoln; drawn from what they have read about the Warren Commission Report the warm reassurance that the catastrophe could just as easily have smitten any other country; and already begun comfortably to forget the ugly exhibitions that surrounded and followed Kennedy's death. Insulated within their illusion, they can leave vocal expressions of concern to that last section of the population which feels the wrong kind of concern: those who believe in a kind of national philosophy of corporal punishment, and call on the rest to meet threats with threats, violence with violence, strength with strength. "We believe that the future safety of the United States depends on a responsible citizenry skilled in the safe and effective use of personal firearms and alert to the threat of extremist groups that would change our form of government. . . ."

The reflection that this may be the voice of America makes, to say the least, an unsettling thought.

10 ⁂ The Gold Behind The Curtain

> *"What kind of a country is this, then, unknown to the rest of the world, and where all nature is of a sort so different from ours? Probably this is the country where all is well; for there absolutely must be one of that sort. . . ."*
>
> —VOLTAIRE,
> *Candide*

This is one of the magics of America: that in the middle of harsh winter you can by stepping on an aeroplane find yourself transported to a different world within the same land; a kindly world, where the air around you is warm and gentle as it was biting in the December north. And the people in the corridors of the Miami airport terminal are in shirtsleeves and cotton dresses, their skin brown; and in the washroom, where the women are labeled "senoras" on the door, there is no hot tap. Nobody needs one.

Under the blue sky, over the bridge into Miami Beach, there are sights curious to those who have come out of the snow: palm trees, deep-fronded, and green leaves and grass everywhere; poinsettias red-dark as in their pots in the northern stores; hibiscus like great glowing convolvulus flowers, and real oranges and real grapefruit really growing on real trees. The wind from the Atlantic blows in to Miami Beach, over small translucent blue

226

jellyfish lying scattered and stranded; past coconuts on a palm with a parking meter underneath. All the way down the beach as far as you can see stretch the tall white hotels, each with its own precious strip of sand and a swimming-pool above surrounded by line upon line of long lying-down chairs. There are no people on the beach this particular morning, the wind is too strong; but the lounge of the great glossy Americana Hotel is full of cheerful tubby Bermuda-shorted men and wives wearing labels: a convention of Stone-Crushers. They sit among the potted tropical vegetation drinking coffee, crushing nothing tougher than sugar; they don't look inordinately wealthy, in this town of sky-high prices. Nor do the open-necked crowds eating corned-beef sandwiches and blintzes and innumerable kosher lunches in Wolfies Restaurant, nearby. But the big cars jamming the streets spell money; and the size and prices of the skyscraping hotels; and the endless familiar willingness in every store to charge purchases if the impulse-entering customer has no money in her purse.

There are islands in the bay between Miami Beach and Miami. Palms and hibiscus grow lush and tropical over them in the lagoon calm, and the big white houses lie sheltered and beautiful, with two or three cars in the garage, Spanish filigree on the patio, and orange trees fringing the road. One island has a guard in a sentry-box, covering the entrance of the only road.

"Where you going?"

"Just to look around."

"Hmm . . . haaa . . . well, don't drive more than twenty miles an hour."

And he peers again suspiciously on the way out, in case one has stolen a small wealthy child, or an orange tree.

But the Keys are not like that. Southwest from Miami Beach, the curved string of little islands stretches round with the Gulf Stream, a solitary necklace in the sea. The Keys are not like Miami; they are not like any other part of the United States. As you drive out to them, the trees change, and there is scrub instead of tropical fern; the wind blows strong, grabbing at the car, and the sun fitfully glancing out through broken cloud glints on swamp, reminding you that the Everglades are not far to the north. From Key Largo the long road runs unbroken a hundred miles to Key West: a made road, linking all the islands, running sometimes on bridge or causeway, sometimes along thin tongues of land where there is little room for anything else. It is scattered with small motels, and a vast billboard always heralding the arrival of each small motel—most of which are fairly similar, with a short terrace of chalet-rooms round three sides of a swimming-pool, and coconuts clustering fat and green on the palms outside each door. "No traffic noise," promise the notices at the head of each driveway; and indeed there is not much. And at night there is only the whoosh of the wind from the Atlantic bending the palms along the shore, twenty yards from the bedroom window. The leaves rattle against one another like the patter of rain.

But there is little rain here in December. In the mornings, the sun blazes up slow and then sudden out of the sea beyond the palms, and at the cafés open for breakfast along the long Keys road, the last fishermen are buying beer and Coke before they go off for the day chasing grouper and yellowtail and sea-trout. "Trout?" says one of the café-owners, who catches his own fish and lobsters and stone-crab to cook there, and says sadly that he wishes he could enjoy them as his customers do—"Trout? I wouldn't touch sea-trout. Full of worms, the flesh is. I wouldn't serve it here. But back there you see it selling in the shops everywhere—" He jerks his head "back there" in the direction of the mainland: back to America. And yet of course this is America too.

The café-owner's son is getting eleven cents a pound for kingfish, he says: pompano is the most expensive fish. "Get a haul of that, and you're set for the season." They lead seasonal lives, these people; for three months of the year they can let their rooms and sell their meals and charter their boats to the Northerners escaping from the snow; and then the heat clamps down, and brings mosquitoes down over the low-lying islands from the

Everglades, and there is only the fishing. But some people will always come for the fishing; there will always be the enthusiasts who live to watch a sailfish jump, or to feel the rasp of a shark's skin.

They fish from the big charter-boats that cost seventy-five dollars a day; from every variety of powerboat down to little outboard dinghies; they fish from quays and causeways and bridges, rows of them standing there patient and sun-brown, perched up on the balustrades as the cars swish close by them on the two-lane road. On each bridge the signs say: "No fishing except from catwalk," but not many seem to see them. The men stand there happy and still, in wide-peaked caps and battered straw hats, T-shirts and blaring bright shirts and no shirts at all. A fair number of women fish too, though often in the cafés at midday you can see gaggles of deserted wives, resigned and brown, discussing their men. Even when you drive past at night, through the warm silver-mooned dark, the fishermen are all still standing there on the bridges, motionless, with their rods and buckets and tackle-bags. Do they ever go away?

One group of fishermen with their eyes on the deep water have chartered Captain Wilbur, a large red-brown Florida sailor with hands like bananas. He treats them with a mixture of friendliness and wary tolerance: anxious to earn their money, but not so anxious that he will risk subservience. Above the television set in his wooden house a sailfish hangs mounted, with its great top fin fanned out glowing blue; every self-respecting house and restaurant on the Keys has its sailfish on the wall, and perhaps dolphin, lobtser, turtle shell, yellowtail, or starfish a foot across.

Captain Wilbur's boat lies moored at a small private jetty: a big white motor-cruiser, forty foot, with bunks, galley, enclosed cockpit and dual steering gear above on the fishing-boat bridge. There are racks of handsome six-foot rods, and two long curved metal outriggers like slim antennae; he slants and shackles these backwards, low-sloping, their tips crossing, until the expedition shall be out at sea. In the early morning sunshine the big boat noses out, deep throbbing, through channels where the mangroves on either side grow thick and green, and in some patches gray and ghostly, with dead leaves and an old crate caught in the bared roots. "That's what the last hurricane did," he says. "Everyone thought the mangroves were all killed, but they're putting out leaves again from the dead patches, see, here and there."

(When hurricanes whirl towards the Keys, everyone puts up his shutters and bars all his doors, and flees to Homestead or Key Largo: two peaceful names for the places near enough the mainland to be sheltered from the worst blast of wind and green water, that rips over all the low islands and breaks plate-glass windows like a hobnailed boot. The last hurricane hurt the Keys people badly; years from now they will still be repairing their restaurants, motels and homes. The Cuban revolution hit them all even harder; suddenly, for three months, they say, nobody came. And a Keys man in a bar, all alone with his wife, drinking beer from a can, before the rows of bottles in the cool Venetian-blinded half-dark, says nostalgically with the single-mindedness of the tradesman that the old days are gone. "We used to get some very nice Cubans here. Lovely yachts they had. The boats would come round and tie up, and they'd come ashore here, and they'd buy a lot. . . .")

Captain Wilbur steers out of the mangroves, and a cormorant skims past. The engine revs higher, and the captain takes a weaving course towards the line of piles that is the road-carrying bridge of the Keys. "There's only one way out," he says; though now at high tide it is difficult to see why, over the open water. Then the boat is clear of the bridge, and the throb changes to a roar and the wash to a wide-splashing wake, and the boat is heading out towards the Gulf Stream. Wilbur swings the outriggers up and parallel, and from a rod at either side the line is drawn up, held lightly by a clothes-peg so that the trout-size fish on the hook, a ballyhoo ("ballio," he says) is scuttering astern over the surface of the waves. They are respectable-size waves, over a heaving swell, so that the standing fishermen clutch for balance at the gunwale. A white feather lure goes down from a third rod in the stern; the three swivel chairs riveted to the deck wait empty, each with a socket for a rod—and then suddenly, still within sight of the thin green line of land that is the Keys, one of the outrigger lines is down clear of its peg, and the rod jerking, and Captain Wilbur has cut the engine and dropped down the ladder from the bridge to dive at the rod with a speed improbable for his bulk. Within five seconds the first grinning New York fisherman is winding tense in a chair, on and on, tougher and tougher, until at last when the line seems endless there is a swirl in the water, under the stern where the captain is waiting with a gaff, and a dark thick shape turning and twisting through the green. Then it is up in the air, black and shining, and down to thwack frantically in the metal-lined box in the stern; it is a big tuna. Before long another man brings in a dolphin, a slender fish two or three feet long, which doesn't fight but comes up through the water without diving deep, to twist iridescent and beautiful through the air until it is down in the box and spattered with blood. For the stranger it seems peculiarly unhappy to catch a dolphin, like shooting an albatross or trapping an otter; but the Keys people have no such qualms. "Good eating, they are," says the captain with satisfaction, and shuts the lid of the box. He grins encouragingly at his clients; all businessmen, and all still white-faced from the sunless New York City cliffs. Only one is a seasoned fisherman; the other two, younger, are clumsier with their rods and less able to hide excitement. It is a little difficult to see what brought them to the remote seaworld of the Keys, since one of them seems never even to have been aboard any boat smaller than the Staten Island Ferry; but each of them is alight with the American's love of activity, and the free outdoors.

Several bonita come fast on the lines now: smaller fish, like a plump mackerel: "rather strong flavor," the captain says. The boat is well out towards the Gulf Stream, past a metal-legged lighthouse. "That's all mechanical now. The last man left it a year ago. Now it's unattended, all works by automation." The water has changed color to a deep deep blue; the swell is stronger, and small rainstorms are walking across the sea. The fishermen catch four more tuna, three more bonita and another dolphin, playing and winding them, grim and concentrated and then laughing like schoolboys; the sun is warm, the wind is fresh, the sky is very blue. A seagull wheels over the boat, dipping hopefully to each skipping ballyhoo bait, but is wiser than to touch. The boat thrums to and fro; tankers pass, and cargo boats, and the rainclouds march close and then away. No fish are biting now, and anyway time is running out. The fishermen had hoped tentatively for a sailfish, which would fly over the surface with its great fin spread wide as they played it in; but even if they stayed out all day, and went deep into the Gulf of Mexico, this is not properly the right time of year. So Captain Wilbur heads for home; the outriggers come in, the boat foams up to speed again, leaving its broad white wake on the waves. A giant turtle kicks hastily downwards out of the way, ghostly through the green water; and a hundred yards away a school of porpoise turn over and over, black humped flashes in the sea that has turned back now to turquoise-green, from the deep incredible blue of the Gulf. And when the boat thrums back beneath the line of fishermen on the bridge, they take no notice, since there is no flag signifying "sailfish" or "kingfish" flying from the bow. "Yesterday," says Captain Wilbur with a faint air of reproach, "someone got a forty-pound king." Beyond the bridge the tide has dropped to show sand and shoal-light water, everywhere around the channel that was concealed before; it is apparent now what the captain meant when he said: "There's only one way out." The boat noses slowly back in to the creek among the mangroves, and then to the jetty; and the fishermen pay up the forty dollars that is the cost of the morning's charter. It is an expensive four hours' fishing; but Wilbur waves a big hand at his boat. "I've got about twenty-five thousand invested in her," he says mournfully. "It's a long time before you see any return." Then he goes back to his little wooden house with the trophy fish on the walls, to wait for the next tourist-fishermen to knock on his door.

The fishermen eat the dolphin for their lunch; the owner of one of the little restaurants cooks it for them, charging them only for the salad, coffee and Key Lime pie they consume at the same time. In exchange he is presented with two of the tuna, which he will not sell as steaks, but keep to make several dozen tuna-fish sandwiches. It seems an undignified end for those handsome, stocky, fighting fish.

But this is an unsentimental part of the United States. People are very matter-of-fact on the Keys, and far less involved in the web of consumer-centered pressures that tugs at life in all directions elsewhere. All the same, there is one commercial pressure they do need: all along the Keys road the sequence of motel billboards makes the way garish and ugly, a strip of unattractive civilization between the beaches where cormorants fly low out over the sea, necks outstretched like duck; or herons swoop stately as eagles, or pelicans sit squatting on poles with their long solemn nose-beaks pointing down. Yet somehow here the advertisers do not seem to splash about in advertising for its own sake; they do what they need to do, and no more. There is not very much to be found on the Keys, in the way of a livelihood, except the businesses of running a motel or a shop or a restaurant, or of catching fish. So there are no jobs, except casual domestic work, unless you invent one for yourself; and often the motels are small family operations, run by a couple who have put all their savings into buying or building the little gaggle of chalets, or the flimsy terrace of rooms round the swimming-pool. Often too they do all the work themselves, with the help of a handyman and one or two maids. For these people it is a matter of survival or bankruptcy to be able to lure in every possible passing holiday-making car; and so the billboard goes up: VACANCIES AT RED TURTLE MOTEL SIX MILES AHEAD. And the driver of the car is in turn glad to know that he need travel only six more miles before finding space at a miniature settlement with "self-contained kitchenette apartments," air-conditioning in case the heat goes above seventy-five degrees; television in case (which is less likely) it rains; and a pool for the fidgety kids. Perhaps the place itself does not live up to its advertised description: well, he can easily go on to the Pink Turtle Motel down the road, he passed another billboard just now imploringly announcing that it was only two miles ahead. . . . Through this kind of competition, the motel-owners become tolerant, amiably cynical people, in succession anxious, depressed or content. Mrs. Myron, who does all the paperwork and all the cooking at the twenty-room motel she and her husband have been running for five years, stands under the coconut palms at her door bartering with four car-borne tourists who have just turned into the drive and are looking appraisingly around. The rooms they would occupy are each twelve dollars a day: "But you wanna stay for a week, I'll give you a reduction." There is a muttering among the heads in the car. It is a large glossy car, with the radio jangling; and this motel is not at all glossy, but peaceful and remote, with no music but the rattling leaves and the breathing waves. The driver, who is spokesman, clears his fleshy throat: "Uh, well, matter of fact we got reservations at a place down the road, but we thought we'd have a look here on the way. Guess we'd better just show up there. And if we don't like it, we'll cancel the reservation and be right back." He flashes a brief dismissive smile. "Okay?" The car crackles on the stony dust of the drive, and vanishes down the long road to Key West.

Mrs. Myron sniffs. "They got no reservation anywhere," she says. "They won't be back either. We're too quiet for them. They'll go someplace else." And for that week the two rooms in question stand empty, each tokening eighty-four dollars that never came.

It is the natural wanderers, seldom downcast by responsibility, who make perhaps the best people for the Keys. In many coves on many islands, they have settled to build their motels, often after restless decades of switching from job to job elsewhere. One of them says he worked in almost every state of the Union before he bought his piece of land and shoreline on one of the Keys, and designed and built every part of his motel from the roof of the main house to the end of the jetty. It looks permanent now; poinsettias grow by the walls, and canaries and parakeets, bright yellow and green, whistle and chatter in an outdoor pen. The owner points a lean finger at the motel in slow enthusiasm: "See those steps up to the doors, I used a hardwood you'll not find often, comes from South America. Eleven years weathering and it's as hard as rock. . . . Those ceilings are concrete inside, got them covered with matting to stop the sound, otherwise they'd echo like an aircraft hangar. Some of the matting I got from Mexico, some from Panama, some from Hong Kong. . . ." He speaks as casually as though he went off in each case to collect it personally, and indeed perhaps he did. Certainly he collected the weird-bleached curlicues of driftwood that are fixed white against the pastel-washed walls. Everything from any natural source is bleached white on the Keys by the subtropical sun; white sand on the beaches, white dead mangrove wood, white broken arms of coral, white shells. Some people gather the shells to sell them to souvenir-hunting fishermen's wives; others dive for unbleached shells for the collectors. But this could hardly be described as an industry; it is done when they have the inclination, and the time.

Nobody hurries, who lives down on the Keys. They work, and exist, and enjoy their islands, and although they are isolated they do not seem so caught away from the world as many parts of America do. Perhaps it has something to do with their quietness, and the sea around them. Out on the Atlantic horizon in the dark, on any winter night on the Keys, the flashing star of the lighthouse comes, glows, vanishes again: the light standing alone in the ocean now with no men to tend it, but only the machinery automatically turning its beacon round and out across the night.

The sea is very dark, out there; darker than the sky, where a clear half-moon hangs. Under the palm trees you can see your own shadow black as space, moving over the soft white sand; and round the clustered dark silhouettes of the coconuts overhead the moonlight glints in streaks on the long leaves. Sometimes in a mutter of breeze the leaves rattle softly, but the night is very still; only the crickets chirrup unseen all around, and a boat creaks on a ripple by the shore.

You can move out along a narrow tongue of rock and coral that reaches three hundred feet out into the sea; the sand swishes gently underfoot, and grass and some small creeping plant grow in dark patches against the white ground. Then when you look back from the tip of the coral spit, there all around, overwhelming, is the moon-washed sky with its constellations tilted and unfamiliar, as if you were looking at them from a banking plane, that keeps its private horizon and overturns the sky outside. And the sea is joined to the sky by the glimmering line of light along the road that links the Keys. America is silent and undiscovered; you can hear nothing out there but the faint wash of water, and the crickets' song more distant now; and once perhaps, in the reeds and scrub, the croak of a night bird. The world is black and white and silver-gray—except in one place out in the southern sky, where golden lightning is flickering in strange wavering bursts above the horizon, giving sudden shape to clouds lost in the dark. You could very easily believe that America is the only land on earth, if it were not for that lightning, the only unquiet thing in the warm, still, summer-winter American night. Once you have noticed the flickering in the south, it does not take any very great sense of symbolism to realise that Cuba is out over there, and Guantanamo. But without that small accidental jolt to the mind, you would never have given a thought to such places at all.

One trouble with America is its beauty: its inexhaustible range of causes for wonder and excitement. No other country in

the world is so much involved in responsibility for the future of
the world; yet in no other country is it so seductively easy for the
individual to escape involvement. There are so many places like
the Keys: so many paradises for the lotos-eater or the would-be
pioneer. The physical activity which is a happy obsession with so
many Americans is not necessarily a Spartan matter of running
six miles before breakfast along gray roads in a drizzling rain,
just for the sake of the running or the satisfaction of accomplishment; it is a more straightforward matter of simple enjoyment.
The sportsmen are not all footballers. They are those who stand
in a trout stream deep in remote woods on a clear autumn day, as
much aware of the golden trees and the flash of a woodpecker as
of the fish they may catch; or who gaze happily out over white
mountains under a brilliant winter-blue sky, before skiing down
through snow-mounded firs and birch. Even the huntsmen, who
kill appreciable numbers of one another each year as well as deer
or duck, often take no more pleasure from the hunting than from
the attendant matter of walking lonely forests or sleeping under
the stars. The occupations of Americans—the occupations, that
is, which are chosen for reasons other than earning a living, or
making a profit—are very often indeed simple and unpretentious, with their own peculiar kind of childlike innocence, and
linked closely with the beauty of the land in which their owners
live. It is easy and no doubt valuable to dig out psychological
reasons for the widespread American habit of going off to live
rough or tough; they need to find a challenge to prove that
they're as full of bold pioneering spirit as their forefathers, one
says wisely; they need an antidote for their soft prosperity; there
is a streak of repressed masochism in them. But the reason could
equally well be much simpler than any of these: that they have
not, so far, found or evolved anything that they enjoy more. The
impact of their surroundings is so spectacular, the possibilities
are so many, that their intellectual needs are satisfied—perhaps
stifled—by an enormous mute sense of delight. The principal
root of Thoreau's great reputation in the United States lies, I

suspect, less in the quality of his prose than in the fact that he expressed a part of this delight. And perhaps we on the other side of the Atlantic have forgotten quite what it is like.

Perhaps too, then, this is one of the principal causes of the barrier of mutual misunderstanding that makes up the Golden Curtain. The world does not properly know the Americans, because America is complex and far away: not expressible in simple images, and not within reach of the ordinary people of other lands. And America does not properly know the world; partly also because it is too remote for its average citizens to be able to travel outside its bounds, but mainly because it does not produce any sense of need. "No man is an Iland intire of it selfe: every man is a peece of the Continent, a part of the maine. . . ." You cannot feel the whole depth of that great humanitarian cry in the United States; you cannot feel, there, a sense of dependence on all mankind. In America, the common expression of the humanitarian impulse is a one-way affair—generosity, the giving of help, the charitable instinct. Even in listening to Americans talking of the conduct of the Second World War, you do not hear any more complex sense of involvement expressed. The American has never really known what it is like to need anyone but other Americans; he is a piece of the continent, indeed, but of his own continent only.

He loves his own land with a deep conviction which is less critical, *au fond*, than the equivalent feeling of men in any other land. You do not often find an American driven to settle in another country because he cannot stand his own, and this is not only because he can so easily find something that suits him better within his own huge boundaries. At heart, however clearly he sees and points out the failings and hypocrisies around him, he is still in love with the dream. He sees America not only as it is, but as it could be; and always, in one way or another, he is paying it respect. This is not just a matter of the pompous patriotic twaddle that is so often pumped out round the Fourth of July, the Flag, Veterans' Day, the Daughters of the American Revolution and the "Battle Hymn of the Republic." These are self-conscious things, and the American's real love of America comes from the subconscious; the emotional roots which hold him bound to the idea of America are even stronger than those which hold most Englishmen to England, Irishmen to Eire, Frenchmen to France. And perhaps his concentric loyalties—devotion to family, home-town, state, and country—take up so much of his emotional re-sources that he has none left even for the reflection that he might one day need and cherish further-spread relationships than these.

And so the four corners of his world are marked, geographi-cally, by Boston and Miami, Seattle and Los Angeles; and to some extent these mark the corners of his mind as well. Boston symbolizes what he takes to be English stiffness and reticence; Miami embodies the exuberance of the tropics; Seattle means the distant West, still not yet fully explored; and Los Angeles, to-gether with San Francisco, represents as much of Spanishness and the influence of the exotic Orient as most Americans will ever see. Within these corners of the world, the consumers ride the capitalist system on its merry, prosperous way; the churches thrive and the educational systems struggle to find their proper shape; work hammers and leisure bubbles; the fine arts seek forms palatable to their masters; and the politicians, at the drop of a vote, applaud the whole pattern as something not universal but indigenous: the American Way of Life. "My Fellow Ameri-cans," said John Fitzgerald Kennedy, "ask not what your country can do for you: ask what you can do for your country." He said many things of wider import; but this is the one which Ameri-cans instinctively selected to remember him by. And if the most obvious reason was that he himself was killed while serving his country as President, there is still the deeper reason that the idea of the country as an ultimate value dominates most American minds. It does not do, in the United States, to set beside Ken-nedy's words the famous challenge of E. M. Forster: "If I had to betray my country or my friend, I hope I should have the courage to betray my country." If the friend were an American, would he value the sacrifice?

The American does not notice his insulation, any more than he notices the composition of the air he breathes. It is the foreigner, living in America, who discovers the sensation of being cut off from the rest of the world. I am English; I live in America; and I have, I think, as much contact as most Americans with the other side of the Atlantic, through reports, letters, visitors, visits and so on. Yet for all this I know that I have no real idea of what is being said, thought or done in London, Britain, Europe; of what the present emotional climate there is like. There is no sense of being within the same family. I have felt as isolated in the U.S.A. as in the U.S.S.R.; for though in Russia one is cut off from any source of home or international information except the occasional *Daily Worker* or the militant effusions of *Pravda* and *Isvestia*—even so, the sense of being enclosed within a distant, alien world is no greater than it can sometimes be in Texas, or Ohio, or Alabama. Nor is it different in kind. There is the same awareness of living among people who know little about your own background, and who care less; whose world ends at their own national boundaries. And if we are all to consider the non-Communist world, the West, as a distinct entity, surely this should not be so?

It is not deliberate; it is not isolationism. But the Golden Curtain does exist, enclosing America in accidental separation, and it seems to me inexpressibly important that we should admit this, and begin seeking ways of tearing the barrier down. There is small comfort in the fact that Senator Barry Goldwater, high priest of insulation, was defeated at the polls; the alarming thing was that he should have got there in the first place. The conflict within the Republican Party which ended in his gaining the Presidential nomination was a microcosm of the conflict which divides the whole of America—not into political camps, but into the camps of those who would keep her insulated, and those who would draw her into the international mainstream. For certainly she can be drawn out. The openminded American, who has by care or happy accident never been constricted by the effects of insulation, is a fellow of infinite capacity. The image of President Kennedy held in it all the qualities of this openmindedness, which is one of the reasons why so many Europeans were utterly dismayed by his death; and in every part of the United States the insulated American has his counterbalance. And there are many points on which you can generalize about the second, as about the first. The Open American, for instance, is no less patriotic than his insulated fellow, but when he supports the American Way in argument, he tends to be upholding not wholesome American youth, Christianity, or capital gains, but his own interpretation of the democratic ideal. When he thinks of Europe— and he does—it is not only as a market. He is a tolerant man. Sometimes he has unexpected reasons for his tolerance; he may be someone who has suffered from the prejudices of other Americans: the member of a minority group, or the liberal who was once investigated—unprofitably—by the Un-American Activities Committee. At one extreme he is a wide-eyed Anglophile; at the other, the kind of conservative Republican who shuddered and departed from the brand of conservatism preached by Mr. Goldwater's camp. He is not proud of the methods which Presidents have to use to reach the Presidency, but he was shattered by Kennedy's death. He supports the United Nations Organization. He can understand the resentment which many Canadians feel towards America, even though he does not sympathize.

Whatever his newspaper, he reads widely; perhaps the *Saturday Review*, the *Manchester Guardian Weekly,* and magazines ranging from the *Nation* to the *New Yorker*. Sometimes he may even read verse. He has a strong sense of humor; a peculiarly American kind of leg-pulling wryness. He has catholic tastes, he asks questions, he likes to listen as well as to talk and explain. He may make a great deal of money, but is unlikely to own a Cadillac. If he makes personal enemies, he does not develop an ulcer over the fact. He may have more children than he can afford, but does not think this a disaster. He is more likely to drink Scotch or Bourbon than Martinis or Manhattans, but however much he drinks he does not give the curious impression of *needing* it which many insulated Americans do. He worries sometimes whether foreigners have the right idea about his country. He knows the meaning and sensation of the word *Angst*. You are much more likely to find him in New York or San Francisco than in Washington, but you may also find him driving a cab in Chicago, or teaching classics in a small college in Iowa. He is easily recognizable, and the most recognizable thing about him is that always he will contain a large amount of the unexpected. . . .

Of course, there is no one such person; as there is no one prototype insulated American. But all these qualities exist, scattered throughout America, and are good for her. And among all the real individuals, the two hundred million permutations of both sets of qualities, there are to be found one or two other things in common: notably the fact that most Americans are friendly, warm, and eager—almost anxious—to be liked; and that most are indeed likeable. This is perhaps the greatest enigma of the United States. Seen properly in context, the Americans are an enormously attractive people; prosperity, unlike poverty, creates an atmosphere in which generosity, hospitality and benevolence can easily breed. "Life, liberty and the pursuit of happiness . . ." the faith is still tangible in the air, among insulated and open minds alike. Yet somehow that faith is becoming inbred, curiously oppressive; one can love America, and most Americans, but at the same time feel an ominous air of impending disaster about the combination of the two. You are wonderful people, you have a wonderful country; but what are you doing to it?

In Britain, we too are by temperament and position isolated—but because we are islanders, we know it. We have had to force ourselves into extroversion: the state of understanding the need for things like NATO and the European trade groupings.

We sit in our small sea-defined land, eyeing our dozen neighbors, and although at heart we should probably still prefer to keep ourselves to ourselves, centuries ago we learned the need for external relationships. One day we may even really get around to building that Channel Tunnel. Perhaps we are lucky in the knowledge that although we may have stood alone against monstrous odds in 1940, we could certainly not stand alone now.

But nine out of ten Americans, if challenged, would state a firm belief that their country could quite easily stand alone. You do not envisage this happening, of course; you see yourselves as the leaders of something called The West, though many of you are not too clear about the way The West is made up. But you have, as a nation, no real sense of needing anybody else, and so there is no natural spotlight—of concern, self-preservation, alarm—to illumine for you the fact that in almost every matter except that of defense, you have become strikingly cut off. Where we have always known about our tendency to remoteness, you have never been aware in the same way of yours. Politically you are not now isolationist—far from it. By temperament you are almost too open. But your own openness is too often all that you see. When you reflect on your national values and preoccupations, of the kind I have tried to show in this book, you do not see in them the symptoms of withdrawal from one another, from your national ideals, and from the rest of the world. All these have accidentally begun to develop, yet you do not know; you have not noticed the Golden Curtain growing gradually across the Atlantic in the last twenty, fifty years. But it has grown, and still grows.

There you sit, the Americans: anxious but complacent, loveable but disturbing; and we do not properly know you, nor you us, at a time when real knowledge and understanding become more important every day. We see only your self-made images of the United States, each partly valid but each incomplete. And behind the curtain which these weave, the real America goes its way, in the long unwitting conflict between those who are trying to tear the barrier down, and those who are dedicated to weaving it thicker still. Perhaps the main thing for all of us to remember, on either side of the Atlantic, is that at least the conflict is there.